ADVANCE PRAISE OF

RESILIENCE

"Les Wright's style of writing is clear and concise, intimate, honest, and emotionally charged at once. His childhood was lonely and isolated, even in the midst of a large family from whom he felt alienated very early. Like many gay kids, Les became fascinated by secret codes and languages, thus German language and culture became a part of this secret intimacy and he lived in Germany for a number of years. This is a moving book that slices you open with its rare insights and naked truthfulness. Wright spares very little—he is at times very hard on himself, but never gives into self-pity. He deals with his own alcoholism, his struggles with drugs and HIV, his conflicts with people who label themselves 'progressive,' but are basically cold and feckless, and his survival in the closed, cut-throat, and entitled backways of academia, that often coddle people from the upper middle classes, which he was not. The book is shockingly frank sexually, but even more important, it is emotionally unsparing, rare in gay books that often shy away from the most genuine, painful, and raw feelings. Les Wright does not, but embraces these feelings with extraordinary craft and skill." —Perry Brass, author of *A Real Life*

"*Resilience* offers a searing portrait of queer life in the latter half of the 20th Century through the eyes of Les Wright, a pioneer of Bear history. Wright takes readers on a journey from the suffocating conformity of the 1950s in rural New York, through the radicalism of gay liberation and the trauma of AIDS, all the way to our ambiguous present. Written in an intimate and uncompromising style, *Resilience* unfolds the pleasures and pains of gay life and raises challenging questions about sex, suffering, and the failures of queer revolution." —Tyler Bradway, coeditor of *Queer Kinship*

"Wright takes the reader on a Dantesque journey from the backstreets of pre-HIV sex to the aeries of academia. Through the gay enclaves of Europe and the US, the story echoes of Lars Eighner." —Bo Young, former publisher of *White Crane Journal* and LGBTQ+ historian (gaywisdom.org)

"This daring confessional spills the tea about bad behavior in gayborhoods, and about gay-on-gay sabotage in politically-correct universities. Ranging across AIDS, pompous queer theory, and the Bear movement, Professor Wright teaches an authentic crash course in what gay folk don't learn in school and need to learn to 'know themselves.' Self-knowledge is his survivalist message. Slumming like the transgressive Charles Bukowski and naming names like Truman Capote, he takes no prisoners as he reveals who did what to whom in the shocking dark underbelly of gay life.

"I could not resist the truth and visions of his Dantean tour through sex, drugs, and rock-n-roll. The analytical author hits high notes of insight as he narrates coming out from boyhood incest and rape to find and frame and free his gay-ghetto self in the wider human context of world history and the international pop culture of books, films, music, travel, and camp that gayfolk use to construct queer identity. Wright's comedy of errors and eros is recommended for readers eager for outsider gay history told by an authentic eyewitness survivor and mentor." —Jack Fritscher, Ph.D., founding San Francisco editor of *Drummer* magazine and author of *Profiles in Gay Courage: Leatherfolk, Arts, and Ideas*

"In his fascinating, often wrenching, roller-coaster-ride of a memoir, Les K. Wright takes us through his long-enduring search for love, acceptance, community, meaningful work, and a place to truly feel at home. *Resilience* reads like a history of a half-century of American gay life, condensed into one man's very intimate story." —Wayne Hoffman, author of *An Older Man* and *Hard*

"In this memoir, Les Wright walks us through a life filled with challenges: a sexually abusive father, coming to terms with a condemned sexual identity, the horrors of the AIDS epidemic, and the pull of alcohol, among them. *Resilience* reminds us of the power of the human spirit to survive and thrive even under those most difficult conditions. As told in these pages, Les Wright's life has the power to inspire and give hope." —John D'Emilio, author of *Memories of a Gay Catholic Boyhood: Coming of Age in the Sixties*

"Les Wright's life story confronts the reader with the painful fact that surviving AIDS is neither a happy end nor even an end. And in Wright's case, as it is for so many gay men, it is not even the first survival. That began in a childhood in the 1950s where the flimsy American dream could be ruined like a family Polaroid exposed to soon. There's another tentative survival in school where even the whiff of difference could be a kiss of death without the kiss. Wright's salvation in German literature and Germany gleams like Oz although the witches are always waiting in the interstices of that real dream. Wright takes us with him through the thrills of sex and sexual politics, the majestic promises of culture and the intellect, which makes the horrors of AIDS all the more an obscene violation. Survival becomes an ethical calling, at times an art form, at times a retroactive rescue of the bullied kid, at times a call to a stricken community. *Resilience* is at once the perfect title of the book and a poignant understatement." —Earl Jackson, author of *Strategies of Deviance: Studies in Gay Male Representation*

"In his memoir *Resilience*, Les K. Wright maps out the ways in which exclusion as a social practice—in one's own family and personal relationships as well as in academic, gay, and even recovery communities—can work to wear us down and leave us stranded late in life, dispirited. In resonant prose, Wright documents one individual's history of disconnection and disaffection, and relays to the reader how he has been able to resist the forces that isolate us and to re-engage with what makes his heart sing. As a long-term survivor on many counts, Wright has much to teach us about persistence in the pursuit of peace and kinship, and he does so carefully, lovingly, inclusively." —Chael Needle, co-editor of *Art & Understanding: Literature from the First Twenty Years of A&U*

"What Les K. Wright has accomplished is much more than a personal memoir. It's a story about the complexity of one's life and of American life. He shows courage in revealing himself, sharing his perceptions of gay men following World War II. His life through the frightening HIV epidemic speaks to other survivors still grieving those years and to the young generations who know AIDS only as a historical fact. Wright writes in an open, simple, fluid style. This is perhaps the most detailed, deep story I have ever read." —Walt Odets, author of *Out of the Shadows: Reimagining Gay Men's Lives*

RESILIENCE

The Bear Book
Readings in the History and Evolution of a Gay Male Subculture

The Bear Book II
Further Readings in the History and Evolution of a Gay Male Subculture

RESILIENCE

A Polemical Memoir of AIDS, Bears, and F*cking

LES K. WRIGHT

Bearskin Lodge Press
Cortland, NY

for

Ruth Lehmann

PREFACE

I began this memoir in 2014. I had recently moved from San Francisco back to my childhood home in Central New York. I soon discovered SAGE Upstate in Syracuse, New York, which had a gay writers' group. In the course of a year with the encouragement of group members, Akosua Washington-Woods, Chris Thompson, and Kim Dill, I wrote down my bare-bones memories, unearthing a lot of long-buried pain in the process. I realized many memories had faded or become blurred with the passage of time. The weekly deadlines and the unwavering faith of these women in the power of the story I was revealing to them kept me going.

Over the next ten years I worked on the manuscript, a bit at a time, only to set it aside again in frustration. When Ruth Lehmann, my long-time friend from graduate school days in Tübingen, heard I had given up, she rallied me back to the project. With her support, I approached an old friend, Raymond Luczak, to see if he would be my editor. He agreed and directed me to some dozen or so memoirs and autobiographies.

I continued to wrestle with vague and mixed memories, finding how selective my memory was and taking time to verify dates, names, and events. I settled on a subjective account, realizing the contradictions between reality and how I remembered it. I worked my way to the bottom of Raymond's reading list, and then I read Perry Brass's memoir *A Real Life*. This was the breakthrough I had been seeking.

I have always admired John Rechy's writing style and especially his novel *City of Night*—the rich detail, the immediacy of his prose, the intimacy of drawing the reader into his confidence. This novel had a powerful effect on me. It was my first guide, exposing me to the vast American gay underworld I was joining.

Perry Brass, writing in his own unmistakable voice, exerted a similar power on me. Both authors wrote about a postwar, pre-Stonewall gay underworld, now long gone, where my earliest days as a gay man had begun. What they both described rang true for me. The breakthrough for me came with Brass's explicit commitment to tell the truth. My project here is to tell the truth—or at least, some of the truths about the world and myself I have come to understand.

Once I came out to escape the living hell of being in the closet, I became a blatant, militant homosexual. Years later, when I got sober, I became open about my drinking and my recovery. When I was infected with HIV and later diagnosed with full-blown AIDS, I was open about that too. Any time I tried to keep any of these facts about my life a secret, someone inevitably tried to blackmail me or otherwise use that information against me.

In writing this book, I wrestled a long time with the question of my anonymity as a member of Alcoholics Anonymous (AA). Every few months, nowadays, one or another public figure in entertainment or the sports world comes out as a recovering member of AA. The Eleventh Tradition states that AA's public relations policy is one of attraction and not promotion. The Twelfth Tradition reminds its members to place principles before personalities. Much of my path in recovery has involved being a member of AA and practicing the principles of AA. Wherever I speak of my experiences in these pages, I do not speak for AA (no one individual can). For the most part, I have not revealed identities of people still alive in the text. Any potential "public controversy" discerned here reflects on me, and on me alone.

LES K. WRIGHT

PROLOGUE

In 1953, Hugh Hefner published the first issue of *Playboy* magazine, featuring Marilyn Monroe on the front cover. Julius and Ethel Rosenberg, accused of being Soviet spies, were executed. *The Crucible*, Arthur Miller's allegorical play about McCarthyism, opened on Broadway. As one of his first acts in office, the newly inaugurated President Dwight Eisenhower, World War II war hero, signed an executive order to have all known homosexuals fired from federal jobs. The American Psychological Association defined homosexuality as a mental illness. Freud had theorized that male homosexuality was caused by having a domineering mother and an absent father. The homosexual man lived in a state of arrested psychological development.

In a 1953 TV commercial, Dinah Shore, long rumored to be a closeted lesbian, beckoned Americans to "See the USA in your Chevrolet." Car design in the 1950s, with ever higher tail fins, emphasized high-speed aerial flight. The front grills resembled human faces, suggesting each model had a distinct personality. The rapid changes in design compelled drivers to buy a new car every year. For those who could not afford this, repainting their car was popular. The 1950s cars had large, upholstered interiors that felt like the family living room and could be driven to the local drive-in movie or hamburger joint. Germans called these behemoths *Straßenkreuzer*—"road cruisers."

Post-World War II Americans subscribed to the belief that everyone could get ahead and climb the social ladder by working hard. They showed off their affluence with more and more consumer goods—from suburban tract houses and automobiles to rabbit-eared black-and-white television sets and TV dinners in aluminum trays to eat from while watching TV. People still dressed up when going out, whether going to church, going grocery shopping, or even going to the local movie palace.

PART ONE

1

My parents were high school sweethearts and married at 19. When Mom married Dad in 1950, he was a smooth-chested redhead. His body hair grew over time. Mom found hairy men repugnant.

Dad was just young enough to avoid serving in World War II. He joined the Army National Guard in Syracuse. When Dad came back from summer Guard drills at Fort Drum and sported a moustache, Mom refused to kiss him and ordered him to shave it off.

Dad's first full-time job out of high school was selling shoes in Johnson City, over fifty miles away. Although I was too young to have any memories of this, my dad's absence would become a hallmark of his relationship with our family. Dad's father worked on the railroad, East Syracuse being the site of switching yards for the New York Central Railroad. Neither Dad nor Mom went on to college. For many years Dad would have one low-paying job after another, with stretches of unemployment in between. Mom hoped to become a gym teacher. But after briefly attending the state college in Cortland, she left, unable to afford college.

Both of my parents came from big families. Both were middle children. Dad was one of seven kids, and Mom was one of four. My dad's father was called Rasty because of his red hair. He worked as a stoker when trains were powered by coal. When I was born, East Syracuse coal-powered steam engines had given way to diesels and Rasty rode the caboose as a flagman. Grandpa Wright eventually died from lung cancer caused by the coal dust he inhaled on the job. When I grew up, the neighborhood was no longer dark and dingy from coal smoke but smelled of gasoline and diesel exhaust.

Mom's mother, my Grandma Newkirk, was a flapper in the 1920s. She had an almost Parisian flair for making herself look smart even in her simplest clothing. Her first husband, father of her first child, had been a bootlegger. He abandoned her and their infant daughter, leaving her to find whatever work she could find.

While working as a maid in the upscale Eastwood district of Syracuse, she met and fell in love with a handyman. His name was Andrew. They had three children. Their marriage lasted some twenty years before Andrew fell to his death in a work-related accident. The scaffolding supporting him while he was painting a downtown office building gave way and he fell four floors to the sidewalk, dying instantly. It left Grandma Newkirk and her children homeless. This I learned when I came across a newspaper clipping Mom had tucked away. No one ever talked about the Great Depression.

My earliest memory of Dad was him playing horsey with me on the living room floor. He'd tickle me until I screamed in a mix of pain and pleasure for him to stop. He also played a war game with me, where Dad would hide behind a wall or door and suddenly burst out of hiding, shooting me "dead" with a toy machine gun. I would run screaming from the ambush. I carried the memory of two snapshots of me and Dad together from this time. In one, Dad is dressed in a pea green T-shirt, a memento of the recent Korean conflict, and is holding me by the hand. We were about to walk down to the corner store; Mom had come outdoors and stopped to capture this moment of paternal warmth. In the other photo, Dad is standing in front of his army jeep in khaki fatigues and mirror sunglasses. He is holding me in his arms, I am wearing his military cap, and I am smiling. Dad is beaming with pride.

I recall my early childhood as a time when I felt cocooned in the warm comfort of feeling loved. My fondest memory of Dad then was getting a postcard from him in the mail from Olean, New York, where his job had taken him. I became fascinated by postcards.

As I got a little older, Dad grew distant. He stopped playing with me. He never taught me how to play baseball. I never learned the rules for baseball, football, or basketball. At school I dreaded being forced to play these sports in gym class. I was inevitably the last picked to be on a team. He also never taught me how to use tools. When he asked for my help, I would usually screw up and be recriminated for not knowing how to use any tools.

By the age of nine, I found that Dad had stopped talking to me. If he had anything to say to me, he would tell Mom and she would tell me. She always prefaced this with "Your father wants you to know ..." When I was middle-aged, Mom told me that she and Dad had pretty much figured out by the time I was five that I was homosexual.

They were very involved when I was a Cub Scout. Mom became a Den Mother. Dad helped me with my wooden racing car for the Pinewood Derby. After that he stopped attending the important events in my young life. He was not available to come with me to a father-son dinner where Larry Czonka, a pro football player, was the guest speaker. A friend's father brought his son and me, as their guest, to the dinner.

I loved Grandma Newkirk. She rented an apartment in her daughter's family house. It was tastefully appointed with a violet davenport, white sheer curtains, and an antique radio cabinet, the most elegant piece of furniture in the living room. Like the way she dressed, she had a flair for making her home attractive and cozy.

She sometimes allowed me to share her bed when I stayed overnight on Fridays. I would put on my pajamas and watch her brush her long, long grey hair. I would be awakened in the middle of the night by the cuckoo clock. This left me feeling safe, imagining myself in a cabin deep in a dark forest. On Saturday mornings Grandma Newkirk made me breakfast— cinnamon toast and hot cocoa. I watched shows on TV—*Sky King, My Friend Flicka, The Roy Rogers Show*, and cartoons. I remember her taking me to Eddie's Restaurant in Sylvan Beach on the eastern shore of Lake Oneida, New York, and to the boardwalk in Asbury Park, New Jersey.

When Mom was pregnant with me, she went through a baby names book. The name she wrote in the margins was Geoffrey Gregory. Instead, she chose Leslie Kirk. I was born on a bitterly cold Saturday morning in January. As an old rhyme has it, Saturday's child must work hard for its living. When a nurse from the delivery room brought me to Mom (as she told me years later), she yelled, "Take it back. I want a girl."

2

I remember most of my childhood in photographs. I recall in snapshots swimming at Jamesville Beach. I remember Mom sending me to Gus's corner market for milk, being sent to Rothschild's Drugstore to buy her cigarettes. I remember watching an intricate Busby Berkeley dance number on TV. I remember crying in my crib while Mom listened to a Patsy Cline song.

I remember climbing small trees with my cousin Greg, trees on the edge of a swamp behind my school building. One afternoon I got it into my head to climb a tree and, holding onto it near the top, jumped off without letting go. The tree bent down without breaking. I repeated this again and again, laughing and squealing with intense pleasure.

I remember my cousins—so many cousins from our building—playing in the street. I remember me and my cousins Greg, Danny, and Rich playing in the used Chevy car lot behind our building, breaking into cars and trucks, rummaging under the seats and in the glovebox for whatever we could steal. Sometimes we went down to the railroad switching yards to play on the tracks until the railroad dicks chased us off the property.

I remember the swiveling metal magazine rack full of comic books at Rothschild's. When Mom gave me extra money to buy her candy bars I would be careful to see there was enough change for me to buy a comic book. My favorites were *Dennis the Menace, Little Lulu, Nancy, Donald Duck, Superman, Batman, The Justice League of America*, and *The Illustrated Classics*. I escaped into these worlds, and the characters became my friends.

I drank root beer soda because that was what Dennis the Menace drank. I read *Illustrated Classics*, which was my introduction to Literature.

I remember myself in two photographs, but with no emotional connection to them. One photo was a studio portrait in sepia tones of me at age three. I am sitting on a blanketed cushion. I am wearing a fringed cowboy shirt and waving a cap pistol in my right hand. My hair is dark. (I was so dark at birth that family members joked I was not a Wright.) There is a twinkle in my eye. I note, as if looking at someone else, that I am strikingly handsome, in a way that boys who grow up to be gay sometimes are. "You're too pretty," one aunt told me to "be a boy." The photo hung in the dining room of our apartment. It got lost in a later move.

In another photo I am trussed in a leather harness and tethered to the back porch railing with a white clothesline. I am standing at the edge of the porch, my arms outstretched. I appear to be reaching for my cousin Greg McDonald, who is standing on the sidewalk at the bottom of the stairs. He has a flat cap on his head and has a sucker in his mouth. He is staring into the camera. Greg has large pouty lips. He looks like Jackie Coogan in a famous movie still of him and Charlie Chaplin in *The Kid*.

Another memory is not a photograph, but an image frozen in time. Three of my cousins—Ted McDonald, Simon, and Bernie—are walking across the dirt of our side yard. They are all around the same age, maybe 11 or 12. Tony is wearing blue jeans and a white T-shirt. Simon is bare-chested, and Sandy is carrying a baseball bat. His T-shirt is dirty and torn. When I laid eyes on this sight of my cousins, I was caught unawares, captivated by their maleness.

The image I still carry from our swimming trips to Jamesville Beach is of the men's changing room. This was the first time I had ever seen men naked. The changing room was a large, drafty wooden structure that was one open space. It smelled of men—sweat, deodorant, aftershave, and cigarette smoke. They were in various stages of undress, some completely naked, some naked and talking to each other. I saw their cocks, all different from each other and all surrounded by a small patch of hair. I was filled with a feeling of incredible excitement. These naked men with their naked cocks fascinated me, filled me with rapture—feelings I didn't know what to do with or what they meant. But instinctively I knew not to tell anyone about these feelings.

I remember other incidents. One Saturday morning I went next door to get Greg to come out and play. His oldest brother Ted was sitting in his undershorts in the dark living room watching a Three Stooges movie on TV. He told me to come in and watch TV with him.

He pulled his cock out of his boxer shorts It was hard and so large.

I had never seen a cock hard before and was amazed at how big it was. He told me, "Suck it." I was both terrified and thrilled at the same time. "Put your mouth over my dick and move it up and down." He grabbed my head and began moving it up and down over his cock. After a little while, he let go of my head and said, "Now you." He began sucking on my little prepubescent cock until I couldn't bear it anymore. He jacked himself off.

This happened more times than I can recall. My only other memory was of the time he made me suck his dick in his bedroom. I tasted it and was disgusted. "It tastes like soap," I said. He let me go. I was maybe nine and he had to be fifteen.

One summer evening after dinner I was walking across the dirt side yard. The Morgans' kitchen window was open and the Morgan boys—Ted, Alan, Greg, and Ray—were washing their supper dishes. Some of their toys were lying on the ground below the screened window. Something possessed me and I started stomping on the toys, breaking every one of them. Greg yelled out the window, "Why are you breaking those toys, Les? Stop it!" But I couldn't.

My parents took me to the movies all the time, even when I was too young to understand them. As children of the Depression their generation had grown up going to the movies every week. They bought a TV set as soon as they became available. I grew up swimming in a sea of mass media images.

I loved going to the movies. Mom and I walked the three blocks from our building to the East Theater on West Manlius Street. I remember seeing *Old Yeller, Around the Worlds in Eighty Days*, and *Bambi* there. When Kevin Corcoran was forced by his dad to shoot his dog Old Yeller, I cried. I cried and cried and cried. I also remember *Shane*. I was drawn to Shane just as Joey, the little boy in the movie, was. I was electrified by the closing scene. Shane is leaving Joey's family ranch and Joey calls out, "Shane, come back!" I was much too young to understand what was going on. But I also felt Joey's grief at the loss of the man he had worshipped and loved. I cried then and now sixty years later I still weep over this scene. In retrospect, I knew you never get over the loss of such love.

Mom and Dad took me to the Wescott, where I saw *The King and I; Bell, Book, and Candle*, and old Francis the Talking Mule movies. Grandma Newkirk took me on the bus to Loew's State Theater downtown. I no longer remember any of the movies we saw, just the palatial opulence of the theater itself. When I was eight, Mom gave me money to take the bus to Eastwood to see Saturday matinees at the Palace.

We went as a family to the drive-in, mostly to the Dewitt Drive-In on Erie Boulevard East. It was there that I saw the Doris Day-Rock Hudson comedies. I adored Doris Day, her startlingly blue eyes and almost white, blond hair, her 1950s-smart fashion, and her soft voice. I loved her singing. Compared to Doris Day's onscreen presence, Rock Hudson was much more real to me. He looked like a Real Man. He had a very handsome face, a very warm smile, and seemed so friendly and welcoming. When I saw him in *Lover Come Back* with a full beard, I was smitten.

Television fed my soul in the same way the movies did. I laughed myself silly over Lucy's antics in *I Love Lucy*. I wanted to have "the Beave" in *Leave It to Beaver* and Chip in *My Three Sons* as my friends. Though I didn't know at the time there was a name for this feeling, I had a crush on Cubby on *The Mickey Mouse Club*. I hankered hopelessly for Timmy on *Lassie*. The mournful theme song made me cry every time.

When I was nine, a TV show called *Fair Exchange* began airing. This show was something new and different. The story followed two teenage girls, the daughters of two World War II vets, one British the other American, who swapped places to spend a year living with the other's family and learning how to live in a different culture. I didn't take nearly as much interest in the story lines as in learning about English culture. The program awakened in me a deep desire to live abroad and experience a different culture.

I remember looking forward to starting kindergarten. Mom said I talked about it for weeks. I was so excited. I remember the black-and-white photo of me, standing in the driveway in my Sunday best clothes, about to go to my first day at school.

When I got to school and saw all those other kids, total strangers, I panicked. When Mom told me she was leaving, I started screaming. She stayed for a while until I calmed down. Then she left.

I was afraid of the other kids. I found it hard to play with them. One kid stole a toy I had picked out of the large toy chest. I remember that moment, but I don't recall how Miss Sykes had come over and comforted me.

I remember I broke Mom's large yellow mixing dish, which I had brought to school for the day we were going to make cookies. I cried and cried. I was terrified of what would happen when I told Mom I had broken her bowl. I refused to go home, and Miss Sykes had to call Mom to come and get me. When Mom got there, she told me, "Stop being such a crybaby."

Things got somewhat better when I started first grade and the kids all had to sit at their own desks. Learning to read came easy to me. I was very annoyed when the teacher gave another kid a ruler to hold under a line of text so he could read it. He then threw up all over the book and the whole class was stunned into silence. The kid was sent to the school nurse and a janitor came in, and cleaned up the puke.

Miss Rawlings was my favorite teacher. She was our second grade reading teacher, and we went to her room for class. Her hair was short in a sort of military cut that women didn't wear in those days. She always seemed to have a deep tan. This made her coral red lipstick stand out. She often wore clunky jewelry. I remember a necklace of large white chunks of stone, and her metal bracelets made noise. She wore print dresses with large leaves and flowers. She liked to laugh and found so many things funny. It was like she was the only person in on the joke.

Miss Rawlings had a roommate she always talked about. Her roommate had been in the first Peace Corps group to serve in Kenya. Our class was invited to a color slide show Miss Rawlings put together of her visit with her roommate and their travels together through East Africa.

I tried to make friends with a kid in my class named Randy. He was loud and always making funny remarks. Our teacher called him the class clown. That made him stand out. Mom had told me to make friends at school and stop relying on my cousins. I sometimes walked home with Randy. His house was two blocks over from mine.

I asked him to ask his mother if he could come over to my house to play. He said she said yes. So we played in the dirt side yard. Randy wanted to get up on the roof of the neighbor's garage. We found a ladder stored behind the row of garbage cans lined up along the side of the garage. Randy and I lifted it and tilted it toward the roof. Randy suddenly dropped the ladder and it fell into a window. The glass shattered, and Randy ran away.

The neighbor lady came out and yelled at me. Mom came out then and yelled at me too. I told them I didn't do it, to no avail. Mom paid our neighbor for the broken window out of her coin jar, where her cigarette and candy money came from.

I was pretty sore at Randy the next time I saw him. We headed home after school as usual. Then he called me a "sissy." What I remember most was my furious rage. I punched him and knocked him into the bushes next to the sidewalk. I kicked him and I cried. I ran home. I never spoke to Randy ever again.

I had been called "sissy" once before. I had never heard the word and didn't know what it meant. One day as I was walking home alone, two older boys, maybe 12, were suddenly there. Just there, as if out of nowhere. "Hey, show us your boner, kid!" one of them shouted. "I bet you don't even know what a boner is." (I knew what it was, but I didn't know the name for it.) "Aww, you're just a sissy," the other boy yelled. They pushed me into the bushes and ran off laughing.

I went home crying and told Mom what had happened. All she said was, "You're going to have a hard life."

Then I discovered a new interest. Grandma Newkirk gave me a postage stamp. It was a brand-new stamp the Post Office had just released, a blue-and-yellow Project Mercury stamp, the yellow space capsule against a blue deep space background, honoring John Glenn's orbit around the Earth. Our class had followed Glenn's flight on TV. This stamp was a Big Deal for me. Grandma Newkirk explained that the Post Office issued new commemorative stamps all the time. She would be sure to get one whenever a new one came out.

I asked Mom for the stamps on her mail. Uncle Dick brought home envelopes of mail he got at his office so I could have the stamps. Mom gave me money to buy five-cent and ten-cent packets of foreign stamps. I spread my treasures out on the living room rug, sorting them alphabetically and wondering about where stamps called Nippon, Suomi, or Shiqipëri came from, and daydreamed about far away and exotic places.

Then the outside world came crashing in. In 1962 everyone became very scared. I heard radio reports that something terrifying was happening in a place called Cuba. I had a few stamps from Cuba, so I knew it was a country. For some reason, I don't recall hearing any of this news on television. Something terrible was happening there, and it was all the fault of a guy named Fidel Castro. He was threatening to harm America. "Castro," I remember telling Mom, "is an evil man."

A few months later my dad's youngest brother Uncle Earl was killed in a fiery car crash. It made huge headlines in the Syracuse newspapers. All of us cousins knew Uncle Earl was home from the Marines. He must have been drunk. The papers reported he had dropped a girlfriend off and then drove his car into a tree. The papers played up the fact that he was trapped in the wreck, which caught fire. He burned to death. One newspaper reported that people heard him screaming, "Help me! I'm dying!" Funny how no one in the family ever mentioned what happened to Earl.

Only weeks later Mom got an unexpected phone call. I saw her answer the phone and from the way she was acting I knew something bad must have happened. She was sobbing on the phone. I prayed it wasn't Grandma Newkirk. But it was. She had suffered a burst aorta and died in the ambulance on her way to the hospital.

I was ten. I had believed life for everybody was just like my own.

3

And then Dad totaled the family car, a two-tone green 1958 Chevrolet Biscayne station wagon with its happy face grill and taillights, driving home drunk on a Friday evening. Dad was working full-time for the Army National Guard unit in Cortland, an hour's drive south of Syracuse. Dad stayed at the house of a buddy from the Guards, and came home for the weekend. Cortland County was full of family-owned dairy farms and had a few factories. Smith-Corona typewriters were made there.

On Fridays Mom made us supper, we watched some TV, and I was sent to bed by 8:00 PM. Dad got home after my younger sister Sylvia and I had fallen asleep. One Friday Dad didn't come home. The next morning Mom broke the news to us that Dad had been in a bad car accident. He was "okay"—he survived and was in the hospital in Cortland. The family car had been totaled. He had tried to pass a tractor trailer, failing to see the truck driver was signaling a left turn and had already started to make it. Dad broadsided the trailer. Only after Dad had been released from the hospital and was back home recuperating did I realize he had been drunk at the time.

I was more upset by Dad totaling the Chevy. I loved our car and all those other 1950s cars with chrome, tail fins, and the expressive faces of their front grillwork. Most of them appeared to be smiling, reflecting the optimism of the Fifties. Erie Boulevard East in Syracuse had been built up in the early postwar years for the burgeoning car culture. Everything was shiny and inviting to the mobilized shoppers. Driving down Erie Boulevard always filled me with visions of the exciting future just around the corner. I was captivated by *Here's Hollywood*, a TV show where movie and TV stars were interviewed in their homes in Los Angeles. The show opened with a drive down Hollywood Boulevard. I wanted to visit all those famous people living in the middle of where America's future had already begun.

Dad was bedridden for several weeks. His driver's license was suspended and we no longer had a car. Mom announced that we were going to move down to Cortland. When Dad was back on his feet and back to work, he also looked at a new place for us to live. I must have been oblivious to what this meant. Dad enticed us kids with the promise that we would have our own rooms. I shared a small bedroom with Sylvia in separate bunk beds. I was ten and getting to be too old to be sharing a bedroom with my sister.

My excitement over the impending move was dampened by my sadness at saying goodbye. On the last day of school, we met with our new teacher and classmates. Two of my cousins would be in the same class with me. I would miss my cousin David. We shook hands and said goodbye.

Mom told me Dad wanted me to go with him to Preble and get the house and yard ready for our move. We left early on a Saturday morning. Dad let me pick out a station on the radio. I was grateful for the music. I didn't have to sit through the silence of the hour ride.

It was a very strange day. It was the first time I ever spent any significant amount of time alone with my father. Except for giving me assignments, he didn't say a single word to me all day.

We moved to Preble because Dad was working at the Cortland National Guard Armory. He soon left that to take on a series of dead-end jobs. He was periodically unemployed. The worst time was when he was unemployed at Christmas and my parents borrowed money from Dad's parents to buy food. (I got so sick of eating fried spam.) Eventually, Dad landed a more secure job at Smith-Corona, the typewriter factory. He also went back to the Guard. This began his work routine for the rest of his employed life. He was at the factory all week. He came home and slept on the living room sofa. He was at the Guards all weekend. We never saw him. I was under the impression he was avoiding his family.

As I said, the earliest memory I have of music, recorded music, not the lullabies and children's songs I sang at school, was Patsy Cline singing "You Belong to Me" (I imagined myself among the pyramids along the Nile), "She's Got You" (I noted the things young lovers shared with each other), and "Sweet Dreams." The lush opening strains of violins in cascading glissando pulled me into a world of longing and loss.

These sounds resonated in my soul. The melodies were laden with bittersweet melancholia, anticipating either the betrayal of dreams of love or the failure of love to ever come true. The songs that I lost myself in were the Phil Specter "Wall of Sound" songs, emotional and honest, about teenage love—dreamed for, thwarted, mourned, or shattered. Lesley Gore wailed over teen heartbreak. "It's My Party" recounted her birthday party where her boyfriend Johnny has left the party, and her girlfriend July has also disappeared. They returned with Judy wearing Johnny's ring. In "Judy's Turn to Cry," Lesley Gore rejoiced in her revenge when Johnny leaves Judy to come back to her. The Chiffons paid tribute to the "designing women" Mom kept warning me about. In "He's So Fine," the Chiffons assured the listener how she will one day make the man she has targeted her boyfriend. In "One Fine Day," the Chiffons confidently announced how the man she has targeted will become hers. With the Ronettes' "Be My Baby," my own feelings were most clearly articulated. I longed for a certain someone (I didn't know who) I hoped would come, feared would not come, who would probably break my heart. My unfulfillable longing was filled nostalgia for a love I had not yet lost, the deep sorrow of a heart that had not yet been broken, an anticipated struggle for the life ahead of me that I could not yet see. I lost myself in this fantasy world, where love meant pain—Bobby Vinton cried out "Lonely." Gary Puckett bemoaned the fear of betrayal in "Woman, Woman." Even in old age I still cry when I hear Andy Williams sing "Moon River," describing an ideal love, "two drifters off to see the world/there's such a lot of world to see." The achingly sad melody belied the hope.

As "Moon River" finished, Dad pulled into the driveway of the empty house. Its cedar slats, stained green, were weather-worn. White paint was peeling off the window frames. The two-story box-shaped house, built before the Civil War, had a flat roof. While the flat roof was cheaper to build, it was a bad choice given the heavy rainfall and many feet of snow that falls in upstate New York. The house looked south, facing into the strong winds that frequently blew up the valley in the winter. The property stood on a quarter-acre of land. A two-story barn behind the house served as the garage, and our landlord used the second-floor space to store hay. A dilapidated chicken coop was behind the barn. The grass had obviously not been mown once that summer. The country air was rich with the smells of summer in the country—freshly mown hay, fresh cow manure spread on the fields, air free from city pollution.

"You mow the lawn," Dad ordered me as we got out of the car. "I'm going to start cleaning out the barn." I got the gas can out of the trunk and went to the barn, where his dad had stored a lawn mower he had bought at the Montgomery Ward store on Main Street in Cortland. I wheeled it out into the dirt driveway and pulled the starter cord. After several yanks it sputtered into life. I began mowing along the circumference of the yard, in ever smaller concentric circles. Meanwhile, Dad had disappeared into the house.

When the sun was high overhead, Dad drove up Preble Road to the general store at the four corners where Preble Road crossed Route 281. He bought thinly sliced bologna and American cheese, a loaf of Wonder bread, and half a dozen bottles of Hire's root beer for our lunch. We made ourselves sandwiches and sat in the shade of the wrap-around porch and ate in silence.

We moved into the country house in late August. I stayed in my bedroom reading comic books, enjoying my first brush of privacy. After a week of this, Mom shouted up the stairs at me, "Go out and play. There are kids down the road. Why don't you go out and introduce yourself? They won't bite you."

4

Caving in to Mom's pressure to socialize with our new neighbor kids on one late August morning I stepped out into the summer heat. I walked up Preble Road. About a half a mile up I saw a girl about my own age playing in her front yard.

"Can I play with you?" I asked.

"Where are you from?" she replied, ignoring my question.

"Syracuse."

"My daddy's a truck driver." She ignored my answer.

"My dad is a soldier in the Army," I volunteered. "If you want, we can play in our barn."

We started walking back up the road to my house. The girl followed in silence.

When we got to my house, I led the girl to the barn out back and we went up the stairs along the back wall. The sweet smell of the newly baled hay had already dissipated—filled with now old, dry hay. It was hot and stuffy in the loft. We climbed up on a cross timber above the hay, which was several bales deep.

"Jump!" the girl said. "Watch out for the hay bugs. They bite!"

"Are they dangerous?" I asked, alarmed.

"No, silly," she laughed. "I was just fooling. There are no hay bugs. Boy, you city people sure are stupid."

Then she jumped into a pile of loose hay. I jumped behind her. We jumped several times, rolling down through the loose hay, laughing. I really enjoyed this new game. It reminded me of jumping off trees with my cousin David.

"I gotta go home now," the girl announced.

"What's your name?" I called after her.

"Sally."

The next morning, I pedaled my bike down to the Tioughnioga River, which was a shallow creek when it flowed through Preble. An old house stood beside the creek. The white paint was peeling off the walls. It had a screen-in walk-in porch. There was an old-fashioned doorbell, the kind you ring by turning the brass key. A boy lived there with his mother. I twisted the doorbell key. A middle-aged woman, her dirty blond hair gathered and tied behind her head, came to the door.

"Hello," I said. "My mom said your son collects stamps and I should meet him. Is he at home?"

The woman remained behind the screen door. "Who are you?" she asked.

"We're the new family here. I live up the road in the Knapp house."

"Royce isn't home right now. Come back tomorrow."

I came back the next evening after supper, and Royce was home. He was in his early teens. He was sitting at a table in front of the TV, pouring over some stamps. "Are you the new neighbor boy?" Royce asked.

"Yes, my name is Les."

"You like stamps?" Royce asked.

"Yeah, I collect them too."

"Sit here next to me and we'll look at them together. You can have some of my duplicates."

The living room was dark and musty. Knickknacks cluttered every shelf and yellowed lace doilies lay atop the living room chairs and sofa. The color TV set chattered to itself. My mom did not believe in color TV. *The Wild Wild West* was on when I sat down. I loved the show. The main character James West, played by Robert Conrad, was handsome, wore very tight pants, and had a hairy chest. The writers contrived scenarios requiring Conrad to appear barechested as often as possible.

Royce went through his stamp stock books, lifting various duplicates out with a pair of tongs. He worked away in silence, placing the stamps into little clear glassine envelopes, separating them by country. When Royce had finished going through his duplicates, his mother put out a bowl of potato chips and lemonade for us. *The Wild Wild West* ended, and I thanked Royce and his mother for everything. I headed home in the dark.

I never saw Royce or Sally again.

I found my summer days long and increasingly lonely. I rode my bike to the hill on the east side of Preble and spent days alone playing in the woods on the hillside. I chose a spot halfway up the hill where I created a "fort" for myself. I cleared the leaves away in several spaces and pretended they were rooms in the fort. Then I would take my clothes off and hike through the woods.

On other days I rode up to the general store to buy Mom candy bars and cigarettes and for myself penny candy and comic books. The county library sent a bookmobile to Preble once a week. I checked out mostly science fiction novels. Robert Heinlein quickly became my favorite author.

I started with *Citizen of the Galaxy*. The story opens with a young, strong-headed slave, who is sold at auction to Baslim, a disabled man. Baslim educates the boy and has him run secret missions. Thorby eventually learns Baslim is involved in a secret society fighting to end slavery throughout the galaxy. Thorby becomes ever more entangled, and Heinlein introduces challenging cultural questions. Like a good fairy tale, Thorby also learns of his actual identity and the great things that call upon him to do for the good of the galaxy. I fantasized that I too had real parents and I would be rescued from the Wright clan.

Heinlein's narrative presence, the way he took me, the reader, into his confidence and trusted me to let my assumptions about my culture be challenged, endeared him to me. I was open to the challenge of being forced to rethink so much and raced through one novel after another. I read all his juvenile novels and then moved on to *Stranger in a Strange Land*. (Both of these books were inspired by Rudyard Kipling's books.)

In *Stranger*, an Earthling is born on Mars and raised by Martians. As an adult Michael Valentine Smith is brought back to Earth, and the reader sees Earth culture through the alien's eyes as he learns about human culture. Through this outsider Heinlein introduces the ideas of free love (physical and emotional), non-monogamous marriage, and nudism, challenging body taboos all the while. Heinlein sends up organized religion, while stressing the importance of individual liberty and self-reliance. By speaking Martian, Smith can do what looks like magic to Earthlings. Heinlein's point is to show how language itself shapes reality. I adopted the verb "to grok."

Heinlein challenged the reader's assumptions over and over. At one point, Jubel Harshaw, Smith's iconoclastic mentor, points to a statue of an old woman and says she is beautiful. When asked why, he explained that he saw the young woman still inside that old body. The legal system employs people who are called "the Witness," whose role is to witness what is actually seen and lay bare the personal and cultural assumptions being read into the situation.

Showing how the social outsider Smith is able to rise above society's tendency to repress nonconformist thought set a great example for me how to think for myself and persist in the face of social deterrence. Reading through a dictionary of foreign terms used in English, I came across Socrates' phrase "know thyself." It triggered an epiphany in me and I seized upon it, writing it in large letters on my notebook. My history teacher spotted it and asked me what it meant. His only comment was, "You're going to have an interesting life."

Other juvenile novels spoke to me deeply. In Madeline L'Engle's *A Wrinkle in Time* a magic door in my own backyard in the country could lead me into other-worldly adventures and be guided by my own Mrs. Whatsit, Mrs. Who, and Mrs. Which. I found myself drawn to mentors who would help me grow the way my teachers, but not my parents, did. In Richard Matheson's *I Am Legend*, Earth's people all turn into zombies and a single man survives, fighting them. I read this as an allegory for what it's like to be a homosexual in a heterosexual world. Scott O'Dell's *Island of the Blue Dolphins* recounted the real life story of a young girl who was accidentally left behind when her tribe relocated to another Pacific island. I followed how she recreated the world of the adults and survived all alone for many years until missionaries found her. I became absorbed by science fiction novels about nuclear holocaust, a very real fear in the 1950s and 1960s, and was instructed in how to survive in total solitude as the last man on Earth. I did not realize I was learning how to be a survivor.

One day when I was returning to my homeroom after gym class, an unexpected announcement came over the speaker of our school's PA system. President Kennedy had just been shot. We were all stunned. I went home and went to bed with a pounding headache that lasted for a week.

5

The Labor Day weekend could not come soon enough. With the start of school, my summer of solitude came to an end. Homer Central High School was a half-hour bus ride away. Our house was the first stop and I sat in the front seat where I could see everyone who got on the bus. From kindergarteners to seniors Preble had a couple of kids in each class year.

I looked forward to school every day. I liked learning and enjoyed most of my classes—English, history, math, and German especially. Most of the teachers seemed to love their subject matter and teaching. I was placed in the Regents classes, which concluded with New York State Regents exams for college-bound students. Many of my classes were for the college-bound and I became a member of the social circles that grew out of this daily familiarity. I ate lunch with these friends.

We had one daily period of study hall, where I usually completed my homework, and a free ninth period, when student clubs met. I joined both the chorus and the band. Both used ninth period for rehearsal. All of us students loved our music teacher and chorus director Mr. Byrd. He was passionate about music and seemed to connect directly with every student in his classes. He was short and slender and hunchbacked, something his impeccable suits could not hide. He sometimes told us stories of his girlfriend in far-off Scotland.

I joined the band because I played the French horn. Mr. Caputo had started me out on the cornet but had me switch to the French horn. This was how he populated the band with needed instruments. Back in East

Syracuse Mom talked me into taking piano lessons. Grandma Wright had an upright piano I could practice on. This lasted two lessons before Mom realized they could not afford my private lessons. She had coaxed me to learn the cornet when I was in elementary school. I hated having to stay inside and practice. After several of my crying fits, she let me give up. When Mom took us kids to see *The Music Man,* I was so excited by the spectacle of the shiny, jubilant marching band at the end of the film that I begged Mom to let me take cornet lessons again. She and I loved Herb Alpert, and she encouraged me to aim for proficiency on the trumpet. Once I could read music, I tried to teach myself how to play it. Using sheet music for the Hammond chord organ Mom once owned, I slowly and choppily worked my way through songs like "Ghost Riders in the Sky," "Les Feuillies Mortes," and "Sometime I Feel Like a Motherless Child," a sad, soulful tune that spoke to me.

Several high school teachers stand out in my memory now. Looking back, I realized that Mr. Byrd had been a closeted homosexual. My history teacher Mr. Hubbard had also been gay. One day he simply disappeared from the classroom and school officials never said a word about him or his disappearance. He was simply erased. Years later, I learned that he had written a love note to another male teacher.

My strongest subject was math. I always got A+. I assumed I would major in math at college, even though I had no idea what I would do with a degree in math. (In the 1960s few people knew that computer science would be the future.) Mr. Shattuck, my geometry teacher, put an end to that vision. Rather than concentrating on his teaching, he used our class period to talk sports with the jocks and flirt with the girls. (He was eventually let go for getting a 15-year-old girl pregnant.)

My classmates called our world history teacher Mrs. Adams "Screaming Jean." I, however, loved her. Although the course was taught for the Regents exam, which emphasized people, places, and dates (which she made sure we memorized), she went into some detail into what these events meant, why they had happened, and what she hoped we would take away from that. Her husband had been a Hitler Youth in World War II, which she talked about freely—not out of any Nazi sympathizing, but rather because it was something he was forced to do against his will. As was the law in New York State in those days, she showed us documentaries on the Nazis' Final Solution and its concentration camps as well as the bombing of Hiroshima and Nagasaki and the nuclear arms race between the US and the USSR. (I became fascinated with the Soviet Union and wanted to study something that was so other, so alien to me.) I can still remember her drawing a circle on the blackboard to explain the range of political tendencies. She placed democracy at the top. The ring around the right led to fascism. The ring around the left led to communism. As she pointed out, the most extreme ends merged—the ultra-radical right and ultra-radical left became the same.

A foreign language was required for Regents students. Homer High offered Latin, French, and German. I chose German because of my family's German heritage. My great grandfather, Mom's mother's father, Karl Heckbarth, had been an immigrant. He had fled Germany to escape being conscripted into the Kaiser's army at the start of World War I. All the Heckbarth descendants owned a photo of a small castle in East Pomerania, which was claimed to have belonged to the Heckbarths. Karl had been a stowaway and arrived penniless in America. (Many years later, when Uncle Deforest did a family genealogy, it turned out our minor royal had in fact been a stableboy for the actual Count.)

My German teacher Frau Klemperer was from Germany. She and her husband had grown up during the turbulent 1920s. As Dickens would say, it was the best of times, it was the worst of times. Frau Klemperer told of how out of control inflation was that it took a wheelbarrow full of paper money to buy a loaf bread. By the next day that might not be enough money. She talked, rather vaguely, about the exciting nightlife. Berlin never slept. People were very free. I got a taste for something special. Weimar Berlin spoke to me directly. (Not until college days would I learn how wide-open Berlin had been, a city of social and sexual experimentation. Openly homosexual men and women had their own clubs and bars. People were so poor that, among other things, young working-class men sold themselves for sex to other men.)

Frau Klemperer and her husband were university students in Berlin when Hitler came to power in 1933. They knew that was the end of the Weimar Republic so they emigrated to the United States. Her husband became a doctor. He had two brothers who became famous—Otto Klemperer became an orchestra conductor and composer, and Werner became an actor and played Colonel Klink in *Hogan's Heroes*, an American sitcom that satirized Nazi Germany. The Klemperer family was so appalled that Werner, a German Jew who fought on the American side, would play a Nazi for laughs that they disowned him. She told us she refused to ever step foot in Germany again.

German grammar fascinated me. It seemed like a sort of mathematical system—declensions, conjugations, sentence structure, all followed their own sets of rules. But words said so much more than numbers. Vocabulary fascinated me. At first it was like learning a secret code. As I progressed, I learned more and more words that did not have direct English equivalents. I began to get snatches of insight into seeing how words shaped my perceptions. I got glimpses of how Germans saw the world through a different lens.

Frau Klemperer taught units on German history, culture, and literature. I was hooked on the travel films. They highlighted beautiful landscapes, quaint villages, famous landmarks, and German customs. The film portraying German Christmas customs, the history of "*Stille Nacht*" (silent night) and "*O Tannenbaum,*" and the Christkindlmarkt (Christmas Market) in Nuremburg cemented my desire to live in Germany. Frau Klemperer tutored me in third-year German while taking second-year German in school. She also encouraged me to go to West Germany as an exchange student.

The devastation wrought by World War II and the massive rebuilding efforts across West Germany were left out of our education. We were living in the midst of the Cold War, so a lot of that information was common knowledge. We did see a short film documenting the 1948-49 Berlin Airlift, *die Luftbrücke,* at the start of the Cold War. Frau Klemperer also related how when President Kennedy went to Berlin and said, "*Ich bin ein Berliner,*" Germans repressed a snicker, since what he actually said was, "I am a jelly donut." (Frau Klemperer cited this also as a lesson in German grammar.)

Mrs. Perfetti, our English teacher, asked our class one day if any of us had ever been to New York City. We all answered no. "Well, then," she said, "We are going to New York." And so the whole Regents English class went to Manhattan for a weekend. I stayed in a hotel room for the first time. I shared my room with Jim Owens, who would grow up to become a preacher. His mother was the school librarian who directed me to many great books and other Heinlein novels. I spent a Saturday on the Owens' chicken farm; Jim had asked me to bring the record of my favorite trumpet music. (He played cornet in the school band.) I brought one of Mom's Herb Alpert records, excited to share it with Jim. He played a recording of Baroque trumpet music. I was embarrassed by my poor taste in pop music and ignorance of classical music. I was ashamed that I was such a country bumpkin.

In New York I ate in an automat for the first time. We went to Mama Leone's for dinner. We climbed to the top of the Statue of Liberty. The real treat was seeing the original Broadway run of *Mame*, with Angela Lansbury playing Mame, at the Winter Garden Theater. I had seen the film of *Auntie Mame* with the wonderful performance by Rosalind Russell. I had seen it several times on TV. I fell in love with Mame and wished I could have an aunt just like her. "Your Auntie Mame, Patrick, will open doors for you, doors you never ever dreamed existed." I longed for someone so fabulous to introduce such wonderfully eccentric people and open some of those doors for me too.

In similar ways I was captivated by *The Wizard of Oz* and *The King and I.* Judy Garland sang "Over the Rainbow," which expressed my own longing to escape my family and Preble. I wanted to land up in a phantasmagorical place like Oz. Once I got there, I would be so happy to stay. Dorothy could keep her dreary, depressing, black-and-white Kansas. I also dreamed of being like Anna in *The King and I*, invited to be a teacher and live in a king's palace.

Learning German gave me strange dreams. I was often plagued by insomnia with German verb conjugations going around and around in my unsleeping mind. In one recurrent dream I found myself on a six-lane highway driving across a bridge. The bridge was very high over a body of water, which seemed to be a large lake or a bay. Traffic was thick, fast, and dangerous as if it were rush hour. I felt both excited and terrified—excitement because I felt I was going somewhere important, and terror because I felt certain I would be killed behind the wheel.

In another dream I found myself in a maze in a warehouse, much like the one I had seen in *The Three-Penny Opera*, having sex with Bobby Darin. I thought Bobby Darin singing "Mack the Knife" was the coolest thing, the hottest thing I had ever seen. I woke from this dream to find my groin covered in cum. This was my first wet dream.

In a third dream I found myself in an apartment. It is dark in the apartment. I am looking through a floor-to-ceiling high bookcase with no back. I can see through it to the apartment door. It is evening. I have a sense of immense well-being. I am anticipating the arrival of a man. The knowledge of this man's arrival fills me with a sense of safety and warmth.

In the most intensive repeating dream, Dad surprises me by bringing the soldiers under him in his platoon to our house in Preble. At my request they are all naked. I am suddenly naked too. I join in with them, feeling my flesh hot and rubbing against other men. I am grabbing cocks and stroking them. I then woke up to find my crotch wet from my own cum.

LES K. WRIGHT

6

"My ears are frostbitten!" I had just walked into the meeting room in the back of the Preble fire station. It was January and it had been snowing lightly all day. If the snow had been bad enough, I was going to cancel going to the Boy Scout meeting. As it was, the bitter cold should have kept me home. Everyone in the room looked up at me momentarily and went back to what they had been doing.

The heat was on full blast and the meeting room felt cozy. Three boys about my age were talking. A wiry, hairy man with bushy eyebrows in his mid-30s told them, "It's time. Let's get the meeting going." One boy set up two flags. Two more boys came from outdoors.

The man waved me to come over and join them.

I went and stood beside a blond-haired boy wearing glasses. "Hi," he said. "Are you the new boy from Syracuse?"

I replied in the affirmative.

"My name is Tom." He smiled, revealing deep dimples.

"I'm Les."

At 7 p.m., the meeting began with a formal flag ceremony led by the scoutmasters. The boys recited the Pledge of Allegiance, the Scout Oath, and the Scout Law: "A Scout is trustworthy, loyal, helpful, friendly ..." Then Tom collected money for summer camp. "We save up to go to Boy Scout camp," he explained to me. He told me the names of the other boys as well as the scoutmaster, Jude Curry.

Then Jude came over and told me more about the scout troop. They discussed an upcoming camping trip. I couldn't imagine pitching a tent on the snow and sleeping in it.

I continued to observe and passed on the camping trip. I went to the meeting every week. Over several weeks I got to know Tom. We both went to school in Homer. We were on different school bus routes, which was why we had never met before. We were in the same year, but in different classes. When I found out Tom was also a stamp collector, I invited him to my house to look at my collection.

By now it was early March and on warm days that melted some of the snow, the stench of cabbage rotting in the fields filled the air in Preble. Tom showed up at my house after lunch. We went up to my bedroom. Dad was in Cortland at the armory as usual. Mom was visiting her friend Kathleen Ouellette and had brought Sylvia with her.

I closed my bedroom door and pulled a stamp album off a shelf. After Tom leafed through it, I showed him my comic book collection. I didn't know what possessed me, but I asked Tom to lie down on my bed. "Can I pump you?" I asked him.

"What do you mean?" he asked.

I explained how it was done. "My cousin Ted taught me."

We took our clothes off. I saw the hair around Tom's very large cock was blond. I sucked on his cock until it got hard and began stroking it. I didn't know a cock could be that big.

"Let me do you," Tom said, reaching for my already hard cock.

Tom said, "Pump harder." He spit on his own cock and I stroked him harder until he came. He wiped his cum into his hand and stroked me until I came.

We started getting together nearly every weekend. Whatever our activity, it usually included playing with each other's cocks. When summer came, I took Tom to my fort in the woods. We'd strip and walk to the top of the hill, which was a large meadow—an old cow pasture that had been abandoned. We chased each other under the warmth of the summer sun. We rolled around in the grass. We always ended up sucking each other off.

We both found other boys to play with.

Tom started inviting me over to his house, where we listened to pop songs on the radio and had tickle fights. He invited me to Saturday night sleepovers. We watched TV in his bedroom. One evening, when his older stepbrother was visiting, he stuck his head in Tom's bedroom and said, "What are you faggots doing?"

"Watching TV," Tom said, "Get lost."

We spent more and more time together. Tom and I became best friends.

***

Mom's habit of sending me out to buy her candy and soda continued when we moved to Preble. Now it was a mile ride away to Don Wright's store—a combination of corner market, gas station, and motel along Route 281. It also had the only public pay phone booth. I was always careful to get what she specified, no substitutions. I bought myself a comic or two. These comics were cheap, having been remaindered with their front cover torn off.

Mom had gradually put on weight over the years. Us kids were brought up on a lot of sugar, too—cookies, cakes, candy, soda. I don't recall her dieting, though I remember her frequently weighing herself on the bathroom scale.

She had let Sylvia and me adopt a kitten each from the Wright farm down the road from us. I named mine, a female, Blackie. Blackie got pregnant on a regular basis. Mom made me give her away. My math teacher took her. It wasn't long before he complained that Blackie was pregnant when I gave her away.

Mom threw her back out one morning when she bent over to pick a kitten up. She couldn't stand up and called out to me to help her stand upright. By then she had become very fat indeed, which today would be called morbidly obese. She took to her bed. She would spend weeks at a time bed-ridden and described herself as a "semi-invalid." I took on housecleaning, vacuuming, washing dishes, tending her vegetable garden. I helped her with her bedpan. Sylvia must have started helping out at this time too.

It was during this period that my furtive sex with Dad began. He always pretended to be sleeping, and I believed he actually was. This went on intermittently for a few years. For me the thrill of danger from this furtive, illicit act was intoxicating, perhaps more than the actual sex act. I don't know for sure what unconscious drives drew me into this sexual danger. My father never expressed any love for me, which was typical of men of his generation. But he never even acknowledged me, except when I made a mistake, trying to do something he had ordered me to do and which I had never been taught how to do. He was quick to anger and criticized me. Although he never acknowledged our sex play, over time I realized that he welcomed it very much. Pretending to be asleep while I was sucking him off or, later, while he was sucking me off, was pretense to keep me coming back. I fancied he loved me and would imagine how years later we would talk about these private good times.

I attempted to repeat this act with Dad's best friend, Will Davis. I babysat Will and Sonia Davis's kids one New Year's Eve. The next morning, I peered into Will and Sonia's bedroom and saw Will, naked and uncovered.

I approached him and began to touch his cock. Will woke up, terrifying me. I didn't know what he would do. He whispered to me, "Go ahead and suck it. I know you want to." Then he pulled me up to his face and sucked my cock. I never noticed that Pat never woke up.

Will drove me home. On that ride I begged him not to tell my father. He said, "Why would I do that?" After that, whenever Will came to visit my parents, he would come upstairs to go to the bathroom. He would step into my bedroom and have sex with me behind closed doors. This continued until I was 17.

7

I liked to stay up late. Mom accused me of not wanting to miss anything. I read voraciously and often read two or three books at a time. I read through a set of encyclopedia books Mom was buying at the local Grand Union as each new volume came out. I joined the student book club at school. I read all the travel books, full of photos, at the school library. I studied atlases. I dreamed of seeing other countries and wanted to learn as many foreign languages as I could.

In a Sunday *Parade* magazine, I read an article about pen pals, which included contact information for a free pen pal service. I wrote to the pen pal service. They sent me a short questionnaire asking about my interests, my age, my sex, and my hobbies. They sent me the profiles and addresses of three people the same age as me. One was a Boy Scout in Malaysia, one was a girl in Tokyo whose father managed a small shopping center, and one was a boy whose family owned a sheep farm in Queensland, Australia. We wrote each other informative letters about ourselves, our home life, what living in our country was like. Ahmed and I wrote about the Boy Scouts, and we traded stamps. Suzuki and I traded stamps too. She sometimes sent photos. Once she sent me a souvenir from the Osaka World's Fair.

My correspondence with the Australian farm boy, Keith Wallace, was different. We wrote very long letters. We wrote in detail about ourselves, not just what we were doing but our hopes and dreams, our fears. Our handwritten letters sometimes ran to twenty pages. We seemed to be kindred spirits, growing up in rural isolation and longing to see the world.

Keith told me we were "mates"—loyal friends—and that was an important relationship in Australia.

I contacted the pen pal service several more times asking for more pen pals. Many of my new pen pals only wrote a few times. Four of them developed into regular correspondents. Pinsiri went to a boarding school in Ceylon. He once wrote to me of a scandal at his all-boys boarding school. Several boys were discovered having sex with each other. Robert lived in Bulawayo, Rhodesia, and his father was a bank executive. Jürgen lived in Dresden, East Germany and was a stamp collector. Norbert, who lived in Karl-Marx-Stadt, East Germany, read a lot of philosophy.

Later my German teacher Frau Klemperer invited us first-year German students to get a pen pal in West Germany. I jumped at the chance to correspond with someone I could practice my German on. I was connected to two more pen pals—one in Lübeck and one in Burgsteinfurt, near Münster. Werner in Lübeck was also a stamp collector. Alex in Burgsteinfurt played trumpet in his high school band. Max asked me if I would write to a classmate of his, Angelika, and I happily agreed. I practiced my rudimentary German with them. I fantasized about traveling to West Germany one day to meet them.

Frau Klemperer was in her mid-50s. She had long silver hair gathered in a bun. Her glasses had a chain attached to them, and they often rested on her bosom. She began every class with a melodious *"Guten Morgen,"* in what I would eventually learn was a Berlin accent. She enunciated clearly and spoke slowly, necessary for us beginning students, who would otherwise be unable to distinguish individual words. She would model every new vocabulary word, then command us "Alle *zusammen!"* to repeat it. Most of my classmates made no effort to imitate German sounds accurately. They simply kept the umlaut out of ö or ü, substituting the English "o" and "u." She rolled the "r" in the back of her throat (High German). They could not do this. She encouraged them to roll it on the tip of the tongue, as practiced in Austria and Bavaria. (The English "r" is a half vowel that exists only in English. Germans have an even harder time learning this.) Some of my classmates cracked up whenever they heard *womit* ("with what") and *damit* ("with that"), which sounded like "vomit" and "dammit." This irritated me to no end. It seemed childish and I felt frustrated by my classmates' apparent unwillingness to take language learning seriously.

Starting in second-year German classes Frau Klemperer emphasized culture. We learned about the regions and cities of West Germany, how each had a separate and distinct history and culture. She taught the highlights of German history, from the Middle Ages to post-war West Germany. We began to learn about important authors and read short excerpts, including Thomas Mann (then very popular in the US), Herman Hesse, Berthold Brecht, and Rilke. Our class read the entire play, *Aufstieg und Fall der Stadt Mahagonny* (*Rise and Fall of the City Mahagonny*) and learned about the music of Kurt Weill.

Frau Klemperer delved deepest into the life and writings of Franz Kafka, a German-speaking Jew who had lived in Prague. We read his short short story "Before the Law." The story stayed with me. I carry the image of the man at the door to this day, haunted by it.

Before the Law

A doorkeeper stands before the Law. A man from the country comes to the doorkeeper and makes a request for admission to the Law. However, the doorkeeper tells him that he may not grant him entry to the Law at this time. The man thinks about this and then asks whether he might be permitted entry at a later time. "That is possible," says the doorkeeper, "but not now …" Since the door to the Law is standing open, as ever, and the doorkeeper has stepped aside, the man bends to look through the gate into the interior. When the doorkeeper sees this he laughs and says, "If you find that so intriguing, try to enter despite my forbidding it. But take note: I am powerful. I am only the lowest doorkeeper. There are doorkeepers, room after room, one more powerful than the other. The mere look of the third one is unbearable to me." The man from the country had not expected such difficulties; the Law should be accessible to everyone, he thinks, yet now as he looks more closely at the doorkeeper's fur coat, his big, pointy nose, his long, thin, black Tartar beard, he decides it is better to wait until he gets permission to enter. The doorkeeper gives him a stool and lets him sit to the side of the door. He sits there for days and years. He makes many attempts to gain entry and exhausts the doorkeeper with his pleas. The doorkeeper interrogates him periodically, asking him all about where he was from and many other questions, but these are always indifferent questions, such as how great men are made; in the end he always tells him that he still could not be granted entry. The man, who had thoroughly equipped himself for his trip, has used everything he hoped would be useful to blackmail the doorkeeper. The doorkeeper accepted them all, but says, "I accept these things just so you won't think you have missed anything." Over the years the man continues to observe the doorkeeper steadily. He forgets the other doorkeepers over time and this first one seems to be his only hurdle blocking his entry to the Law. In the early years he curses the unfortunate coincidence long and loud, and later, when he has grown old, he would just hum to himself. He would become childish, and over the course of studying the doorkeeper for years, he even recognizes the fleas in the doorkeeper's collar and asks the fleas to help him change the doorkeeper's mind. His eyesight finally grows weak, and he does not know whether it has grown dark around him or if his eyes are deceiving him. Still, in this darkness he sees a steady light shining from the door of the Law. He is not much longer for this world. As his death approaches, all his experiences of this time come together in his mind into a question, which he has never asked the doorkeeper. He waves him over since he can no longer lift his body. The doorkeeper has to bend down very far as the difference in size has changed very unfavorably to the man. "What else do you want to know?" the doorkeeper asks. "You are insatiable ..." "Everyone seeks the Law," the man says, "so how is it that in all these years nobody but me has sought entry?" The doorkeeper realizes he has come to his end, and in order to reach his fading hearing, shouts at him, "No one else could have been given entry here since this entrance was meant only for you. I am going now and closing it."

[Translation by the author]

LES K. WRIGHT

8

Everyone knows the 1960s was a decade of profound social change. Thanks to newspapers, television, popular music, and the movies, its effects seeped into the very fabric of American society. Even rural corners like Preble, New York were not immune. Daily news from the war in Viet Nam was part of the background noise. The assassinations of JFK, Robert F. Kennedy, and Martin Luther King shocked everyone. Czechoslovakia was invaded by the Soviet Union. No one in Preble had heard of the Summer of Love in San Francisco and most were distantly aware of the Woodstock rock concert which took place some 150 miles away on the other side of the Catskills.

Rock and folk music, with an increasingly political bent, ruled the airwaves. Pop songs now carried more serious messages than teen heartbreak. Protest songs energized youth rebellion. When protesters grew their hair long, America's youth did too. Bell bottom jeans, love beads, and Lord Boards became the uniform. Musicians smoked pot and experimented with other drugs. Timothy Leary famously proclaimed, "Turn on, tune on, drop out." We were invited to reject the straight, square world and enter the new counterculture. "Let your freak flag fly." It was a leap in human consciousness. Mahatma Gandhi, Malcolm X, Che Guevara, and Mother Teresa were leaders in this revolution in consciousness.

This new world was far away from mine. The night of the first moon landing I was babysitting a neighbor kid. While watching Neil Armstrong step onto the moon, I heard noises in the back of the house. I found the kid walking in his sleep and peeing on the bathroom door.

Mom forbade me from growing my hair long. My school banned blue jeans and sandals. I was told not to do drugs. I was told I would be judged by the company I kept. Aunt Mona warned me never to ride a motorcycle. She took me to the state fair one year where we saw The Cowsills and Up with People perform. "These are clean cut, decent people. You can be like them," she said.

At school some kids grew their hair long. Mom cut my hair, so I never had the option. Some kids smoked grass. A neighbor down the road from us in Preble came home from Viet Nam a heroin addict. Every summer there were riots in the black ghettoes across America. Whenever Mom drove us up to Mona and Dick's, we had to drive through the South Side of Syracuse, the nearest black ghetto. Mom always ordered us to lock our car doors.

I continued to listen to songs with a powerful emotional punch, like "The Impossible Dream" from *The Man of La Mancha*. Vikki Carr acted out "Let It Be Him" in a TV performance, sitting by her phone waiting for it to ring. I empathized, waiting for a phone call I would also never get.

I became very self-conscious, and I sometimes felt unsafe in the world. For Halloween when I was 14, I went to my first costume party. On a goof, I dressed up in an old maroon brocade dress from Mom's pile of discarded clothes, which were intended for the Salvation Army. I loved the color. I found a white beaded purse and a pair of scuffed high heels. Mom had not worn high heels in years due to her weight. I put on the dress and some old costume jewelry, and carrying the heels, walked the mile up Preble Road to the fire station in the brisk October night air.

There were a lot of people I didn't recognize, or even know, at the party. Almost immediately, a local young farmer in jeans and rubber boots came up to me and began flirting with me, calling me pretty. He scared me—he came on really strong. I couldn't tell if the teen was teasing me or was seriously coming on to me. I thought the guy was attractive, but his public come-on unnerved me. I turned red, suddenly realizing the village folks saw me as a fairy, though no one had ever said so to my face.

The next day Mom asked me if I enjoyed wearing dresses. I felt I was being caught in a trap. I deflected her question, answering, "No. I just thought it was funny." Another time, when I was alone with Mom in the car, she asked me out of the blue what I thought about homosexuals. I panicked, realizing she was trying to find out about my sexuality. "I think they are people too and should be allowed to live their lives as they choose."

I looked up "homosexuality" in the family Funk & Wagnalls encyclopedia. The entry was filled with terminology unfamiliar to me. It stated with authority that "homosexuality" is a mental illness, and a bad one. This was an early step for me in trying to put a name to what I did with Tom, struggling to reconcile the sex play that I took such joy in with this horrid fact that I was mentally ill.

I watched a CBS TV documentary called *The Homosexuals*. Mike Wallace, a widely respected and authoritative voice in journalism, painted a very bleak portrait. (Network news was understood to be the objective truth, so I had no reason to think otherwise.) Wallace told the American viewing public that homosexuals live unhappy, furtive lives in the shadowy underworld of fellow homosexuals. He reported the results of a recent poll that revealed that most Americans considered homosexuality to be more harmful than adultery, abortion, or prostitution. A homosexual man who was interviewed was married and had children asserted that homosexual men suffer from narcissism and therefore are incapable of forming a stable, loving long-term relationship.

Neither I nor any of the boys I played with were anything like the homosexuals who appeared in the CBS documentary. I thought there must be other kinds of homosexuals. I thought they might be like Dad and Will Davis. Maybe they were like that guy who had chosen to marry and have children.

9

When I was 14, Mom sent me to classes to prepare for my first confirmation at Grace Episcopal Church in downtown Cortland. The Greyhound bus came down Preble Road on its route from Syracuse to Cortland. To get to Cortland I flagged it down. I enjoyed my classes on the history and rituals of the Episcopal Church. Father Larkin was a good teacher. Somewhere in this schooling the message was transmitted that homosexuality was a sin, an unforgivable sin. (Many years later as a seminarian I would read Peter Damian's *Book of Gomorrah*, which the professor singled out for creating the doctrine that the sin of sodomy was so bad it was the one unforgivable sin.)

What I had learned about religion at home was that it was really all about social ranking. It was important that we were Episcopalians, at the top of the social pecking order. The only time religion was mentioned at home was when Mom would warn me away from resisting parental authority by citing the commandment, "Thou shalt honor thy father and thy mother." She was also fond of saying, "If you want something done right, you have to do it yourself."

At that time Dad was managing a five-and-dime store around the corner on Main Street. After the bag lunch I brought with me, I'd go see a Saturday matinee at the State Theater, a block further down on Main Street. I'd spend the rest of the afternoon hanging out in Dad's store.

In high school I had a girlfriend. Her name was Julia Jenkins. She had blond hair, which she wore short in a pageboy cut. She had small breasts.

She had proptosis, a condition which caused her eyes to bulge. It left her always looking like she was startled. The less flattering term was bug-eyed. She played bassoon in the concert band. That was where we met. We became boy and girl friends as a result of her scheming. (Julia was what Mom meant by a "designing woman.") Julia's mother saw me as her daughter's future husband and did whatever she could to encourage our teen relationship.

Julia never pressured me for sex. We only ever necked once. She had a small, pointy tongue. When it darted in my mouth, it grossed me out. When we were college students, Julia came out to me as a lesbian.

In the fall of 1969, *Time* magazine published a cover story entitled "The Homosexual in America." Mom subscribed to *Time* and I read it every week. Like the television reporter Mike Wallace, *Time* was considered factual and objective in its coverage.

I read the essay several times, carefully, and looked up a few unfamiliar words. The picture it painted was bleak and mirrored the Mike Wallace program. Homosexual men, it stated were "failed heterosexuals," their behavior was "against the law." Society saw homosexuals as "fairly bizarre." Homosexuals were depressed and guilt-ridden, their jealousy was irrational, and they possessed "a megalomaniacal conviction that homosexual trends are universal." The article stated directly that "63% of Americans consider homosexuality harmful to American life.

A boy became homosexual as the result of an overbearing mother and an aloof or absent father, or not finding a masculine role model in the father. That tallied with my self-examination: Mom was domineering, and Dad was both absent from the house all the time, and definitely aloof when I was around him, including during sex.

Homosexuality was also caused by a "fear of the opposite sex." I did not fear the girls in school. I had several female friends. I just didn't find them sexually appealing. I loved my grandmother and some of my aunts. I had little to do with any of my uncles because they took no interest in me.

Homosexuals, *Time* said, gravitated to certain professions—fashion, art, theater, dance, and music. *Time* described this as a "conspiracy." These homosexuals who infiltrated the arts (which *Time* labeled "Homintern," a word I could not find in the dictionary) were full of vitality and brilliance, but seldom had strength. Homosexuals were to be blamed for "pop" art, because they trivialized art, and for "camp," something that made fun out of bad and ugly and banal things. I couldn't find "camp" in the dictionary, but "camp" stuck with me. The essay had a lot to say about homosexuals and their connection to all things creative.

How would I know how to spot one of "them"? *Time* stated homosexuals were "psychic masochists." I had to look that word up. They were "supercilious" (another word I had to look up), whimpering, and their aggression was fake. Homosexuals were also bullies. They cringed before a stronger person but were merciless when in power and unscrupulous about trampling on a weaker person.

All of this laid out plainly so much of what I feared about me being a homosexual. I loved males and sex was a secret pleasure. But I found it very hard to identify with most of the things that were wrong or unnatural about homosexuals.

But I also read bits of changes in the air that gave me a glimmer of hope. I encountered the word "gay" (meaning homosexual) for the first time. I read about cruising, gay bars, the different types of gay men who each had their own kind of gay bar, and that gay bars were the "center of a minority subculture." I read that major cities were full of gay men and gay bars, that San Francisco was the capital of them all.

I also read that homosexuals had recently rioted in New York City.

Time mentioned the Kinsey study that stated 4% of all men were homosexual. There was a copy of his book in our family library. I read it immediately. "The only unnatural sex act is that which you cannot perform," Kinsey wrote.

The *Time* article concluded on a very discouraging note: "But it deserved no encouragement, no glamorization, no rationalization, no fake status as minority martyrdom, no sophistry about simple differences in taste—and, above all, no pretense that it is anything but a pernicious sickness." Mom kept that issue of *Time* magazine in the center of the living room coffee table. Every time I walked past it, I felt she was pointing a finger at me.

10

I excelled at my studies. I really enjoyed learning. It was the only thing for which I received validation from other people. I always got high grades and was always on the high honor list. My one weakness was science. In my sophomore year in biology, I never got better than a B+. Whenever I brought my report card home with less than straight A's, Mom would tell me, "Just work harder." I discontinued taking science courses after seeing I had no aptitude for it.

School was where I was around other people. The school day ended with a half-hour study period when extracurricular activities happened. I played cornet, and then French horn in concert band. I also played in the marching band, which put on half-time shows.

I tried intramural sports but was very bad at them. I went to wrestling once. I was easily overpowered by the other boys in my weight class. I was always pinned almost immediately. Once I wrestled with Mark Griswold, one of the school's football stars. I found him strikingly handsome and very masculine—short, dark hair, thick, dark brown eyebrows over deep, dark brown eyes. He was already sprouting chest hair. He had a deep baritone voice. He reminded me of Rock Hudson. That one time when Mark wrestled me, he wrapped his arm around my torso and almost immediately pinned me down with his full body's weight holding me. I got an immediate erection. When Mark got off me, I rolled over to cover the bulge in my gym shorts. I headed straight for the boys' shower room and jacked off.

I joined the Debate Club, the Math Club, and the German Club. I was elected president of the German Club. I translated several popular songs, such as "My Favorite Things" and "Raindrops Keep Falling on My Head," into German to the delight of my classmates. For the annual joint German and French Club Christmas dinner, I wrote several skits, directed them, and oversaw the construction of the sets.

I had no idea I was stepping on the toes of Mr. Whiting, the head of the foreign language department, who was also the advisor and director of the Thespian Society. Mr. Whiting wrote and staged a version of *The Wizard of Oz* and oversaw the construction of elaborate sets. Mr. Whiting's expertise clearly dwarfed mine. His *The Wizard of Oz* brought the house down. I felt embarrassed and shamed in front of my classmates and their parents.

I gambled my hopes for proper recognition when, I assumed, I would be inducted into the High Honor Society. This was very prestigious for those who were not football players or cheerleaders or actors or in popular cliques.

Everyone knew I was among the top students academically. There was a kind of informal rivalry between Jon Canale, Laura Gustafson, and me as to who would end up valedictorian. We all expected to make High Honor Society. But that took outside activities to indicate "well roundedness" as well. I knew being president of the German Club and playing in the concert and marching bands were pluses. Since there was no swimming team, I played on the tennis team, earning a junior varsity letter. Playing singles made it a mostly solitary sport, which suited me just fine. I felt secure in the knowledge that I had covered all bases.

High school juniors were inducted into the high honor society in a school-wide event, held during the final class period in the last week of the school year. Afterward, students would go directly to their school buses.

My class was seated in the balcony, which was directly across the hall from our homeroom. After the auditorium lights were dimmed and the principal made his opening remarks, he began the ceremony by first listing a student's accomplishments, allowing students to guess who was being described. As the name was called, the student went up to the stage amid loud applause and took a seat on the stage.

As the principal worked his way through the list of inductees, my excitement grew and grew. I recognized most of my classmates from their list of accomplishments. My name was at the end of the alphabet, so I anticipated being the last inductee.

But before getting to my name, the principal stopped the roll call. He turned his outstretched arm to the chosen few on stage and asked them to stand and prepare to be awarded with their certificates.

I was crestfallen. I felt devastated. I felt humiliated when Ed Wright, who had been inducted and was now back sitting next to me, whispered in my ear, "I'm sorry." At that my tears started flowing—tears of crushing disappointment, tears of shame. I felt publicly humiliated.

As my tears flowed in the darkness, I thought, "This is what people really think of me." As we dispersed and headed home, I wiped my tears off on my shirt sleeve. I rode the school bus home, sitting quietly, looking out the window the whole ride back to Preble. "Know thyself," indeed.

11

My pen pals wrote about their countries, giving me glimpses into worlds I had never dreamed of, feeding my desire to live in another country. Frau Klemperer encouraged me to go to West Germany as an exchange student. I applied to Rotary International to spend my junior year abroad. The Rotary committee received my application warmly but turned me down. They thought I was not mature enough but encouraged me to apply again next year.

This rejection was another blow, but I realized it was a temporary setback. Rotary had recommended I try again for my senior year. On my second try I was more assiduous. The two biggest problems facing society, I wrote, were the threat to earth's ecology (I wrote an essay on the threat to the Everglades for a writing competition held by Sertoma International; my essay won first prize and was published in the *Cortland Standard*) and communism. I made no explicit mention of the war in Viet Nam, as that was highly controversial at the time. But I did talk about Stephen Crane's *The Red Badge of* Courage as one of the books having the most influence on me. I found Crane's poetry and *The Red Badge of Courage* easily accessible, carrying an important message. The war in Viet Nam had been going on forever. Anti-war protesters like the long-haired, pot-smoking, peace-loving hippies, were considered juvenile delinquents. I saw in Crane's book a more powerful anti-war message in his psychological portrayal of the fear-filled mind of the cowardly deserter, who returned to the Civil War.

When asked who my favorite author was, I answered Robert Heinlein, knowing that science fiction was not considered a serious genre, but more on a par with comic books.

I was accepted into the exchange program. They promised to do their best to place me in a German-speaking country. They had located a family in Austria and were waiting for a definite commitment from them. When the Austrians dropped out, I was offered placement with a family in Bolivia. I was discouraged by this prospect, but I really wanted to live abroad, so I said yes. I started learning Spanish from a "teach yourself" book.

As I wrestled with my Spanish book, I got word that a family in West Germany had just signed up to host a student. One of their sons was going to be an exchange student in the US. I was given their contact information and began exchanging letters in German with my new host family. The father, Herr Jochum, also wrote to my parents.

Herr Jochum, who asked me to address him as *Vater*, was the *Stadtdirektor* of Mülheim-an-der-Ruhr, a garden city in the industrial Ruhr Valley. He and his wife had three nearly grown children. The eldest, Rüdiger, was a student at Bochum University. His other son, Markus, who was my age, would be the exchange student in the US while I was in West Germany. They had a daughter Astrid who was one year younger than I.

Vater Jochum sent photographs of his family—*Vater* in a business suit, *Mutter* in a severe, German-looking dress and the three children in fashionably American clothes. They lived in a very large house, what Germans referred to as a *villa*. Like most German houses, it was painted white. I did not know how unusual it was for Germans to own a stand-alone house. It had a large, landscaped garden, which gave the house much privacy. A stone tower called the Bismarckturm was perched on the brow of the hill across the street. The house was located at the bottom of a hill after a steep curve.

My parents borrowed money from Grandpa Wright for my airfare. (This was the only time I recall getting financial help from my parents.) They booked my flight to Düsseldorf and left the return flight open. Mom and Dad bought me two suitcases, which were cheap, plastic, powder blue-colored affairs. When we got home, I immediately started packing my suitcases. I repacked them over and over during the summer, trying to decide what I would wear for a whole year. I kept taking my tennis racket out and putting it back in.

When the departure day arrived, Mom drove me to the Syracuse airport. I carried my luggage from the car. At the terminal entrance a black man in a suit offered to take my bags. I had never encountered a skycap before; Mom gave the man a tip. I thought having someone else carry my luggage when I was perfectly capable of doing that myself as being a spendthrift. This was the first taste of a world parallel to my own I knew nothing about.

I had never flown before and was excited as I boarded the plane. I held on to the arm rests during takeoff, scared by the strange new sensation. At first, I was afraid of the plane falling out of the sky. But I relaxed into the ride and focused on the realization I was going someplace new and foreign. All my teenage years up to that point I had taken care of my mother when she was bed-ridden. I felt the distinct, yet never expressed, expectation that I was supposed to stay home and take care of my mother for the rest of her life. But here I was going someplace far, far away.

I had to change planes at JFK and got onto a much bigger jet. It stopped for refueling in Shannon, Ireland, and most of the passengers got off to buy alcohol, cigarettes, and Irish crystal at a duty-free shop. I sat quietly the whole trip. I brought a book to read. By the end of the flight my throat was parched. The recirculated air had dehydrated me, and I had been too shy to ask the stewardess for a glass of water.

After collecting my baggage and going through passport control, I found the entire Jochum family waiting for me. They met me with beaming smiles. *Vater* shook my hand, and "*Wilkommen! Wie geht's? Wie war dein Flug?*"

After that I barely understood a word.

12

Thick and heavy, shutters in Germany were built into the houses, and are lowered every night, turning the houses into little fortresses. "Guten Morgen, Les!" Mutter Jochum chirped as she raised the shutter of my bedroom window. She threw open the window and the city's morning air came in, diesel and gasoline exhaust overpowering the greenery from the garden right outside.

I got up and showered and dressed and came downstairs for breakfast. Breakfast usually consisted of cold cuts and cheese or jam or *Nutella* on *Brötchen* and eaten open-faced. There was orange juice and coffee. Supper, or *Vesperbrot*, was a variant of breakfast, more open-faced sandwiches. With cold cuts. *Mittagessen* was the hot meal of the day. Astrid and I had a two-hour break for lunch, and Vater Jochum came home from the office.

At my first breakfast with the Jochums, I encountered a strange liquid in a cup at the table I was dubious of tasting. This was my first experience of *Joghurt*. "*Was ist das?*" I asked. I quickly got into the habit of asking for words—heard something on TV or in a snatch of overheard conversation—to be explained rather than looking them up in a German-to-English dictionary.

Vater Jochum often asked me about America. I had a lot of practice explaining American things to my pen pals. But Vater Jochum asked more complicated questions. He once asked me why Americans publicly divulged their political affiliation. Vater Jochum was a prominent member of the CDU, the conservative party. He did not disclose what, if any, party he had belonged to during World War II. (He had served in Hitler's army and was captured by the Soviets. He was very grateful when American forces liberated him from the Soviet POW camp.) I was befuddled by this question and said, "People just do."

With several weeks before the winter semester started my host parents familiarized me with everyday German life. Mutti took me on her errands in the *Innenstadt*. Downtown Mülheim was a pedestrian zone, and I sometimes went window shopping, perused the bookstores and department stores.

Vater took us on excursions to nearby points of interest—*Schloß Broich* (a nearby castle), Xanten (the home of the mythical Siegfried), Cologne to see its cathedral, the hydroelectric power station at the confluence of the Ruhr and the Rhine (which terrified me), a dairy farm, a lock system along the Ruhr, walks in the forests (where I was warned to stay on the paths to avoid stepping on a buried land mine), a walk in our Sunday finest on the *Königsallee* in Düsseldorf, and a walk through the Essen *Altstadt*, where I witnessed a drunken gay couple arguing in the middle of the street.

Vater also gave me weekly *Taschengeld*—a generous allowance of 20 Marks a week. This was a very generous gift that I appreciated. My mom paid me a weekly allowance of 50 cents for doing housework and gardening. The Jochums' upper middle-class lifestyle was a revelation to me. I spent it on streetcar fare, coffee or beer, postcards and postage, stationery, color slide film, books and magazines, records, and *Pommes frites*—French fries with mayonnaise. I continued to collect stamps and postcards and writing to my pen pals. For Christmas Oma Jochum gave me a four-color ink pen. Vati and Mutti gave me a beautiful huge green leatherbound *Schreibmappe*, an elegant writing case to carry and store stationery and envelopes.

I began to dream in German. (They say you have become competent in a language when you dream in it.) I remember saying things in German in my dreams, things I did not yet know how to say. I stared having lucid dreams. In some of them I could fly. I simply willed myself to lift up off the ground. I soared over the Jochums' house and gardens, over the *Innenstadt*, over the Ruhr river. I felt exuberant in flight, and I felt happy being in Germany.

The Jochums introduced me to more, much more. I attended formal functions, wearing a tuxedo handed down from their sons. I went to dance school, where I learned ballroom dances and proper social etiquette. The Jochums took me to a couple of formal balls and was presented as a "respectable young man." They encouraged me to travel, and paid my expenses to go to Berlin, Rotterdam, Rome, Paris. I took the train to visit my West German pen pals in Lübeck, Hamburg, and Burgsteinfurt.

I hung out with Astrid. We played tennis a few times that summer. We went swimming at the Olympic-sized *Hallenbad*. I continued to swim there on a regular basis. (In my weekly *Sport* class, swimming was the only activity for which I showed up constantly.)

While hanging out with Astrid, I met her best friend Eleanor Schmidt. Eleanor was rather short with a brusque haircut that made her look like Mireille Mathieu, the French chanteuse. Eleanor's nickname was *die Nonne*. We went for walks together, stopped for *Kaffee und Kuchen* in the *Innenstadt*, and listened to pop records at the city library and the department store Neckarmann. In my bedroom I listened to BFBS on the radio, the one place I heard English spoken (outside of English class). They played a mix of the Beatles, the Rolling Stones, Procol Harum, Deep Purple, Melanie, Roger Whittaker, and a brand-new singer named Elton John. Oma Jochum, Vater Jochum's mother who lived in her own set of rooms on the second floor, listened to German *Schlager* music on WDR radio while doing housework.

In a matter of weeks, I drifted into a dating relationship with Eleanor. I started going to her house to listen to records with her in the music room. We had long petting sessions, which consisted of kissing. Eleanor's older sister had a boyfriend who slept with her at their house. I was surprised by the openminded acceptance of teenage sex in German society. I never felt the desire to have sex with Eleanor, and she never pressured me. *Gymnasien* were still sexually separated. Astrid and Eleanor were classmates at the girls' high school, and my *Gymnasium* was all male. *Gymnasien* were for the smartest, university-bound students. Classes were rigorous. The course structure was very different from the US. We took a dozen subjects that year. Some courses, like English and German, met three times a week. Others, like religion and philosophy, met once a week. There were no extracurricular activities and students socialized outside of school. Joining my class and being a foreigner made me an outsider. With no school activities to interact with my classmates, I was hard put in breaking the ice. During the free period my classmates gathered out in the street on the sidewalk to hang out and smoke cigarettes. As a strategy to join in I started smoking as well. When a classmate asked me, *"Hast di Feuer?"* I was able to offer him a light. This gave me an in.

Eventually I made two friends among the smokers. Wilhelm Hoyer, pale, slender, tall, with straight fair hair, talked to me first. Wilhelm enthusiastically explained things to me and discussed what we were learning in class. (The concept of "perfection," introduced in philosophy class, was hotly debated.) Wilhelm ended every other sentence with *"Verstehst du?"* which seemed to be rhetorical rather than a serious query about my understanding.

My other friend, Clemens Brinkhalter, invited me to his apartment after classes to listen to pop music on his reel-to-reel tape recorder. Clemens lived with his mother in an apartment in the *Altstadt*, which overlooked a busy intersection. Clemens' home felt *gemütlich* ("cozy") to me. I liked being able to look out into the busy city street, seeing streetcars roll by, hearing car horns, church bells, and the occasional police siren. I felt more alive being in the middle of all that activity. We sometimes stopped for a *Kölsch* at a *Bierstube* after classes.

Once school started, I quickly lost interest in most of my classes. My drive to excel in academics no longer seemed important compared to experiencing German culture, urban life, and my first taste of freedom. Because of the difference in the pacing of learning I found I was way ahead in some subjects like biology and English (and therefore bored) or woefully lacking in knowledge in other subjects, like chemistry and French. A few classes kept my interest—geography, philosophy, and history. In history class we studied original documents rather than reading textbooks doing the interpretation work for us. My class was studying German unification in 1871. My confidence in math failed me. Calculus was the next course for me both in high school back home and in Gymnasium. Calculus was a very different kind of math, and the language of math in German was different from English. (When I was exposed to German legalese, I again encountered this very different vocabulary.) My homework always came back drenched in red ink. I didn't understand the comments any better than the math itself. I had no idea what I was doing.

After a while I started cutting classes—*blau machen* was a sport for my classmates. They ditched a class here and there, without any penalty. I cut more and more classes and was never penalized. My teachers seemed not to notice my absences. Only once did my English teacher greet me after my long absence, mocking me for acting like an arrogant Frenchman, with a sneering, "*Bonjour, monsieur* Wright. Will you be joining us today?"

I enjoyed my solitary walks around the city. Some days are sunny, many more are overcast. Some mornings when I head out, a very light drizzle, more like a spray, is falling. Germans call that *nieseln*. I am always greeted by the industrial city air—a mix of diesel and gas fumes and a hint of the water from the nearby Ruhr. In the winter the air is especially damp, and it stings. But winters are not snowy. Only once, on a Sunday morning, did it snow. There was a light layer blanketing the field of the *Bismarckturm* across the street. Mutti pointed at some kids tobogganing down the gentle slope there and pointed out, "*Guck, das ist eine Rodelbahn.*"

I enjoyed watching people and browsing in bookstores, which became another source of education for me. I listened to records on my own in the department store Kaufhof. I picked up on the German obsession with *Krimis*. I learned about the spirit of May '68—the student uprising in Paris, the story of Rudi Dutschke (a leftist student leader), and the romance of socialist visions for West Germany's future.

I developed a need for these solitary walks, observing city life. This became a lifelong habit. I learned there was a word for it and a long modern tradition—*flâneur*. I first encountered this in Walter Benjamin's *The Arcades Project*. I was a follower of the Frankfurt School and was reading in preparation for my doctoral exams.

In public men's rooms I looked for messages—signs of homosexual activity—hoping to find a phone number or a time and place to meet for anonymous sex. I walked along the promenade along the Ruhr River after dark, looking for men cruising for sex. I never found any evidence of homosexual activity. Today I cannot explain how I happened upon these cruising methods on my own.

In 1970 the spirit of '68 had pervaded West German society. Leftist activism, especially among students, was widespread. A mixing of the rebelliousness in American society and interpretations of Marx, social structures were being challenged. Both of these influences spoke to me. I grew my beard and let my hair grow long. I embraced the rock music of the day that Mom had banned. I embraced the casual dress, imported blue jeans from America and the like. I was only vaguely aware of the youth challenges to adult authority and the West German's nearly American embrace of consumer capitalism.

13

The Jochums indulged my love of movies. I went to the movies every couple of weeks, occasionally accompanied by Astrid, but usually by myself. I had been pursuing my interest in Russian and Soviet history (as a result of visiting the USSR pavilion at the Montreal World's Fair in 1967, a trip organized by the church in Preble). Vater Jochum paid for me to take evening classes in Russian at the local *Volkshochschule*. I was excited when *Dr. Zhivago* came to the local cinema downtown—I saw it the day it opened and went back two days later to see it again.

My interest in Russian history took a backseat to the love life of Yuri Zhivago, played by the dashingly handsome Omar Sharif, his brown moustache, his emotive facial expressions, his deep brown eyes that the camera held as he shed quiet tears. As the tragic story unfolded, my heart ached for Yuri Zhivago/Omar Sharif and his tragic plight. The film was both an epic story of the last days of czarist Russia, the 1917 Bolshevik Revolution, and the tragic story of a sensitive, complicated man.

Zhivago came from a wealthy family, who were reduced to poverty due to his father's alcoholism. Zhivago was a trained physician but also a poet. He was smart, compassionate, and felt deeply and suffered deeply. He married a woman he did not love. Later, while serving as a doctor in the years of turmoil following the Bolshevik Revolution, he met and fell in love with Lara. When peace came, Zhivago returned to his wife Tonya out of loyalty, but never let go of his love for Lara. He would suffer the rest of his life.

In Boris Pasternak's novel *Doctor Zhivago*, Zhivago was a romantic hero who experienced only brief moments of happiness in a life filled with darkness. I identified profoundly with this man, his tragic life, his tragic love, his unfulfilled longing for love. I fell hopelessly in love with Yuri/ Omar (rather somewhat in the way that Madame Bovary had found her way to romantic love by reading novels). After I saw the film for a second time, I started writing poems to Yuri/Omar, divulging all the emotions the film had sparked within. "We two are alike," I wrote. I longed to take Yuri in my arms and comfort him. I cried tears of sadness, both for Zhivago and myself.

When I went on a week's vacation at a large pension in the country outside of Detmold (I had won the trip in a lottery I entered at a tourism fair), I started a diary. I began to explore my feelings toward Yuri/Omar. For the first time I put down in words admitting my homosexuality to myself—a mix of my first romantic feelings for a specific man and the negative reaction of society. For the most part, this was an exercise in beating myself up.

Vater Jochum signed me up with the *Volkshochschule* for a group trip to Rome over spring break. All the other travelers were retirees. The daily schedule was packed tight, taking us to Roman ruins, churches and palaces, statues and fountains, two or three every day. When I tried to enter St Peter's, I was turned away for wearing sandals. We made two excursions outside of Rome—up into the hills to the Tivoli Gardens and out to the coast to Ostia Antica. We stopped to eat and drink wine at so many *tavernas* they all became a blur.

My fondest memories of this were the evenings in the *taverna* next door to our *pensione*. After dinner everyone spent the rest of the evening gathered in German *Gemütlichkeit*, socializing and drinking house wine. I had not experienced this sort of conviviality before. These pensioners accepted me as an adult, as an equal. I made friends with Lambert and Marga Klein—a judge and his wife, which continued until their deaths. I got tipsy every evening and loosened up. I had my first drunk—our tour guide walked me back to the room we shared. He told me to put one foot on the floor to keep my head from spinning. Never once was I tempted to touch my bedmate.

I applied to colleges back in the US in the spring of 1971. I expected that most of the schools I applied to would accept me. I hoped me applying as an exchange student in West Germany would add weight to the seriousness of my desire to major in German. Frau Klemperer had advised me to apply to Middlebury College in Vermont and wrote me a strong recommendation.

She felt Middlebury was the ideal college for studying foreign languages.

I also applied to SUNY Albany, the flagship school of the SUNY system (my second choice), as well as three other state colleges. They all offered me acceptance. I immediately sent my acceptance notice to Middlebury. But when I received notice of their financial aid package—student loan, work-study, and two scholarships—I discovered that did not come close to covering the cost of going there. I was disheartened to have to turn down the offer and, with mixed feelings, accepted the offer from Albany, where tuition was a small fraction of Middlebury's.

Many years later, my first Classics professor, Sylvia Barnard asked me what my first-choice college had been and why I had decided to go to SUNY Albany. She, who was herself a graduate of a private school, Yale, and McGill, told me that what Middlebury had done was a not uncommon practice. Elite universities often accepted working-class students like me with full knowledge that we stood no chance of being able to afford to attend. This information came to me, as I had learned over the years, as yet another example of how the American "merit system" was actually rigged to work for some and against others, while appearing to be equally available to the disadvantaged. Today it makes me wonder how differently my professional (and personal) life would have unfolded had I had this leg up, preparing me to enter the privileged world of the Ivy League.

As my year abroad was nearing its end, I jumped the gun to go back to the US. I was eager to graduate from high school with my classmates. I withdrew from *Gymnasium* halfway through the summer semester. I got excellent grades (1's and 2's) in the classes I had actually shown up for, and "gentlemen's C's" (3's and 4's) in the rest of the classes I was registered for. (Years later I would learn of the custom of the "gentleman's Cs" at exclusive institutions of learning.)

I was leaving with all sorts of new knowledge about Germans and their culture. For instance, I loved the breads. There were many more kinds of breads than in the US, and they were all different, all tasty, and of much better quality. You sank your teeth into German bread, and you chewed.

There were all sorts of German beers, some heavy, some light, and all with the same alcohol content as wine. Astrid introduced me to the *Berliner Weiße*, a wheat beer with a shot of raspberry syrup. We drank it on the Kurfürstendam in Berlin in proper Berliner fashion. In Mülheim, I frequently drank a Kölsch with my school buddies. This was a pale ale brewed in nearby Cologne and drunk in special narrow Kölsch glasses.

Shops closed midday on Saturday for the weekend. Sunday afternoon was spent on Spaziergänge (long, leisurely walks), followed by coffee and cake. German coffee was rich and thick, making American coffee seem like dishwater in comparison.

Germans stared openly all the time. That took some getting used to. At first, I felt they were being rude. I also quickly learned that when a German asks you, "*Wie geht's?*"), they were seriously interested in how you are. Instead of brushing everyone off with a polite "I'm fine, thanks," I learned to pay attention to see if the person wanted more information.

I eagerly looked forward to seeing my classmates back at home and finding out how their senior year had gone.

14

I returned home just in time to take part in my high school graduation ceremony. I had not heard from Tom or Julia while I was in West Germany. Everything appeared to be just the same as when I had left. But something was different.

Almost immediately I missed West Germany. I had never felt homesick for the world of my childhood, so I was surprised that I missed the Jochums and Mülheim-an-der-Ruhr, which now seemed more and more like a dream. When I saw Julia, she spoke enthusiastically about how the class of 1971 had grown close over their final year together. The class was organizing a couple of activities to come together for the last time before most of us would leave to start college. I arrived too late for the first event. The second event was a clambake, which my parents forbade me from attending. They informed me that they knew there would be drinking going on and they didn't want me around alcohol. It did not matter that I had started drinking socially in West Germany or, for that matter, that I was now 18, the legal drinking age in New York State at that time.

What was different about my return was that I had withdrawn emotionally from my parents. They felt like strangers to me. No doubt they also found me changed by my experience living abroad. I was now aware of social class differences, that the Jochums could, and did, provide me with advantages my real parents probably were not even aware of. I also had the experience of living in a loving and nurturing family.

I still looked forward to the graduation ceremony. Mom was well enough to attend in person. (Dad was at work.) My classmates were hanging out ahead of the ceremony. I recognized the kids I had been in Regents classes with. I talked briefly with Laura Gustafson and Jon Canale. I approached a few other classmates, who didn't recognize me. I told them who I was, but they didn't seem to remember me. I was stunned. How could they have forgotten me in just one year?

The principal called our names, and we came up to the stage one by one to receive our diplomas. He also announced each scholarship or award a student may have received. All of us in Regents classes got a Regents scholarship. I was very surprised when it was announced I had won a National Merit Scholarship. (This meant I would not need student loans.) On the drive home, Mom fumed over how the principal had minimized me winning a prestigious scholarship .

Through my dad, I got a summer job at the Smith-Corona factory. By this time, Dad had a white-collar job working on payroll. When I went to the personnel office to fill out paperwork, a guy named Tom Smith handled it. Tom invited me out for a beer at one of the student bars on Main Street in Cortland. It turned out he had been a master's student at Emory University in Georgia and was working for Smith-Corona while trying to get a job in his field. We went out a few times. He even visited me at my parents' house. I suspected he was secretly gay and feeling me out. We went on one movie double-date. He specified that I *had to* bring a date. (I came with a neighbor who, when I called her, thought I was trying to set her up with someone else.)

My job was mind-numbing. I milled strips of steel for eight hours on the midnight shift every night. My pay was rated by the quantity I produced, so I milled as fast as I could. I didn't know that the full-time workers paced themselves, milling at a rate far below my own. The other millers were complaining about my work—I threatened to have their output rate raised. They were looking to see me fired. Tom let me know that the supervisor was saying he was suspicious that I was cheating by secretly loading the pans the strips went into with bricks.

Working nights left me with little chance of a social life since I was sleeping during the day. I had a few beers with Tom Smith on three or four occasions. John Alexander, a schoolmate, gave me free piano lessons. We would become close friends later on after we had both come out.

I gradually sank into a deep depression. Whenever I mowed my parents' lawn, I fantasized pulling the lawn mower over me and letting the blades tear my flesh apart. About a half a mile away Albany Street became an overpass crossing the interstate highway. I would take walks to the overpass and watch the traffic below go by. I contemplated jumping over the railing and falling in front of an oncoming tractor trailer.

Most of the time that summer I stayed home and read. I read voraciously, in part to kill time and in part because I had a newfound drive to try and understand myself through other people's lives. Three works resonated powerfully and have accompanied me throughout my life—Sylvia Plath's *The Bell Jar* (which had just been published), Oscar Wilde's *De Profundis*, and Susan Sontag's essay "Notes on 'Camp.'"

The Bell Jar went to the heart of where I found myself that summer. The metaphor of the bell jar succinctly described my own feelings of being isolated, walled off from the world, trapped in claustrophobic isolation—where I could touch no one and no one could hear me. I too felt a lot of anxiety and disorientation, suspended in that summer in Cortland County, West Germany behind me and the unknown Albany before me. I was obsessed with the idea of killing myself. I knew I was homosexual but was terrified of what kind of life society and the media had told me I would have. The thought of staying in Cortland, working at Smith-Corona for the rest of my life, and living a loveless and meaningless life in the closet terrified me.

I learned about Oscar Wilde in high school. I read *The Importance of Being Earnest* and learned what a "dandy" was. He had lived a scandalous life, which eventually landed him in prison. Although no one ever came out and said it, I knew he was a homosexual. I read *De Profundis* when I learned it was a letter he had written while imprisoned for his homosexual behavior. One lesson I took away from it was that being openly homosexual could land me in jail as well. I also paid close attention to Wilde's quoting of Isaiah 53:3: "He is despised and rejected of men, a man of sorrows and acquainted with grief and we hid our faces from him." This echoed the observation that I was going to have a hard life. I would come to learn that "life is pain."

In 1971 there was a cigar store on Main Street in Cortland that also sold a huge array of magazines and newspapers. It has here that I came across a tabloid called *Screw* magazine. I stumbled down a rabbit hole. *Screw* opened a door for me to a whole underground world that *Playboy* magazine only every hinted at. *Screw* became my companion through several sexless summers. I learned about sadism and masochism from the news of tthe Eulenspiegel Society's founding. Personals sex ads specificized French, Greek, and English schools of sex—oral, anal, and bondage and discipline practices. This is how I first learned about such practices. One issue of *Screw* featured a drag queen named Divine who promoted her film *Pink Flamingos*. All this was stuff happening in far-off New York City.

I fantasized about answering one of the ads, but the advertisers were all looking for women.

That summer I also stumbled upon Susan Sontag's "Notes on Camp." Sontag wrote that "camp" was a sensibility found predominantly, though not exclusively, among homosexual men, which functioned as a secret code. She wrote that it converts the serious into the frivolous and elevates vulgarity and bad taste. I grokked this—it was the flavor of *Screw* magazine, the essence of Divine. Sontag quoted Oscar Wilde, who wrote in *An Ideal Husband,* "To be natural is such a very difficult pose to keep up." My self-monitoring to look for and cover up any telltale signs of my homosexuality—seeking to pass for straight—*was* a very difficult pose for me to keep up. Sontag alerted me to my perspective of the world was that of an outsider. The fun I had had dressing up as a woman, as well as playing house and playing with dolls, learning how to knit and crochet—these were all activities I learned to keep to myself. I relished being an American living in West Germany even as I worked hard at learning how to become German. The life I had led there was an artificial role, so much of it unlike my real life in the US.

Sontag outlined in her 52 "notes" dimensions and examples of camp. Much of it included writers, books, films, art movements, personalities I had not yet encountered. But I got the idea. *Auntie Mame* and *Breakfast at Tiffany's* had moved me deeply. Later I would see *Sunset Boulevard, Mildred Pierce, All About Eve,* and *Some Like It Hot* and know why they were part of the canon of gay sensibility. What budding gay boy wouldn't want his own Auntie Mame?

15

The first time I laid eyes on the SUNY Albany campus was Labor Day weekend 1971. I had come for freshman orientation. I had not given it much thought but had assumed Albany would have a cookie-cutter red brick campus like the college in Cortland. Albany was something quite different.

From the Thruway, the Corning Tower of the Empire State Plaza downtown and the four towers of the high-rise dorms on SUNYA's uptown campus appeared, beckoning visitors to what SUNYA students nicknamed the Emerald City.

These structures were made of reinforced poured concrete. Both were still under construction in 1971. In retrospect both the government complex and the university campus appear as monuments Nelson Rockefeller had built as a tribute to himself. The Empire State Plaza, also known as the South Mall, destroyed much of Old Albany's neighborhoods such as Little Italy and the SRO hotels, inhabited mostly by poor, elderly single men, cutting the downtown shopping district from the old neighborhoods. In a sharply critical article in the *New York Times*, a reviewer castigated the South Mall as a "compendium of clichés of modern architecture" and "not so much vision of the future as of the past." Robert Hughes compared it to the architecture of fascism. Another critic complained the South Mall buildings "loom menacingly, like aliens from another galaxy set down on [a] landing strip."

SUNYA's uptown campus, designed by Edward Durrell Stone, was laid out as an oblong. The Podium, the academic buildings, were connected by a walking surface and a canopy of concrete, which made it appear as a single megastructure. These buildings were connected by an underground tunnel network, not accessible to students. At each corner of the Podium stood a quad. All four-square quads had low-rise dorms connected in the same manner as the Podium. A high-rise tower was situated off-center in the corner nearest the Podium. In the winter the wind whipped through the quads, funneled through the gaps between the low-rises, and blew so strong that it was impossible to open the front doors of the tower dorms. The campus appeared intended for a desert landscape. Over time the individual buildings sank at differing rates, and the harsh hot-and-cold climate caused large chunks of concrete in the outdoor breezeway canopies to fall without warning. Students nicknamed it Stone's Folly.

Our orientation sought, among other things, to lessen the culture shock of student life at a large and anonymous university by fostering connection, trust, and a sense of community. We participated in several small group activities which were intended to help us make friends right from the start. The student population reflected the cultural diversity of New York State—large numbers of small-town and rural whites from upstate, suburban, small town and urban Jews from Long Island and New York City, Blacks, and Puerto Ricans. There was enough culture shock to go around for all of us coming face to face with our fellow New Yorkers.

In the course of three years, I would live on Colonial ("fraternity row"), Dutch, and Indian ("hippie land") Quads. (There was a fourth—State Quad. They were named to identify the historical periods of New York history.) When I lived on Dutch Quad, I saw the social pecking order laid out in where students sat in the cafeteria. The tables were arranged in long rows. The first row, nearest the kitchen, was where the Puerto Ricans and Blacks sat. Next came the generic Upstaters, and then the fraternity and sorority crowd. Next were the mostly downstate Jews. In the last row were the vegetarians.

In one of the new-age exercises in orientation we were asked to close our eyes and feel the faces of the people next to us and keep doing so until we found someone they felt somehow connected to. When they told us to open our eyes, I found myself facing another guy. I scanned the room and saw that everyone else had paired up boy-girl. I could see the fear and panic in my partner's eyes. He no doubt saw the same in my eyes. We quickly stepped away from each other while the other pairs introduced themselves to each other and started talking with each other. Other less dangerous self-discovery and social bonding exercises proved more helpful. I made several new friends.

Dorm rooms at SUNYA were also different. The typical arrangement was a "suite" of six students. Three small bedrooms gave onto a common room and a shared bathroom. My freshman year suitemates included Howie Rappaport (who turned me on to grass our first day together), three guys named Mitch (a lawyer's son from Long Island, a heavy working-class transfer student from Rochester, and an Albany native, who was a cartoon artist), and a white guy with a huge Afro who everyone called "Chief." (Chief introduced me to the Moody Blues, and I would get stoned and listen to *Days of Future Past.*) The first week together my suitemates changed rooms to bunk with a guy they liked better than their assigned roommate. I ended up stuck with the lawyer's son, who was universally despised as being arrogant and overprivileged. I developed a lust crush on Howie, who had very long hair, a very hairy chest, a huge cut cock, and liquid eyes. He liked to be naked in the suite and often played the guitar and played music.

I socialized with the women I had befriended at orientation. Billie Aul and Ellen Bear became fast friends with each other because they looked like twins. Billie dropped the guy she had started dating because she learned he was a shoplifter. I began dating Ellen, but her roommate Beryl had designs on me. Beryl was short and slightly overweight. She had raven black hair and eyes. Her large breasts pointed away from each other—something Beryl focused on obsessively. She constantly sought reassurance from me that she was attractive. She was a graduate of Hunter College High School and was proud to be a "Hunter girl." She rarely drank alcohol and refused to smoke pot because she said it made her paranoid. She was ambivalent about having sex with a goy because foreskins grossed her out. I assured her I was circumcised.

She did not get along at all with her roommate Brunhilda, a Puerto Rican Jesus freak. Beryl made sharing her room with Brunhilda so miserable that Brunhilda moved into a commune of fellow Jesus freaks off-campus.

I jumped into the rich cacophony of student life. We were part of the Woodstock generation. We were latecomers to the hippie revolution, children of the Summer of Love in San Francisco. Change filled the air, and we felt confident social and political revolution was coming. Many students grew their hair long, wore bell-bottom jeans, Lord Boards, and love beads. We smoked pot and experimented with other mind-expanding drugs, participated in the sexual revolution of free love and sexual exploration. Our primary targets were the unjust war in Viet Nam and the failures of our parents' generation.

Anti-war sentiments ran strong at SUNYA. The 1972 *Torch* yearbook, which came out the end of my freshman year, was perhaps the strongest anti-war message to come out of the university. On every two- page spread of the senior portraits six panels in the middle of each page was a photo of a decapitated Viet Cong soldier. (Think Kathy Griffith's severed Trump head.) SUNY Albany now features this yearbook prominently in its history. The editor, Ron Simmons, published the yearbook without informing the Student Association or the student body. Simmons, a gay black radical senior, included 16 pages of gay life on campus. I remember the 24 pages depicting poverty. But to this day, those severed heads are as clear in my mind's eye as the first time I saw them.

Anti-war protests were common. Some of us, like myself, were serious about all of this, but many others were simply rebelling against their parents and relishing their first taste of freedom from middle-class banality. We became the counterculture. We were influenced by the Beat generation— Allen Ginsberg, Jack Kerouac, Lawrence Ferlinghetti, William Burroughs, and others. *Stranger from a Strange Land* became a cult guide. *The Greening of America, The Sorcerer of Bolinas Reef,* Hunter S. Thompson's *Fear and Loathing in Las Veg*as, and the novels of Kurt Vonnegut informed our understanding of the world. *The Teachings of Don Juan* revealed the path to higher consciousness through hallucinogenic drugs. Thoreau's *Walden* and *Civil Disobedience* were our new guides.

The atmosphere was filled with music. The Beatles had recently broken up and were pursuing solo careers. A common question among us was "Are you a Beatles person or a Rolling Stones person?" New albums came out every week, new artists emerged, singer-songwriters and folk music were popular. Bob Dylan had gone electric. The soundtrack of my freshman year was extraordinary. 1971 is now recognized as the pinnacle of classic popular music. Albums included Carole King's *Tapestry*, Cat Stevens's *Tea for the Tillerman*, Moody Blues' *Days of Future Past*, Jethro Tull's *Aqualung*, Santana's *Santana*, Rolling Stones' *Sticky Fingers*, Janis Joplin's *Pearl*, Paul and Linda McCartney's *Ram*, John Lennon's *Imagine*, Joni Mitchell's *Blue*, Carly Simon's *Anticipation*, Harry Nilsson's *Nilsson Schmilsson*, and Yes' *Fragile*.

I shared a passion with Beryl for serious films. She introduced me to Ingmar Bergman (*The Seventh Seal*), Federico Fellini (*Satyricon*), and Woody Allen (*Everything You Always Wanted to Know about Sex [But Were Afraid to Ask]*). We saw American classics *Casablanca* and *Citizen Kane* together. (It was common knowledge that the bisexual professor who taught Introduction to Film, a lecture course that filled an auditorium, only gave A's to students who slept with him.) The Marx Brothers films had cult status, and we got stoned to watch them. I went to see films shown by student clubs—Bollywood movies, propaganda films from China, and films of operas.

One evening I went alone to see *Night of the Living Dead*. I got stoned and dropped acid for it. It was filmed in the countryside outside of Pittsburgh and looked just like Preble. As zombies staggered, unstoppable and already dead, I could well imagine this happening in Preble. One character said, "Yeah, they're all dead. They're all messed up." Because I was "all messed up" from my drugs, I found this film utterly terrifying.

I went to see *Women in Love* with Beryl. The long nude scene in which Rupert Birkin (Alan Bates) wrestles Gerald Crich (Oliver Reed) was intensely erotic. To this day I find this the most erotic scene ever filmed. When I saw the film with Beryl, I listened carefully to the discussion about love between men, which Lawrence has these men describe as the highest form of love. I was not so taken by their idea that such a love should never devolve into anything as tasteless as homosexuality.

I declared my major as Comparative Literature. It was a four-year major, which also meant I could bypass lower division courses in math and the sciences. It permitted me to combine German with Russian and literature in general. The major was modeled on the program at Harvard, and the department chair, a doting fatherly Hungarian, had been coaxed away from Harvard to Albany (which styled itself as the "Berkeley of the East" at that time). My education at Albany would be on an academic par with Harvard. But, as I would learn much later in life, it came without any of the perks affiliated with Harvard.

In the 1970s the Cold War was in full sway, and German and Russian were much in demand. Many liberal arts colleges hired faculty to joint appointments in German and Russian departments. Because of the scarcity of job candidates for this position, this would have made my skills highly marketable.

I found the program exciting. I started out in upper division courses taught in German, Russian literature courses in English translation while continuing with Russian language courses, and Comparative Literature courses, which included literature from the entire Western canon. Freshman year I took the two-semester survey course on literary criticism from the ancient Greeks to the present. Some courses were traditional survey courses, some focused on a specific literary movement, and some Comp Lit courses were organized around a particular theme. My professor of Greek drama had us read three plays a week and taught to the test. That was it, no discussion of plot or character or dramatic conflict—just memorization. Another professor cancelled a month of classes so he could attend a UFO conference in New Mexico. Most professors, however, were very engaging and mixed lectures with discussions of the texts.

The Comparative Literature program was anchored by two texts. One was a two-volume anthology of European literary thought from Plato to Benedetto Croce. The second was René Wellek and Austin Warren's *Theory of Literature*. They divided literary criticism into two approaches—extrinsic and intrinsic. The former included ideal, biographical, psychological, and social approaches and the latter included the rhetoric of language, writing styles, metaphor, and genres. At that time the primary tensions in literary analysis boiled down to reader-response (reception) theory and (text immanent) New Criticism: meaning either comes from what the reader brings to the text or can be discovered only within the text itself.

I soon learned that the way I had read fiction growing up had a name and a sophisticated explanation for what I was doing called reader-response (or reception) theory. In high school we discussed literary texts together, being steered toward close readings focusing on what was actually written on the page. This approach went by the name of New Criticism. I found the most helpful way of understanding what I was reading was when the teacher provided us with personal and cultural contexts. Such contextualizing also came with a range of literary approaches, each having a theory behind it. My Comp Lit courses at Albany were often organized around a particular approach, giving me a smorgasbord of theories to choose from. Unaware of the academic debates and feuds behind proponents of these theories, I took away a very pragmatic understanding—"the right tool for the right job," what purpose did an approach serve and where did it take me?

I took a course on archetypal approaches, a Jungian theory broadened by studying Claude Levi-Strauss's writing on cultural anthropology and Joseph Campbell's *The Hero with a Thousand Faces*. Campbell's cross-cultural studies on myths was coming into fashion at that time.

All these approaches to reading and understanding literature jostled my thinking. Each approach seemed to leave out something important that would open the text up further for me. I took a class on Latin Poetry taught by Sylvia Barnard. As we read poems in class, Sylvia supplied a kind of running commentary, giving us biographical, historical, political, cultural, and other background information. Her approach gave us both a "bigger picture" and—what fed my passion for studying literature—made the poets come alive. With the feel of living in ancient Rome and the earthiness and carnality of Roman life, the poems took on an immediacy I never expected from two-thousand-year-old writings. Sylvia infected me with her passion for literature and classroom teaching. I was so taken by her teaching style that I would base my own style on hers. As it happened, Sylvia was also a poet, and we became personal friends.

Beryl joined the student literary magazine *Phoenix* and coaxed me to join as well. I considered my poetry writing as dabbling. The magazine staff had four editors: Sharon Stonekey, a woman several years older than us undergrads; Sam Steiner, a red-headed fraternity guy; Beryl, and me. Sharon and Sam started dating, and we quickly became a social foursome. We often got together at Sharon's apartment on Lark Street for dinner. Lark Street was Albany's bohemian neighborhood, where writers, artists, drug dealers, gay men, and college students lived. It made me feel like we were being big-city bohemians. To add to the patina of our bohemianism, I secretly lusted after Sam and soon fell in love with him. Sharon, closeted like I was, let me know she found Beryl sexually appealing.

I slept with Beryl in her dorm room. She had chased Brunhilda out and requested no new roommates. We had sex two or three times a week. Looking back, it must have been my 18-year-old sex drive that allowed me to perform. I had no sexual interest in Beryl or in any heterosexual sex. I was attracted to Beryl, as to other women, because she was strong, smart, and articulate. I think I was attracted to women the way straight men might be drawn to other men. Women were all missing the important things—a flat, broad, preferably hairy chest, narrow hips, and a cock. Their shapes were all wrong for me and the missing penis actually disturbed me.

It was sheer serendipity, which Billie Aul pointed out to me many years later, that under my editorship, the *Phoenix* was the first magazine to publish a poem by Gregory Maguire. I had no idea he was gay and no one knew he would go on to write his bestselling *Wicked*.

The Phoenix shared an office with the Gay Liberation Front student group. The GLF, the Gay Activist Alliance, and the Gay Maoist Students arrived on campus at the same time I did. I believe they had all come to SUNY Albany because Albany was the capital of New York State. When I was working on *The Phoenix* and found myself alone in the office, I pawed through the GLF's printed materials. I read pamphlets, flyers, and questionnaires students had filled out. This is where I first read about coming out as a political strategy, and ideas about how the liberation of gay people would liberate all of society. I found a button that proclaimed, "Gay is Good." I read a broadside attacking the American Psychological Association for labelling "homosexuality" a mental illness and for calling us "sick," "deviant," "perverse." This was my first exposure to what *Time* magazine had reported was happening in New York City and what the press was now calling "militant homosexuals."

This was my first glimpse of a new, different, and positive, life-affirming vision of being openly gay. On my own I was having furtive sexual encounters. I found phone numbers scrawled on public toilet walls on campus with messages to call for sex. Once, when I was studying in a corner carrel on the bottom floor of the campus library, the guy in the carrel facing mine somehow reached out with his foot and tapped my foot. I could not see who was tapping my foot. I was alarmed, and excited. I stood up and looked over the divide to see who the guy was. He apparently thought he had made a mistake. He apologized to me and picked up his books and left.

Our literary foursome sometimes went to GJ's Gallery, a neighborhood bohemian bar around the corner from Sharon's apartment. People smoked pot or bought drugs in the bathrooms. Sam started inviting me to his dorm room in the fraternity house, to drink and smoke pot and try other drugs—mostly speed, acid, and Quaaludes. Soon I was hanging out with Sam more often than with Beryl.

I started going to GJ's on my own. Around 10 PM I'd slip out of Sam's dorm room or out of a drinking party at a frat bar. A few times I let a guy pick me up. I'd give him a fake name, go to his house, and after the guy had fallen asleep slip out and go back to campus. One guy fucked me raw. I had never had anal sex before. I thought anal sex was supposed to be painful. It was excruciatingly painful for me.

Tom Smith also came one weekend. He was in Albany for a Republican party function. He invited me to his hotel for lunch and a photo opportunity. (When I saw my photo in the Cortland newspaper identifying me as a Republican I was horrified.) Tom wanted me to take him to a local college bar. I had not yet been off campus at that point and had no clue where any of the bars were.

I looked for the presence of gay men in the novels I was reading in my classes. I found a few examples. *The Portrait of Dorian Grey, The Counterfeiters, Swann's Way,* and *Death in Venice* all presented homosexual experiences that I could not relate to. On my own I read several novels by Hermann Hesse. I found an undercurrent of homoeroticism in some of them.

One day I walked through Campus Center. At the top of the stairway in the lobby I saw two men kiss each other. It was unmistakable. The kiss was long. And in the middle of a crowd! People had to step around them. I had never seen two men kiss before. I was shocked.

16

I went back to my parents' house for the summer following my freshman year. It was a repeat of the previous summer, mowing the lawn, tending Mom's garden, working the graveyard shift, and reading. On Saturday evenings I would go out to the student bars on Main Street. The bars were quiet, and I drank by myself.

I saw Tom a couple of times over the summer. Julia asked me to join her group of actors who were rehearsing a play. I bowed out since I was at the factory when they met.

One weekend Tom was available to hang out. It just happened to be the same weekend Beryl had invited me down to visit her in New Jersey. (This became a frequent pattern in my life that probably happens to everyone else. I'd go for weeks with no appointments and then suddenly be expected to be in two or three places at the same time.) I decided to go out drinking with Tom. Late that evening, when I was fairly drunk, I remembered Beryl and called her from a pay phone in the bar. I told her I was out with my friend Tom and was not coming down to New Jersey. Beryl was furious; no one had ever treated her like this before. She screamed over the phone, "You're a faggot, aren't you?!" and slammed down the phone. These words stung me. I remembered a message on a bathroom wall that went, "The definition of a 'faggot' is 'the homosexual gentleman who just left the room.'" And I remembered Mom once telling me to stop crying, "Sticks and stones can break my bones, but words can never hurt me."

I never saw Beryl again. When I got went back to Albany in late August,

I learned from Sharon that Beryl had transferred to Rutgers. None of us ever heard from her again.

Two other graffiti scrawled on that bathroom wall have stuck with me. "'God is dead. —Nietzsche' and 'Nietzsche is dead. —God'" and "I am a beggar, always on the outside looking in."

That fall I had a new roommate. Bob McCarthy was an ex-Marine I had met at GJ's. We had a friendly talk. Bob was living in the Lark Street neighborhood, struggling, and not making it as a writer. He planned to go to SUNYA to get a business degree. We agreed to be roommates if he got in.

I quickly realized I needed a job. The only job on campus I could find was washing pots in the Campus Center snack bar. The work depressed me; the pay depressed me even more.

Finding myself unattached with Bob never around, I started hanging out with Sam and his best friend and roommate, Carl Andrews. This meant drinking and smoking grass with their frat brothers every night. I often overslept, and sometimes woke up still drunk from the night before. All my courses were graded pass/fail that year, so I could afford to cut classes and do crappy work, and still pass most of my courses. (Pass/Fail was an experiment the student body had convinced the university to employ. The theory was it would free up students to take more academic risks and not worry about GPAs. The university countered that it would make it more difficult for seniors get into grad school. After two years the experiment was declared a failure.) My strategy was to sign up for a course overload, taking a sixth or seventh course, and then dropping any I was failing in, stopping at the four-course minimum to maintain full-time status and not lose my scholarship money. I prioritized partying and boozing over my academic work.

But all that booze and all those drugs did not mask my ever-deepening depression. I let my hair grow and stopped shaving. I grew a beard. I looked unkempt. Sam once grabbed me by my T-shirt and told me, "Clean yourself up. Put on something better. You look like a slob."

One night I trudged back to my dorm room on the other side of campus. It was late. Bob was gone for the night. I tried sleeping. I remembered the night earlier that semester when I stepped quietly over to Bob's bed and gently touched Bob's hard-on. I was scared shitless that Bob would wake up. I thought to myself, "I can't do this. I just can't do this anymore." And I loathed myself for being such a pervert.

I went into the bathroom. I took the blade out of my razor. I slashed my face several times with the razor blade. The blood began to flow down my cheeks. Then I filled the bathtub with warm water and lay down in the tub. I made deep cuts into my wrists. And waited.

17

I woke up, disappointed I wasn't dead.

I washed the caked blood off my face, dressed, and walked over to the snack bar to work in the kitchen. The manager stared at the slash marks on my face wordlessly. I started in on a huge stack of dirty pots and pans.

When I got off work, I went to the snack bar for coffee and a donut. Sam and Carl came in to buy coffee to take to class. Seeing me, Sam exclaimed, "What the hell happened to you?"

I wasn't about to admit to my failed suicide attempt. The first thing that popped into my head was, "I was attacked by a gang of lesbians outside GJ's last night." Neither of them believed this. I could read disgust on Carl's face. But they did not say a word.

Over the next few days Sam arranged for me to move into the fraternity dorm. My room was across the hall from Sam and Carl's room. Sam urged me to rush Beta Phi Sigma. Sam also got me a new job, staffing the university's Information Desk in the lobby of the Campus Center. The building manager, a roly-poly thirtysomething redhead named Clancy Wilhelm, gave hiring preference to Beta Phi Sigma guys and their women friends. (They called him "Nancy" behind his back. But he could always be counted on to help "his" frat boys out.)

The Sam, Carl, and Les party went on. Sam brought two more artsy guys into the fraternity. He recruited Ritchie Welton, who had recently joined the *Phoenix* staff and was studying to become a librarian. He found Steve Berch playing piano in the dorm's common room. Steve was getting a degree in Business Administration, although he was very talented as an

LES K. WRIGHT

artist and musician. (Ritchie became a librarian and drowned in a freak boating accident at the age of 41. Steve would move to Boise, work in high tech, and become a politician in state government there.)

We all gathered in Sam and Carl's room after dinner and homework to party. Two frat brothers, Ken Stokum and Bowen, were drug dealers and kept us supplied with speed, sopors (downers, like Quaaludes), and acid. We got drunk and stoned, goofed off, and listened to records. I became "famous" for performing my version of a "dancing zucchini." I acted "spastic," jumping and flailing my arms. Carl cackled with glee. I had to be fairly drunk before I could be persuaded to make a fool of myself. Carl shouted, "Do it again, twatface, do it again!" We listened to records: Aretha Franklin, Traffic, Jefferson Airplane, Moody Blues, Elton John, Neil Diamond, the Rolling Stones, Yes, and the Hollies.

Some evenings our gang went off-campus to the Cellar Bar at the hotel on Western Avenue. This is where I began my practice of slipping away and going to GJ's by myself. From the gay men I met there I learned about the Central Arms on Central Avenue. The Central Arms was typical for its time. In the middle of a boarded-up storefront was a door with a peephole. You rang the bell; someone inside would give you a look-over. If you looked gay, they buzzed you in. Inside the jukebox blared old hits, lots of the Supremes and the Temptations. A mirror on the wall behind the bar ran the whole length of the bar. It allowed patrons to watch the crowd without being detected looking. A huge pink and orange cardboard sixties hippie flower with a large clock, covered in twinkling pink Christmas lights, hung in the center of the mirrored wall.

My first time there I found mostly working-class men in their 30s and 40s who were pretty drunk and "touchy-feely" with me. I hadn't yet learned that I was "chicken." One guy sitting on the barstool next to me offered to buy me a drink. He reached over and began rubbing my thigh. "It's always Christmas in here, darling." He stuck a bottle of poppers under my nose. I inhaled deeply and held my breath. A huge rush filled my head and I felt ecstatic. The guy kissed me hard, sticking his tongue in my mouth. I got hard and was ready to go home with him.

Back at Beta Phi Sigma, I suspected my homosexuality was now an open secret. They seemed to tolerate it as long as I didn't bring anyone back to my dorm room or talk about my secret life. The only explicit comment came from Tom Kemnitzer, a frat brother with dark hair and a twinkle in his blue eyes. He was very hairy and suggested Robert Goulet to me. We both loved the same 50s love songs.

One day Tom came out of his dorm room and looked me right in the eye and said, "I wish I could give you what you want. But I can't."

18

Sam and Carl both graduated in the spring of 1974, and both were accepted into the Criminal Justice graduate program at Albany. Sam wanted to become a cop, and Carl simply followed Sam. The three of us shared a small three-bedroom apartment a block away from the downtown campus. A free shuttle bus ran between the two campuses, so I was able to get to classes. The Lark Street neighborhood was within walking distance.

I continued to work for the Campus Center and was promoted to the position of night manager. It was an easy job—except for when I had to throw people out of the building. Wilhelm gave Sam the use of a university jeep for the year. What caught me off-guard was when Wilhelm invited me up to the university's Saratoga Springs campus in the Adirondacks. It turned out to be a trap. When Wilhelm pressured me into having sex with him, I saw no alternative since we were way out in the country, and I had no means of transportation. I submitted. This was the second time I was raped. And again, at the time I did not realize it for what it was.

I tried to take academics in my junior year more seriously. Being in grad school, Sam and Carl tried to buckle down. Coursework kept us busy. In the apartment we cooked and ate separately. Sam and Carl piled their dirty dishes up in the sink. I complained to no avail, and often ended up washing the dishes. The kitchen was infested with cockroaches.

Carl complained about the downstairs neighbors, grad students from Nigeria. I learned quite a few new pejorative words for Blacks from Carl's rants. I also learned about anti-Puerto Rican racism. (If someone blew their car horn down in the street, Sam would mutter "… goddam Puerto Rican doorbell.")

I decided to go back to West Germany for my senior year. This meant I had to get better grades. I took courses heavy with reading, and I spent many evenings reading novel after novel, at a rate of two or three a week. Within a four-week period I read *Emma* (Jane Austen), *Madame Bovary* (Gustave Flaubert), *Effi Briest* (Theodor Fontane), and *Anna Karenina* (Leo Tolstoy). They were all about 19th century women and the social constrictions they faced. This was the entirety of my exposure to feminism as an undergrad.

Nonetheless, our partying continued. We often walked to the Washington Tavern, a student bar round the corner, to drink. I continued my pattern of slipping out to look for sex.

I was now putting on a lot of weight and had a growing beer belly. When I bent over to tie my shoes, I got winded. I signed up for a Water Safety class. It was time for me to renew my WSI credential and swimming laps daily would help me lose weight.

Getting back into the practice of swimming felt great. I enjoyed the endorphin high it gave me. It wiped out any residual feelings of a hangover.

I used to stare at a furry, bearded bodybuilder, who was probably a graduate student. He sat for hours at an empty table in the Campus Center, reading. I could never bring myself to speak to him. I was surprised to see him turn up in my WSI class. We paired up for exercises practicing how to break the hold of a panicking drown victim. This guy chose me. He played the role of a drowning victim and got a firm hold on me. He pulled me down, my head underwater. I started to panic. I couldn't break out of his hold. He was drowning me.

And then he relented. I realized he had taken revenge.

I continued to drop my beads in spite of myself. Sam took a phone call at our apartment from a guy looking for sex. "Where did you get this number?" Sam demanded. "Off a shithouse wall" came the reply. Sam was still fuming when he recounted this call to me.

Then he took another call from a guy who said he'd found my wallet in his car. The guy had picked me up at the Washington Tavern. He drove us out into the country on a hill overlooking Albany, and he started giving me a blow job. Suddenly there was a flashlight on us. A cop made my trick roll down his window, asked for his driver's license, and asked him what we were doing. After the cop ran his license, he came back to the car, handed the license back, and said, "Don't come back." I was shaken. I panicked over the realization we were about to be arrested for committing a homosexual act. But that didn't happen. My trick said, "He saw I work for the police department and could have blocked his report." My wallet had fallen out of my pocket when I dropped my pants. I told Sam, "It must have fallen out when a guy gave me a ride home."

I researched several study-abroad programs and decided to go to Tübingen. I was excited to go back to West Germany. (Martians, according to *Stranger in a Strange Land*, would simply pick up and move elsewhere when the place they were living in had become intolerably saturated with experience.) I believed the move would also take me away from the drugs I couldn't stay away from. This would be my senior year and complete my BA at SUNYA. I would be in a new place where no one knew me. I planned to arrive in West Germany completely out of the closet. I could make a fresh start as an openly gay man.

Dr. Spalek, the chair of the German Department, got wind of my decision to go to Tübingen. One day on the lunch line in the Campus Center, Spalek came up to me and in a quiet voice asked me to reconsider the SUNY-Würzburg program. On the spot he offered me a full scholarship to persuade me.

During this time the *New York Times* published the "Pentagon Papers," exposing the government's lies about the Viet Nam War. The Watergate scandal, when the Nixon administration covered up a break-in to the Democratic National Committee's offices in Washington, D.C., outraged the American people and deepened mistrust in Nixon (who responded by claiming, "I am not a thief").

On August 8, 1974, Richard Nixon resigned as president of the United States. I packed my bags to fly to West Germany, vowing never to return.

19

The city of Würzburg, the cultural capital of Franconia, was the crossroads of central Europe during the Middle Ages. The Inquisitors' guidebook— the *Malleus Malificorum*, or the *Hammer of Witches*—was used to identify, interrogate, and punish witches. The Würzburg witch trials of 1625-1631 are among the biggest witch trials, followed by one of the biggest mass trials and mass executions in European history. Some 1,120 men, women, and children are believed to have been executed or to have died in confinement. The *Marienkapelle* now stands in the middle of the *Marktplatz* on the site where a synagogue once stood and was burned to the ground during a pogrom. It is believed to have been erected in atonement.

Würzburg was once ruled by a prince-bishop. During the Baroque period, a beautiful *Residenz* (palace) was constructed to house the ruler. In an act of retribution for the Nazis' bombing of London, the British bombed Würzburg into the ground during the final weeks of the World War II, something that the local residents never forgot because by the time of this bombing, the Germans had clearly lost the war. West Germany was in the midst of a reconstruction boom, restoring the old parts of many German cities and town, erasing the signs of war damage. Most of the city was rebuilt in the styles it had been in before the war, preserving the Baroque beauty of Old Würzburg. Only the *Dom* (cathedral) is a modern monstrosity. In 1974 there were still individual bombed-out buildings amidst the restored architecture.

Würzburg was also in the middle of the Franconian wine-growing region. Franconian wine was very much like Alsatian wine. It was *herb* (dry and fruity), bottled in the characteristic *Boxbeutel* (like the shape of Mateuse wine bottles, an immediately recognizable bulbous oval shape). The countryside surrounding Würzburg was blanketed with vineyards. Würzburg was now the start of the Romantic Highway, a route that winds through picturesque southern German towns and cities. I began my introduction to appreciating wine with the unusual *Frankenwein*.

I was about to begin studies at the Julius-Maximilians-Universität. The dozen students in the SUNY-Würzburg program arrived in the early summer for an intensive language course to bring our fluency up high enough to pass. Like with *Gymnasium*, the academic university year also began in October. I started with the summer language course, but quickly got bored. I was already fluent enough. I started skipping classes.

In the first weeks I hung out with the other SUNY students. We ate lunch together at the *Mensa* and went for coffee at the *Studentencafe*. In the evenings we went dancing at the *Studentenkeller*. This was the height of disco and ABBA's music was everywhere. Novelty dance songs were also popular. We danced the Bump and the Hustle, being the first to bring it to the university crowd. Donna Summer, with her erotic moaning, was also huge, claimed by West Germans for her "Munich sound."

We all lived in *I-Haus*, the international student dormitory. To encourage the international students to get to know each other, the *I-Haus* director organized a dance. The nationalities did not mix: the French congregated in one corner, the Brits in another, the Americans in a third. The one person who mingled freely was Amon, a law student from Egypt. He was old for a student—40. He was the son of Egyptian diplomats, who supported him. He invited everyone to his room for pizza after the dance. Amon enjoyed playing host. His pizzas were famous—black from the thick coating of hashish on top. He was also an alcoholic.

Jim May, a pudgy, pasty guy with long curly hair, came out to me. We hung out together and set out to find out if there were any gay bars. We found a place called Jalousie, a dark, cellar-level bar with red-flocked wallpaper, had an all-lesbian jazz band from Prague, and overpriced, watered-down drinks. We were almost always the only customers in the place. When we realized it was a hooker bar, we stopped going there and decided to keep looking for a gay bar.

We went to a local disco called Odeon 2000, hoping to find gay men there. There weren't any. I mustered the courage to ask one of the bartenders if there were any gay bars in Würzburg. She gave me directions to the Flocon, located on the far side of the Main River.

I started going there by myself. On one of my first visits, I met a guy named Manfred. He was husky, hairy, and older—pushing 40. (I was 20.)

Manfred took me home and we were up all night having drunken sex. In the morning Manfred shared his life story. He was a *Lebensborn* child. *Lebensborn* was a Nazi program where single German women—preferably blonde and blue-eyed—mated with German soldiers to bear racially "pure" Aryan children for Herr Hitler. The children were immediately sent off to be raised by approved Aryan Germans and often members of the SS. The mother was expected to come back to mate for another child. The children never knew their biological parents.

After the war *Lebensborn* children were stigmatized—called "SS bastard," "Nazi child," or "rat." After the war ended many of them spent their childhoods in mental institutions. Manfred had grown up in a mental institution in Würzburg. The Aryan breeding program had failed miserably in Manfred's case. He was neither blond nor blue-eyed. He was also bald, which I discovered the next morning when I woke up. Worst of all, he was homosexual. In 1974, homosexual acts were still illegal under Paragraph 175 of the German penal code.

I declared Manfred my boyfriend. The relationship lasted a week. Manfred's lover Peter found out about us at the same time. Peter screamed at me to get out. As I left, I could hear Peter and Manfred yelling at each other at the top of their lungs.

One Saturday evening early in September I went to the Flocon as usual. As I was sitting at the bar the instructor from my summer language program, Dennis Anderson, walked in.

I panicked. I thought Dennis had come to the Flocon to track me down to find out why I was cutting classes all summer. "What a surprise to see you here," he said.

He sat next to me at the bar. Several men said hello to Dennis. Seeing that he was well known at the Flocon, I was surprised we had never crossed paths there before. We chatted a bit and, after a few drinks, Dennis invited me back to his apartment in the *Innenstadt*. His building looked like an American motel. The building was flush with the side street it faced, and the tenants' parking lot was in an interior space. An exterior stairwell led up. Each floor had an exterior walkway. The apartment doors faced the interior courtyard.

Rob's one-room apartment was sparsely furnished—a mattress on the floor, a wooden table against the window facing a bottle-washing plant, and a Scandinavian modern desk and chair next to the window. The kitchenette had a stove and a sink, but no refrigerator. Otherwise, the apartment was bare.

We had quiet sex. I drifted off to sleep, spooning with Dennis. In the morning I was awakened by a loud clanking sound from the bottle-washing operation. I didn't count this first night together as the beginning of our relationship. For me it began the night I showed up drunk and lonely at Dennis's at 2 AM. Dennis let me in, and I never slept in my dorm room again.

We began spending time together. Dennis introduced me to the Jazzkeller, a live music club in the cellar of a large pre-war building. English and Irish folk singers dominated. We went to the movies, seeing mostly classic Hollywood films dubbed into German. I saw *Who's Afraid of Virginia Woolf?* for the first time and was spellbound by it. For a course I even wrote a paper on sadomasochism in *Who's Afraid of Virginia Woolf?* I read Martha and George as gay men. It carried echoes of what I had seen of Manfred and Peter's relationship. Once, after a night of heavy drinking, Dennis warned me, "If our relationship ever becomes like that, it will be over."

Edward Albee repeatedly and vehemently rejected the claim that George and Martha were actually a gay couple. "If I wanted to write about a gay couple, I would have," he has been quoted as saying. In fact, Aaron S. Lecklider has identified the models for Goerge and Martha on two American leftists, bisexual Communist poet Willard Maas and his wife Marie Menken, also an artist and filmmaker. Albee's rejection of being labeled a gay writer was made publicly very clear. As a guest speaker at an OutWrite conference in San Francisco, he took the opportunity to declared there is no such thing as gay literature.

We never discussed our relationship or set any boundaries for it. I continued to trick with other men. I cruised the train station after midnight, when prostitutes and gay men drank coffee in the station restaurant. Once I inadvertently outed a guy when I slipped out of his apartment after sex and tried to leave the building. The front door was locked. I had to ring the doorbell to wake the guy up to let me out of the building.

I brought an American GI back to the apartment once when Dennis was out of town. All the bars, the Jazzkeller, and some other places were officially "off-limits" to the American military (on grounds that the soldiers often started fistfights). This included the Flocon, which was periodically raided by American MPs—at the time homosexuality was grounds for immediate expulsion from the Army. In the morning the GI would not leave until I gave him 20 marks for the taxi.

At another time when Dennis was out of town, I got drunk with Jim May on sweet vermouth and then went out to the Flocon. I remember leaving the apartment. The next thing I remember was coming out of a blackout and finding Jim sucking my cock. I had always turned down Jim's requests for sex.

On another occasion a black GI picked up Dennis and me. He drove us to his apartment, which was located out in the country. All the GI did was watch us having sex.

Then I contracted the clap. Dennis took me to a doctor, and she treated both of us. Treatment was a shot in the ass that ached for days. German law required anyone being treated for a venereal disease to give the names of their sexual contacts and to abstain from sex until they were cured. I always said I had had sex with GIs who never gave their names.

20

There was a *schwarzes Brett* near the entrance of the *Mensa*. One day shortly after the winter semester began, a large hand-written sign appeared, announcing the first meeting of WüHST, giving the date and listing a phone number for meeting location. I jotted the number down. WüHST stood for *Würzburger homosexuelle Studenteninitiative*. The name was a pointed play on the word *wüst*, which means "desolate."

I called the number from a public pay phone after lunch. I told the guy who answered I had seen the sign and wanted to come to their meeting. He asked me a couple of questions and we chatted a bit. He was clearly screening me and, once it was clear I was gay, he offered me encouraging words about the group, which offered a safe place for men coming to terms with their homosexuality to meet and talk with other *schwule Männer* (gay men). They were a support and social group.

I went to an apartment building practically across the street from the *Mensa*. I rang the doorbell. Someone looked through the peephole and asked me what I wanted. I mentioned WüHST and was then let in.

There were eight other men in the living room, sitting on a sofa, a couple of *Sessel*, and on some chairs dragged in from the kitchen. Some were drinking beer from a bottle; others, coffee. A few were talking quietly with each other. Some sat in silence. The guy who answered the door introduced himself to me. Everyone used first names only and we addressed each other with *du*, the informal "you." This was the custom among university students and gay men alike, whether they knew each other or not.

The meeting began as an informal social gathering. The organization was informal, and the two gay men who had founded it two years before explained they had two goals—to create a safe space for gay men to provide each other with support and to push for public visibility. In the course of my year with my fellow WüHSTlings, I learned about Paragraph 175, a law which criminalized homosexual behavior in West Germany, the pink triangle and how gay men had been imprisoned and murdered in Nazi concentration camps, and the goal to remove Paragraph 175 and to fight to end the social stigma of being gay. Similar students were being organized at other West German universities.

WüHST embraced the American tactic of "coming out," for which there was no German term. Instead they said, "I publicly confess to my homosexuality." "Das Coming-Out" eventually took root in German, as did so many other words in the process of Americanizing German culture. "Gay liberation" was translated as "*Schwulenemazipation*." (The term "*schwul*" specifically meant "gay *men*.")

A couple of the men were law students, actively exploring ways to change the law. Paragraph 175, first introduced in 1871 shortly after Germany's unification, was still on the books in 1974. (Resistance to this criminalization led to the rise of the first modern gay movement.) In 1935 the Nazis broadened the law and forced over 10,000 homosexual men into concentration camps. After World War II, West Germany kept the law on the books and convicted 50,000 gay men. This law was not completely repealed until 1994, lowering the legal age of consent for homosexual sex acts to the age of 14, the same as heterosexual acts.

I found the men at WüHST congenial. Of course, we were all looking for sexual partners.

But this was the first time I made *friends* with other gay men. Over time I got a sense of the gay subculture in Würzburg. Some men had to be discreet. Known homosexuals were banned from the teaching profession, for example. In December, WüHST held a dance, which was widely publicized, and drew a large crowd.

WüHST tried to reach out to older gay men who had been persecuted in Nazi Germany. The older men refused to get involved; some got quite upset and expressed concern that we might all end up persecuted again.

The men who were prosecuted under §175 and 175a during the Nazi period were a mixed bunch. Some were ashamed, others were unashamed but concerned that they might be prosecuted again, and some were both unashamed and unabashed enough to go to court to try to get justice from the West (and East) German governments. Some even went beyond the German courts to European courts. Sadly, all their court filings were rejected. Some tried to get recognition from the postwar organizations that were created—especially in East Germany—for the victims of fascism, so that they would get certain privileges, such as speedier access to apartments, telephones, cars, and so on—all the things that were in short supply. They were immediately turned down by those organizations.

During the dark, bleak February *Ferien* (holidays) the university's International Student Office sponsored a trip to West Berlin, paid for by the federal government. In those days the government promoted West Berlin, in part for educational purposes and in part to attract people to live there. I shared a room with Jim. We got free theater tickets to a Brecht play, which we missed because we showed up on the wrong night.

Instead, we ended up going to see *Cabaret* dubbed in German. I found the film electrifying, from the performances of Joel Grey and Liza Minelli to the musical numbers to the story itself. Seeing this film for the first time in West Berlin, in the context of this divided city peppered with the bombed ruins from World War II, was unforgettable. Among post-war concrete high-rises, hastily built out of necessity, many signs of the war still lingered—vast empty lots waiting for new buildings, the ruins of bombed-out buildings, the ruins of the *Gedächtniskirche* on the trendy Kurfürstendam, permanently left standing as a reminder of the destruction of war.

I went to see *Carabet* again the following evening when it played in the original English. The original included a scene with the Hitler Youth anthem "Tomorrow Belongs to Me," a Nazi song banned in post-war West Germany. I had an acute awareness of myself living in history, seeing the politics of Germany and this new West German gay liberation in a new light. I could feel how things were changing, with me in the midst of that change.

Jim and I spent our last night in a *Tuntenkneipe* ("fag bar"), full of old queens. The place was very festive. Karneval ornaments festooned the bar. The jukebox played corny *Schlager* (German pop) songs, some with campy gay lyrics. Drag queens mixed with butch, working-class men. Everyone drank *a lot*. The bartender gave us American boys a few drinks on the house. The good times seemed to go on for a very long time. When last call came, I discovered it was 6:00 AM and the first light of dawn awaited us outside.

Rob was passionate about American country and folk music. He had a record player so we listened to a lot of Bob Dylan, the Carter Family, Linda Ronstadt, and John Prine. He made friends with two German students, Udo Bayer and Felix Seehausen, who were also Dylan aficionados. Felix invited us out to his and his American wife's apartment in Randersacker overlooking hills covered with vineyards.

Even though I was directing so much of my energies, mental and social, to my exciting "real world" life, my academic work progressed well enough. I continued with Russian, German, and English courses, and got high marks. One feature of the study-abroad program was that my German grades were translated into American grades, and I got official credit from SUNYA. These were the last credits I needed for my BA. I scored very high on the German GRE. I was accepted into every graduate Comparative Literature program in the US I had applied to. I corresponded with the chair of the German Department at Bloomington, Indiana about a graduate teaching assistantship there. The chair denied my request and took the opportunity to let me know he thought my German couldn't be proficient enough to teach elementary German language courses. In the end, I settled on Chapel Hill, North Carolina.

Rob interviewed for a position in the American Studies Department at Tübingen, which his good friend Glen Burns was about to leave. It was a non-renewable five-year contract.

Late that April I once woke up in the middle of the night. I got up to take a pee. Before climbing back on the mattress Dennis and I shared, I looked at his naked form stretched out in the dim moonlight. His body was very thin, and he looked bony. In my mind I saw a photo of Dennis's body lying among other emaciated dead men, naked and bulldozed into a pile, as I had witnessed in a documentary film about the Holocaust. While my sexual attraction to Dennis died in that moment, seeing him through those eyes so fragile, the love I felt for him deepened into a kind of sadness.

A few days later Dennis and I listened to AFN radio's live broadcast of the last Americans being helicoptered out of Saigon, signaling the end of the Viet Nam War.

21

Rob and I had left everything open-ended when I went back to the US. It looked like I would be going down to Chapel Hill. Dennis was waiting to make plans, depending on what happened with Tübingen. I just assumed our relationship was over and we would each move on.

The day Dennis was hired to teach in Tübingen he phoned me. We had a very long, heart-to-heart talk. Dennis invited me to return to West Germany and move with him to Tübingen. I accepted his offer—to continue with our relationship and to start my graduate studies in Tübingen. That part was easy. I was able to transfer to Tübingen based on my year at Würzburg, and Dennis vouched for my financial support.

I was ecstatic. I had found my life partner. I was going back to West Germany. I was officially beginning the training for an academic career. I was excited at the prospect of living in Tübingen. I had seen the university town on visits to Glen Burns.

Tübingen, a medieval university city, is located on the Neckar River, about 25 miles south of Stuttgart. It sits between the Black Forest to the west and the Swabian Alb to the east. One of those rare finds in Germany, a city untouched by the World War II bombings, Tübingen is beautiful, charming, quaint, and noted for being tolerant. The Romantic poet Hölderlin went mad there and was kept in a tower right on the Neckar. Other Romantic writers are associated with the town, and even Karl Marx attended the university for a while. As you walk from the Lustnauertor on the river's edge, you go up a steep pedestrian zone street to the Holzmarkt, from where four more streets lead to other parts of the *Altstadt*. One street continues as a pedestrian zone. Here, the unique, half-timbered *Rathaus* overlooks the square and the daily produce market. Above the Altstadt stands a castle, on the highest point of the hill, with views of the city and surrounding countryside.

During the 1970s West Germany was at the peak of pouring much of its postwar wealth into refurbishing its infrastructure. Tübingen's *Altsadtsanierung* (renovation of the old town) made it a showcase of interior renovation and medieval external architecture. Tübingen's Altstadt was a charming place to spend a day poking about, visiting shops, and walking the odd twists and turns of its streets. This medieval university town was a dramatic change from the kitschy ornamentation of Baroque Würzburg. Würzburg's student body blended in with the mid-sized city's population. In Tübingen you knew when the university was in session—its population doubled, and the town, sleeping in the summer, bustled with foot and car traffic.

My fantasy-filled vision of living in Tübingen hit reality as soon as I got there. I had expected Dennis would have sorted out our living arrangements—found an apartment, bought a car, and be settled in. Instead, Dennis had waited for me to arrive so we could do that together.

Rob was living in a room on the top floor in the back of a ramshackle building in the *Altstadt*. The room was dark and hot, its air stale. It overlooked the *Innenhöfe* and roofs of the buildings behind it. Down the hall were the toilet and a shower that everyone on the floor shared. The other tenants were all Turkish *Gastarbeiter,* younger men or middle-aged men who did the manual labor Germans were not willing to do. They sent most of their earnings back to their families in Turkey.

Not permitted to cook in our room, we ate modestly. We bought fresh bread and sliced meats, yoghurt, and fruit. We went out for coffee and occasionally ate in a *Gaststätte*. Dennis pored through the classified ads in the *Schwäbisches Tagblatt* looking for rental properties. Dennis adamantly refused to go through a *Mackler* (property management agent), dismissing them as money-hungry vultures. In our free time we explored the *Altstadt*.

Rob found a listing for a furnished one-bedroom apartment and called. I came with Dennis. The apartment was on the second floor of a large house, perched on the lip of a hill north of the Altstadt. The apartment had a breathtaking view of the city and the Neckar Valley.

The landlords, Herr and Frau Frieß, preferred to rent to professionals and were thrilled to rent to Americans. It was obvious that we were a couple. No mention was made about that. The apartment was *unterm Dach* ("under the roof") with a sloped ceiling on the north side. It had windows on three sides, and the place was sunny and cozy. Its view looked over the vineyards below them, and beyond to the university hospital complex, and beyond that to the *Altstadt*, the medieval castle on the horizon.

We loved it. Dennis signed the rental contract. The last step to make it official was to register our residence with the local police.

The Frieß family was a powerful force in local politics. They had both served on the *Stadtrat*. They were well-connected and seemed to know everyone of importance in Tübingen. The university's guest house bordered the Frieß's house on the east. Visiting VIPs stayed there. These VIP guests could be seen sitting on the large *Dachgarten* taking in the sun and fresh air. Once I thought I saw the Israeli prime minister Menachem Begin sunning himself. Glen had assured us that the local police had checked us out thoroughly when we moved in.

The Frießes were uncommonly kind and generous to us. Over time the Frießes came to not only trust us, giving us use of their country house on weekends, but also having us look after their house when they were away. When they went to Oklahoma (where they owned property), Dennis was left in charge of any banking or other emergency business. (He got an idea of just how rich they were.) I was left in charge of watering the plants and bringing in the mail.

In a cheerful, chirping voice, Frau Frieß took to calling us her *Hausmänner* ("house husbands"), a word she made up.

We soon began to make friends. We met Hel and Muriel Karlstadt, who were Glen Burns's upstairs neighbors in Ofterdingen. Hel was working on a doctorate in Philosophy. Muriel worked as the secretary for the English Linguistics Department, which was opposite the elevator and a few doors down from Dennis's office in the American Studies Department. We saw each other every day.

Glen had grown up in San Francisco in the aftermath of the Beat era and was something of a bohemian and party animal. He and Dennis had met on a transatlantic trip and discovered they had a lot in common— poetry, American music (especially Dylan), and smoking pot. Glen and his current (second) wife Dorothea had a small boy. She went by the nickname Dodo, and he called their son Cool Breeze. Glen wore glasses and had a bushy black beard, flecked with silver. To me he looked a lot like Allen Ginsberg. I imagined Glen was what most San Franciscans must have been like.

At the end of the summer, Glen threw himself a large farewell party and invited his friends and his students, who all seemed to adore him. This was where Dennis and I met Greg Benzow and his girlfriend Marlene Kirsch.

Like Glen, Muriel, Dennis, and myself, Greg was an American transplant. He and Marlene lived in a *Wohngemeinschaft* in a village on the outskirts of Reutlingen. Marlene was studying biology and Greg, who was majoring in English, seemed to be enrolled at the university mainly to stay together with Marlene.

It turned out that Brendan Donnellan, who had been roommates when they were both in grad school at SUNY Buffalo, was also teaching in the English Department in Tübingen. Brendan's family came from Ireland, and he had grown up in England. He and Dennis had completed their PhDs in German. Brendan's interest was in German philosophers, mainly Nietzsche. His wife Linda was from Buffalo.

Rob befriended Michael Schmidt, a doctoral student in the American Studies Department; he would later found a school to teach German as a Second Language to *Umsiedler*, ethnic Germans from Poland who were resettling in West Germany. Michael's parents were refugees from Hungary, and he was fluent in Hungarian, Swabian German, and American English. He lived above Pub 13, Tübingen's only gay bar. At one time he had been lovers with the owner of the bar, a guy named Rainer, an alcoholic. Michael's current lover was a guy named Alexander, who was also studying in the American Studies Department. Dennis and I often dropped in at Michael's after an evening at Pub 13 to drink more and smoke hash.

We befriended three other people who joined our circle. Elsa Lattey, another American transplant, taught linguistics in the English Department. Muriel introduced us to her. I met Clancy Clements in a German literature seminar. I met Bernd Müller when I got involved in the gay activist group. (As in Würzburg, Dennis kept his distance from the gay activists, finding them all to be "too gay.")

This rounded out our circle of friends in Tübingen. We saw each other every day. We got together socially once or twice every week. Muriel had me and Dennis over for dinners. Sunday evenings we watched *Tatort* on their color TV. We often went on Sunday *Spaziergänge* together and coffee and cake somewhere in the country. Our most common activity was to get together to listen to music and smoke hash and drink wine or beer at our place. At that point Dennis and I were writing poetry, and we'd have an occasional poetry reading in our place.

A social evening at our apartment inevitably included Hel and Muriel, Greg and Marlene, Michael, and others. As is the German custom, everyone brought a host gift, usually a bottle of wine, occasionally a simple bouquet of seasonal flowers. Hel sometimes brought the latest album he had bought. On my weekly grocery shopping trip to Multimarkt I would get a crate of pilsner beer and three bottles of white wine. (I drank half of the case of beer all by myself.) We pooled our hashish. (Pot was not available in West Germany at the time.) We smoked hash in a small hash pipe or mixed it with tobacco, rolling it into a cigarette.

Rob always had Bob Dylan's music to play. He was working on a book on Dylan's reception in West Germany. Hel usually had something new to share. His downstairs neighbor, a Dutch guy named Hans (who moved in when Glen and Dodo left), owned Rimpoladen, a record shop that sold rock, pop, and folk music. Hans was up on everything new. Sorting through the record bins I discovered the Doobie Brothers, the Eagles, and Bruce Springsteen. Dennis collected early American folk and country music. What Hans couldn't order for him, Dennis bought by mail order from the US. Dennis and I listened to AFN and SWF3 radio stations, which kept us informed of the newest releases. SFW3 played a wider range of popular music and often filled in its history and context.

When the winter semester began, we were both plunged into academic activity. I also got two part-time jobs. I was hired as a *Hiwi* (graduate assistant) working for Muriel's boss Bernie Drubig. I also started teaching evening ESL classes at the DAI (*Deutsch-amerikanisches Institut*).

22

In my German literature seminars, I encountered several critical and theoretical approaches. We were expected to read the critical sources on our own. I was familiar with reader response and phenomenology from SUNYA. I had also had limited exposure to structuralism. In German the reader response theory is called *"Rezeptionstheorie,"* and was introduced by Hans Robert Jauss. This approach was particularly important to West German intellectuals because it spoke to the social, political, and intellectual instability of the country at that time. Edmund Husserl founded phenomenology. It is the study of phenomena, of how we perceive and understand phenomena and what they mean in our individual subjective experience instead of asking about what we really are and what meaning phenomena have in our subjective experience.

Structuralism and Semiotics began in France. The Swiss linguist Ferdinand de Saussure argued that a word's meaning is based less on the object it refers to and more in its structure. It focuses on the (unconscious) regularities of human expression—language is a self-contained relational structure. I had encountered the anthropologist Claude Levi-Strauss's theories of structuralism at SUNYA.

Semiotics focuses on how signs and symbols create meaning. Glen Burns introduced me to Roland Barthes's *Mythologies*. I was intrigued by Barthes's essay on "The New Citroën" in his *Mythologies*. Barthes interpreted the French car as the embodiment of so many space-age values and why some celebrated it as the "most beautiful car ever built." Barthes became an entry point into seeing how modern mythologies arose.

The most useful theories I found came from the Frankfurt School. My anchors were among the theorists of mass culture and the Marxist social theories applied to literature. Major writers include Theodor Adorno, Walter Benjamin, and Siegfried Kracauer, among others. They showed how literature, as part of a larger network of human experience, embodied and transmitted cultural meaning and values. Proponents of the Frankfurt School studied mass culture, which they saw as producing desires, dreams, hopes, fears, and longings, all of which were driven by consumer capitalism. This culture industry produced cultural consumers who would conform to the dictates and behaviors of mass consumer society. In this mass consumer society, Theodor Adorno argued, individuals became unimportant, being instead categorized, subsumed, and governed by highly restrictive social, economic, and political structures, which fed the ever-expanding capitalist machine. In "Culture Industry: Enlightenment as Mass Deception," Adorno argued that the commodification of culture was the commodification of human consciousness. Mass culture industry did away with independent thinking and criticism and reinforced the (bourgeois capitalist) social order. An allegory for this was visualized in Fritz Lang's *Metropolis*, where workers fed Moloch, according to Marx, the god of money.

In *The Work of Art in the Age of Mechanical Reproduction*, Walter Benjamin argued that the aura of the work of art, the irreproducible specialness that derives from the uniqueness of a work of art, withers in mass consumer society, where anyone can buy a copy of it. John Berger popularized Benjamin's argument in his popular book *Ways of Seeing*, which supplemented the broadcast of a British television series of the same name he had written, as a response to Kenneth Clark's *Civilisation* TV series. Berger challenged the traditional views of the Western artistic and cultural canon by raising questions about the hidden ideologies in visual images. The book introduced what became known as the "male gaze," a feminist concept for reading visual arts, cinema, and literature, which gained currency in American feminist thought.

In his unfinished *Arcades Project*, Benjamin elevated the status of the *flâneur* in his examination of the Parisian shopping arcades built in the early nineteenth century and how they contributed to the distinctive street life of Paris. He considered their role in a habitat for who strolled there to experience the place.

Siegfried Kracauer argued that capitalism used the natural human instinct to save work by optimizing work processes. The employer's effort was to increase production to maximize profits. Pure profits had taken the place of ownership, and the process of capitalist production, Kracauer argues, had become an end in itself. Capitalism fetishized commodities.

Consumers lived oppressed by the regimentation of the capitalist social hierarchy. Employers lived in constant fear of the uprising of the oppressed. They pacified the masses by supplying ever more commodities to consume. Consumption assuaged political resistance.

In *From Caligari to Hitler*, Kracauer examined the development of the early decades of German film. He considered the trends in the German film market as well as the underlying German social politics. A significant chapter examined *The Cabinet of Dr. Caligari* as an allegory for German social attitudes. It revealed an underlying mentality of an autocratic ruler (Dr. Caligari), who violated all human rights and values in pursuit of power.

Louis Althusser was the guru among West German academics for Marxist literary criticism. Marxist literary criticism existed in several divergent schools of thought. Althusser was studied by many students of literature. In his most influential essay "Ideology and Ideological State Apparatuses," he argued for how society made the individual into its own image. A literary work produced ideology and messaged the reader that ideology (in the case of modern Western societies, bourgeois ideology). In short, (modern Western) literature relayed ideology as the "natural" order of things, instead of revealing the ideology that had created that order. Literature was a bourgeois practice.

I spent many hours browsing in bookstores, an activity which broadened my education. In *Osiandersche Buchhandlung* I came across Michel Foucault for the first time. It was the English translation of *The History of Sexuality, Part One*. Foucault argued that homosexuality became medicalized in the nineteenth century, transforming sex acts into a social identity.

Picking up nuggets from West German gay activist publications of early German writings on homosexuality, I tracked down several works in the University of Tübingen's library. Karl Heinrich Ulrichs wrote about *der Urning* and advocated that sexual acts between men be decriminalized. I read Magnus Hirschfeld's *Jahrbuch für sexuelle Zwischenstufen* and other writings, sweating through the *Fraktur* print. I encountered his theory of *das dritte Geschlecht*. (*"Geschlecht"* translates as both "sex" and "gender.") Both activist-authors—Ulrichs the lawyer and Hirschfeld the sexologist—made the case that same-sex desire is normal (natural). In 1970s West Germany one of the meanings of "normal" was "heterosexual." Both fought against the medicalization of homosexuality, a century ahead of Foucault.

23

On a trip to the US, Dennis and I visited his sister in Minneapolis, Minnesota. We went to the Gay 90s, which was really two bars. On one side was a disco. The other bar was very cruisy. The trim bodies of the dancing men made me feel uncomfortably aware of my own small but growing beer belly. I struck up a conversation with a guy in his thirties, who invited us back to his apartment for a threeway. We smoked a lot of pot, which triggered a panic attack in me. I hid out in the bathroom until it passed.

When we got back to Tübingen that summer I vowed to exercise and lose weight. Dennis and I began a daily routine of swimming before breakfast. We drove down the hill to the university indoor pool and swam laps. The pool was always very crowded, mostly with students. We often ran into Jackson Janes, the director of the DAI, in the locker room. I swam a kilometer every morning and started my day with an endorphin high. My morning swims always cleared my hangovers.

Two other local men, a gay couple, also swam with the 6 AM crowd. They were in their 30s and, although they never went to IHT (*Initiativgruppe Homosexualität Tübingen*) meetings or Pub 13 or were known to ever have had sex with other men in Tübingen, they were well-known in gay circles. Both were strikingly handsome, tall, beefy, hairy, bearded, and well-endowed. The object of much envy, they were known for their aloofness. Dennis and I were subjected to this aloofness in the locker room. I reacted to their unapproachability with my own envy. The mere sight of them sparked anger in me. Privately I called them "Froggy" and "Wasserbüffel" (Water Buffalo).

***

Kino Arsenal, an arthouse cinema, opened around the same time that we moved to Tübingen. The theater was divided into two rooms. You entered through the bar, where tickets were sold. You were allowed to bring your beer with you and to smoke cigarettes in the movie theater as well.

Arsenal showed all sorts of arthouse films—European classics (Fellini, Truffaut, Goddard) and new releases, documentaries and oddities (such as the porno film *Mit Hund und Schwein*), cult films like *The Rocky Horror Picture Show* and Tod Browning's *Freaks*. Best of all, the 1970s was the era of the New German Cinema. West German directors, committed to artistic excellence over profit, received funding from the government, freeing them up to make their films without being restricted by the need for commercial success. Young directors, like Werner Herzog, Volker Schlöndorff, Margarete von Trotta, and Wim Wenders, owned their own film companies. The movement catapulted West German film into international success, not seen since the early days of Weimar-era films.

I appreciated the films for their beautifully framed cinematography, the acting, the focus on West German social issues, psychological complexity, and probing of modern German history. Homosexuality was an issue explored in several films as well. *Die verlorene Ehre der Katharina Blum* was an indictment of West Germany's tabloid press' sensationalization of the public's fear of domestic terrorism. *Jeder für sich und Gott gegen alle* retold the famous nineteenth-century story of Kasper Hauser, a feral child who turned up one day in a small town. *Aguirre, the Wrath of God* and *The Tin Drum* were international successes.

In my book, none of these directors could hold a candle to the Douglas Sirk-influenced Rainer Werner Faßbinder, the openly and in-your-face gay *enfant terrible* of the movement. He made movies at a seemingly impossible rate, often two a year. Dennis and I were always on the lookout for Faßbinder's latest film. Most were brilliant, moving, and insightful. But he also churned out the occasional clunker. *Faustrecht der Freiheit* (*Fox and His Friends*) riveted me. In the film, Fox (played by Faßbinder), a rather naïve working-class man, wins the lottery. He falls in love with the son of an industrialist, who exploits Fox's love, secretly using up Fox's lottery winnings for his own purposes. I read it as a straightforward morality play about how capitalists exploited workers. Common to many of his films, Faßbinder indicted Fox for being an active participant in his own victimization. I appreciated Faßbinder's realistic, if pessimistic, portrayal of West German gay culture.

24

Sometimes I spent the night at my trick's home. Sometimes I walked home at 3 or 4 AM. Sometimes I brought my trick home. We would have sex and sleep in the living room. I missed swimming when I didn't come home. I would come home to an empty apartment. Dennis and I never discussed our sexual arrangements. He never said a word about my bringing men home or staying out all night. He would go swimming and head to his office, getting his breakfast from the vending machines in the Bert-Brecht-Bau (the informal name students gave to the *Neuphilologicum*).

I cooked dinner every evening. I did the weekly shopping, usually on Thursdays. Saturdays we both did housework and then headed down into the *Altstadt* to buy fresh bread, cheeses, and sliced meats, for little treats from a specialty shop. Our shopping ended at Hanseatica, where we bought fresh coffee beans and had a coffee there. Hanseatica only had *Stehtheken* ("standing counters," which became popular in the US decades later). In the evening, after company had gone home and Dennis headed to bed, I stayed up and drank by myself. I fell asleep listening to records. I told myself I had insomnia.

Dennis and I never argued. We never discussed my sex life. We never discussed money. We never discussed the future. We never discussed my drinking. Dennis never criticized me, except for once. One evening I had drunk myself into a maudlin stupor, and complained to Dennis that he didn't love me. (To this day I don't know where that came from.)

Dennis shot back, "I won't live with an alcoholic."

Despite my relationship with Dennis, our circle of interesting, warm, and trusting friends, and my studies, both in and outside academia, keeping me busy, I felt profoundly lonely. My self-confidence came increasingly from other men finding me sexually desirable, which fed my unquenchable thirst for a steady diet of sex with strangers.

Dennis rarely had sex with other men. He only ever mentioned that when he was working on his dissertation in Stuttgart, he had anonymous sex in a city park.

On a few occasions we had sex with other couples. On one occasion we made contact through a personals ad with a gay couple in Stuttgart. One partner, Bernd, was married, and the gay couple lived with the wife. The other guy, Axel, owned a tobacco shop in the Stuttgart *Innenstadt*. He did not drink and explained that he was in AA. As the couple served us all the beer we wanted, I suspected Axel was counting my drinks. I felt very uncomfortable.

We periodically went to Bonn to visit Dennis's former host family, Gwen and Dieter Gescher and their teenaged children. Dieter was a senior diplomat in the West German diplomatic corps. Both came from upper middle-class families in the Rhineland. The house Gwen grew up in was now the Belgian embassy. They lived in a Bauhaus-inspired house Dieter had built for them. It was perched on the crest of a hill, overlooking pastures and the village of Oberbachem below. They were both fluent in several languages; they were art collectors and patrons of the arts, supporting painters and classical musicians. Gwen's best friend was an openly gay and noted sitar musician from India.

They accepted me as Dennis's partner and treated us both as family. Dieter was especially attentive to me. At his behest he would choose a novel for the two of us to read and then discuss on our next visit. We shared a taste for nineteenth-century European novels, and discussed Dostoevsky's *The Brothers Karamazov*, Goethe's *Elective Affinities*, and Balzac's *Père Goriot*.

Gwen and Dieter once came to Tübingen to visit us. They stayed at a nearby hotel. That Saturday they came to our apartment for coffee. Then Dennis announced that he and Gwen were going shopping in the *Altstadt*. Dieter stayed behind.

When Gwen and Dennis had left me alone with Dieter, he started praising me for my attractiveness. He gently pulled me to him and began kissing me. I never suspected Dieter was gay; I found him very unattractive. As I acquiesced to Dieter's come-on, it dawned on me that the three of them had agreed upon this secret tryst.

When Dieter finished with me, we got dressed and met with Dennis and Gwen for lunch at an outdoor restaurant. I was so upset with having to have sex with Dieter that I got royally drunk on white wine, became very loud, and made lascivious remarks, intending to embarrass the three of them.

Rob only ever stayed out all night once. I became intensely jealous and so enraged that I threw every bottle of wine in the apartment against a kitchen wall and passed out. The next morning, I woke up to find Dennis quietly picking up all the shards of broken glass. He never said a word to me. Thanks to the thickness of the walls, our landlord never heard a thing. For months afterwards I would find bits of glass in the house plants, under the rug, and behind books on the bookshelves.

25

One evening Dennis and I watched an old black-and-white American film on TV, a film he had recommended I see. It was called *The Lost Weekend* and starred Ray Milland. It had won a Best Picture Academy Award. In *The Lost Weekend* Don Birnam, the protagonist, steals money intended to pay his cleaning lady and uses it to buy two bottles of liquor. The next evening, at a bar, Don tells a friend he is going to write a book about his drinking. He recounts how he met his wife and how sneaking alcohol had complicated things. He stays sober when he starts dating the woman, but soon goes back to drinking, and drinks up all his money. Unable to start his book, he tries to pawn his typewriter for money to buy more alcohol. But it is Yom Kippur, and all the pawn shops are closed. The scene of him going from one closed pawn shop to another, growing more and more desperate, haunted me for years.

In desperation Don goes to another woman, whom he had jilted, and begs her for money. She gives him money. But he falls down the stairs in the hallway of her apartment building, which knocks him out. He wakes up in an inebriates' ward. He refuses treatment and sneaks out of the hospital. He gets drunk again and suffers delirium tremens and terrifying hallucinations. (This scene also haunted me.) The next day he steals his wife's coat and pawns it for a gun. Then he goes back to his apartment, where his wife stops him just as he was about to kill himself. He stops drinking and resolves to write his book. The film ends on a positive note, suggesting that Don's willpower will keep him sober.

The film was notable for its realistic portrayal of the experience of suffering from late-stage alcoholism. Ray Milland spent a night in the alcoholic ward of Bellevue Hospital to get a feel for what his character Don went through. Bellevue allowed the ward to be filmed for the one and only time.

The Lost Weekend was based on the eponymous novel by Charles Jackson, who based his portrayal of Don on his own experiences as an alcoholic. The novel ends on a less than optimistic note. Don has a few drinks and crawls into bed, wondering why his drinking was such a big fuss. And this after a counselor at Bellevue had told Don the truth: "There isn't any cure, besides just stopping. And how many of them can do that? They don't want to, you see. When they feel bad like this fellow here, they think they want to stop, but they don't, really. They can't bring themselves to admit they're alcoholics, or that liquor had gotten them licked. They believe they can take it or leave it alone—so they take it. If they do stop, out of fear or whatever, they go at once into such a state of euphoria and well-being that they become over-confident. They're rid of drink and feel sure enough of themselves to be able to start again, promising they'll take one, or at the most two, and—well, then it becomes the same old story over again."

In the film adaptation of Jackson's novel directed by Billy Wilder, every allusion to Don's closeted homosexuality is left out. In the film Don is unquestioningly heterosexual. In the novel, allusions are made to Don being a closeted homosexual. He is kicked out a fraternity after he writes a love note to an upperclassman. Elsewhere the narrator notes that homosexuality is "a blind alley, not shameful, but useless." In Jackson's second novel, *The Fall of Valor*, he openly explores his own homosexuality, drawing again on his experience as a closeted homosexual in the 1940s and 1950s.

Jackson was writing against the literary tradition of authors like F. Scott Fitzgerald and Ernest Hemingway, who embodied the notions that heavy drinking was a sign of a "real man" and that alcoholism was the dark key to their tortured genius. Jackson, Lowry, Fitzgerald, and Hemingway, like so many of their male literary ilk, had their creativity destroyed and met with the alcoholic's early and miserable death.

I justified my own excessive drinking to being a sensitive, creative soul. I welcomed the conceit that my drinking was a sign of my unrecognized genius. My growing sense of loneliness and pessimism, my suspicion that my life was a cosmic tragedy, despite the obvious good fortune of my life in Tübingen. I found my sense of myself in the life and writings of Charles Bukowski, who felt slighted and being overlooked by the more successful Beat writers. (Bukowski considered himself a fellow Beat.)

Bukowski wrote about the seedy side of Los Angeles in his autobiographical novel *Factotum*. He wrote volumes of poetry in the same simple language, belying the depth of insight, revealing the beauty in ugliness, matter-of-factly recounting his profligate sex life, and always the boorish party-crasher. Bukowski reveled in his low life and excessive drinking. I felt a soulful connection, almost even a political solidarity with his marginalized, blue-collar existence.

Excessive drinking had a long history of being seen as a sign of a weakness of character or a lack of willpower. This perception shifted in the mid-twentieth century. As the result of what has been labeled the "Alcoholism Movement," alcoholism became medicalized and the alcoholic a victim of a physiological or psychological aberration.

One school of complicated psychoanalytic thought posited a link between alcoholism and homosexuality. (*The Lost Weekend* had been written against this backdrop.) The Freudian argument asserted that all men had latent homosexual tendencies, which society teaches men to repress and sublimate. When intoxication reduces these inhibitions, these homosexual instincts surface. Hence the expressions of deep affection, even physical intimacy among otherwise straight men. This was shrugged off with a dismissive "Let's forget last night. We were both drunk."

Another psychiatric argument asserted that alcoholics had had overindulgent and protective mothers and cold, distant fathers. (This was the same Freudian explanation of homosexuality.) Lightyears away was the notion that alcoholism in gay men could have arisen either as a coping mechanism arising from the cognitive dissonance of leading a closeted double life or from the habit of drinking in gay bars, the only place gay men could safely socialize.

The most significant manifestation of the Alcoholic Movement's "disease" model was the self-help program of Alcoholics Anonymous. Alcoholism became destigmatized, largely by AA's promotion of the disease model and their own success in helping hopeless alcoholics achieve long-term sobriety. The alcoholic individual could be successfully treated, rehabilitated, and reemerge as a productive member of society. In a study from Harvard published in 2011 researchers reported that, in part, AA succeeds by surrounding the alcoholic in early recovery with other sober alcoholics, finding support among members in abstaining in social situations, changing social networks, and increased spirituality.

Gradually rehabilitation programs for alcoholics became widespread, as health insurance companies started to pay for the cost of these programs, which hired professionally trained and certified specialists to administer counseling, behavioral therapies, and medications to treat the alcoholic. The professional world replaced total abstinence with harm reduction and considered relapses a normal part of recovery. The professional world developed what might be called a hostile attitude toward AA.

New York State legally ruled Alcoholics Anonymous a cult and banned AA materials and practices from rehab programs. Rehabilitation programs evolved from requiring their counselors to be members of AA to banning all AA literature and philosophy, not even permitting AA to be mentioned. In *Alcoholic Anonymous*, the primary text of AA, the word "God" appears in five of its twelve steps of recovery. The anonymous author states "reliance on a Higher Power, whom we choose to call God." The Big Book, which this book is referred to among AA members, also states that you are free to believe in any Higher Power of your choosing or to have no belief in a Higher Power. It further suggests "Take what you like and leave the rest."

In the 2020s, chronic alcoholism continues to be a problem in the queer community at a rate higher than the general population.

26

In Würzburg I had found understanding and acceptance, made friends, and received guidance in gay activism in WüHST. I sought out the *schwulenemanzipatorisch* group in Tübingen. The first sign was a handwritten placard announcing a Gay Dance at the start of the winter semester.

Rob and I went. The dance was held in a large auditorium, and over a hundred gay men showed up. I got picked up and went to the guy's apartment. He turned out to be a "sniffer," jacking himself off while smelling me head to toe. He told me about the IHT (*Initiativgruppe Homosexualität Tübingen*), which sponsored the dance, and gave me the address of where the group met.

The IHT met monthly for support and discussion in the Schlatterhaus (in the Altstadt), the meeting place for the Protestant student group. The IHT had the feel of a loosely-knit social group with overlapping friendships. I made friends with Bernd Müller and often hung out with him. He sometimes invited Dennis and me to go up to Stuttgart with him to go disco dancing at The King's Club. The camp name for the disco was "KZ," the slang term for *Konzentrationslager* (concentration camp).

I attended meetings regularly, but Dennis declined because he did not care for activist gays. He felt his own homosexuality was not a problem and saw no point in being in other people's faces about it. As an upper middle-class Minnesotan of Scandinavian descent, he expected and found his colleagues and friends to treat him as an equal. This had not been my experience growing up.

In fact, I saw how this difference in our perspectives played out on two occasions. During our stay in Minneapolis, friends of Dennis's invited us to a buffet dinner at their apartment. When I was standing in line for the buffet a woman asked my what my relation with Dennis was. I told her, "We are lovers." In a flash, the expression on her face turned to one of utter disgust and contempt and she said something very hateful to me. My mood turned to intense anger. I went straight to Dennis and demanded, "We need to go. We need to go right now." Dennis tried to brush it off. But I would not budge. I walked out the door and waited outside while he apologized for my behavior.

The IHT held consciousness-raising groups, which in practice were coming-out support groups. The practice was borrowed from American gay liberationist practices, which had been borrowed in turn from 1960s American feminist activist groups. This American gay liberationist coming-out strategy was embraced by West Germans.

The IHT was actively supported by Christoph Müller, the progressive, well off, and openly gay co-owner and editor-in-chief of the daily newspaper *Schwäbisches Tagblatt*. He and his lover owned a small castle outside of Tübingen, which they had renovated. Müller came from old Tübingen money. He was a noted art collector, patron of the arts and godfather of gay Tübingen. He knew all the other (mostly lesbian) movers and shakers in the city. He had a reputation across West Germany for publishing a very progressive newspaper. He published lots of pro-gay letters to the editor. (I learned about his policy after the *Tagblatt* published my letter protesting the TV broadcast of a documentary *"Der schnelle Mark am Bahnhof"* ["The Quick Buck at the Train Station"], which painted young gay men as hustlers at train stations.)

Founding organizer Reinhard Brandhorst was a very earnest and serious person. He was stout and bearded and looked like the like Protestant pastor he would eventually become. His lover, Karl-Heinz, a queeny silly-goose kind of guy, lanky and given to giggling, was studying to become a school teacher. Both were in the closet as homosexuals and were banned from their chosen professions. Reinhard worked behind the scenes to change the *evangelische Kirche's* position on homosexuality in the church. He effected several significant changes and ended up hired as a pastor. He became the most well-known activist from the IHT.

Occasionally we read and discussed something one of the guys thought would be informative for us. We discussed articles in the West German gay press. For one discussion session I brought in Carl Wittman's "Refugees from Amerika: A Gay Manifesto," which I translated for the group.

I read this as carefully as I could. It was a radically different message from the mass media (*Time* and the television networks), which I had been taught was neutral and objective. Wittman said, clearly and directly, that all that was lies. Consciousness raising was key to the counterculture's effort to change—or "liberate"—American society as a whole. This was the first time I saw how these politics applied directly to me. Supporting anti-war efforts, women's liberation, Black liberation, all the stuff I felt I should support, suddenly included me as a homosexual man.

Politics suddenly became personal.

Wittman said, "Homosexuality is the capacity to love someone of the same sex." Having grown up in an emotionally cold family, I longed to be loved all my life. I was obsessed with being loved by a man. I felt I did not deserve what I longed for. I believed no man could love me because I was gay. I liked Beryl as a person, but I certainly had no romantic attachment. I experienced my relationship with Beryl as fulfilling a social expectation. And here was an openly gay man, who rejected everything I had been trying to do: "Gay is good."

Wittman wrote about joy and self-acceptance, about building political coalition with other groups in the struggle for liberation, about rejecting the heterosexual script. He called marriage part of the oppression. I was taken by Wittman's description of a gay ghetto and his call for gays to move to San Francisco. After our discussion meeting, I contacted Wittman, who was living in Wolf Creek, Oregon at the time, and we struck up a correspondence.

The IHT held a public screening of Rosa van Praunheim's *Nicht der Homosexuelle ist pervers, sondern die Situation in der er lebt* (*Not the Homosexual is Perverse, But the Society in which He Lives*). Von Praunheim (whom all the local gays called "*die Rosa*") introduced the American gay liberation model to West Germany in his book *Armee der Liebenden oder Aufstand der Perversen* (*Army of Lovers or Uprising of the Perverts*). Die Rosa had begun his filmmaking career as a member of the New German Cinema. His gay work led to the founding of gay activism in West Germany, Austria, and Switzerland. There was a little resistance from some West German gay activists to his appropriation of American culture. During the 1970s West Germans couldn't get enough of American culture.

The IHT hosted a one night only performance of *Brühwarm*, a satirical gay comedy show from Berlin. The program notes included a *Wichstuch*—a paper towel cum rag, and an LP recording of their comedy called *Mannestoll* (man crazy).

Our most ambitious undertaking was the weekend conference the IHT organized and to which gay activists from across the country were invited to attend. We held two days of workshops and CR groups. In one of the CR sessions I met Wilfried Eißler, a Swabian native who was living in West Berlin and was active with the Homosexuelle Aktionsgruppe Westberlin (HAW). I had read his study, which would later be published by Rosa Winkel Verlag as *Arbeiterparteien und Homosexuellenfragen: zur Sexualpolitik von SPD und KPD in der Weimarer Republik.* We hit it off and he invited me to visit him in West Berlin. We began an affair. I visited him several times in West Berlin, where he introduced me to the gay subculture there.

The weekend culminated in a *Fummelrevue* (drag show) that we called *"Das kann doch keine Tunte erschüttern"* (*That Could Never Shock a Queen*) and we invited the general public. Bernd Müller was our impresario. He encouraged us IHT folks to perform. He recruited drag friends from other parts of the country. He even got his friend Ferie (pronounced "fairy"), a professional drag queen in West Berlin, to join us. (Ferie came from Lebanon and his parents were diplomats.)

We rehearsed for four months. This was my first time doing drag. A few of us kept our beards, which was called genderfuck drag. I was a little taken aback to see how a wig, make-up, a dress, and high heels could turn so many gay men into screaming queens. Bernd gave me the drag name Cora Tschitterbäbb. He also cast me as the biker on the "Leader of the Pack" number. In another number I was cast as the stud desired by the queens cruising a public toilet. (Bernd explained to me that "All the guys know you're the slut from America.")

My biggest first-time challenge was having to go and buy all my *Fummel* (drag costumes). I went to Multimarkt, where I did the weekly food shopping, and got all my women's clothing there. It was very hard to find high heels big enough for my feet. Multimarkt was much like the later Walmart, part supermarket, part department store.

I had removed most of my clothes for the cruising number. I remained semi-naked in the closing number. Our surprise ending was to all jump off the stage and run into the audience. This remains a warm memory for me. Being gay among fellow queers was much more fun than being given the homophonic cold shoulder by a bunch of Dennis's social-climbing friends.

27

I usually ate lunch in the *neue Mensa*, halfway between the Bert-Brecht-Bau and the *Altstadt*. One day I went into the *Altstadt* to pick up some books from the Gastl bookstore. (Many years later I learned that Gastl was owned by a lesbian couple and hosted a monthly invitation-only literary salon.) That day I went to the *alte Mensa* for lunch. Student cafeterias were subsidized by the government and meals cost next to nothing.

Food tray in hand, I entered the dining area, scanning the room for a place to sit. A man, clearly not a student, caught my eye. He was in his fifties with a full head of close-cropped hair. He had a pair of mirrored teardrop sunglasses perched on his head. His tight white T-shirt marked him as an American and showed off his arm muscles.

The man caught me looking and waved me over. I sat across the table directly in front of him. He introduced himself as Tad Baugh and asked me if I was a student. The mutual sexual attraction was electric and immediate.

Tad taught German and Russian at a private high school in Marin County and lived on Castro Street in San Francisco. He had sold two properties he owned in the Castro to pay for a year in West Germany. He was living in Munich at the time and had come to Tübingen for a few days. I told him some of my story and offered to show him around my Tübingen.

Tad planned to spend the second half of his year in West Berlin. He invited me to visit him in Munich. He told me about San Francisco, the Castro, how gay San Francisco was. He said "everyone" was moving there, and suggested I consider moving there too.

In short order I made the first of several long weekend visits to Tad in Munich. He took me to the leather bars and introduced me to the leathermen he knew there. We ate dinner at the *Deutsche Eiche*, popular with the Munich leather crowd. One evening Tad introduced me to Rainer Faßbinder, a regular there. Tad told me he was not well-liked.

Tad introduced me to a German guy named Horst, who was an architect. He lived in a very gay neighborhood and was on a first-name basis with all the gay shop owners. Our sex quickly went from what he called "vanilla" to bondage scenes. Tad became my first leather master.

When Tad moved to West Berlin, our relationship continued long-distance. I continued to see Horst. Tad and I wrote each other frequently. When Tad got back to San Francisco he began sending me a column from the *San Francisco Chronicle* called "Tales of the City." Its author, a gay man named Armistead Maupin, drew me into his version of San Francisco. Tad assured me what Maupin wrote about San Francisco was all true. Maupin typically described events that had taken place a few days earlier and his gay readers were seeing their own lives reflected back to them. Soon this version of San Francisco seduced me just as Tad had done. I understood why Carl Wittman had written so passionately about San Francisco.

I began to accumulate boyfriends (which I learned later would more properly be called "fuck buddies") as I had pen pals. In addition to Horst in Munich, I got involved with a fellow gay activist in West Berlin. I had two fuck buddies who lived way out in the Swabian countryside. When Dennis and I traveled to other countries, I made sexual connections there too.

After the Bicentennial hoopla in the US was over, we took a long trip stateside to visit friends. We had celebrated America's birthday with Hel and Muriel with a trip to Strasburg. Muriel had made her "special" brownies for the trip. (They were laced with hash.) We spent the weekend stoned. My only "memories" came from the photographs I took during the trip. I don't remember visiting the cathedral, but I have photos I took from somewhere high up inside it.

Our stops included Boston, Albany, New York City, Cortland, Chicago, and Minneapolis. I brought Dennis home to meet my parents. I had already come out to them in a letter I wrote to them explaining why I had moved back to West Germany. Meeting me with my male partner must have been quite a challenge to them. But they were quite friendly to Dennis. They gave both of us Christmas presents they had been holding since the previous winter. (Dennis later complained that they gave me much nicer presents than they gave him.) The only hint of discomfort Mom displayed was when she saw us kissing on the living room couch. Out of the corner of my eye I could see she looked unsettled.

We stayed with Dennis's sister Gail in Minneapolis and stayed overnight at their parents' house out on the prairie. Gail and Dennis were close, and she was very welcoming of me. Dennis had not come out to his parents. His mother put us in bedrooms on different floors the night we stayed there.

Our first stop was Boston. We stayed with Dennis's friends Jim and Susan Mayer. They were dorm parents and lived on Harvard Yard. Jim was working on a doctorate in history and Susan was completing an MBA. They showed us around their Boston, mostly meals in fancy restaurants and drinks in tony watering holes. They talked favorably about Elaine Noble, then the first openly lesbian elected to public office. They introduced us to the Eagles and *Hotel California*.

Rob was also friends with Jack Armstrong, a poet and owner of Stone Soup Gallery, where he hosted poetry readings and rented out to other community groups. Jack was a well-known figure in Boston, one of its last bohemians. He invited us both to read our own poetry at Stone Soup. He showed us around his Boston, including a diner breakfast in the Combat Zone.

I found Boston to be very gay and very cruisy. We visited the gay community center on Beacon Street. We saw the empty brick houses in the South End, one of which could be bought for a dollar if you promised to refurbish it. Gay men were beginning to take up on the offer. We went to Glad Day, a gay bookstore on Boylston Street. I bought my first copy of *Fag Rag*. I got cruised every time we rode a streetcar. A guy told me about Provincetown, a place that was totally gay on the tip of Cape Cod.

It was during this stay that I met Larry Salmon. Dennis and I went to Sporter's, a neighborhood gay bar on Beacon Hill. I was quickly drawn to a handsome dirty blond guy with a full beard sitting at the bar. One thing quickly led to another, and when he stood up, I was surprised to see how tall he was. We went back to his apartment and continued to talk way into the night. I found him to be a very sweet, sincere, and warm man. We became friends. In the future I would stay with him on my visits to Boston. Larry would be the first person I knew who died of AIDS.

28

I always checked out the local bookstores when I traveled. I used the Bicentennial trip to buy every gay newspaper and book I could find. In the aftermath of Stonewall, numerous gay newspapers had sprung up and gay small presses formed and published gay and lesbian books. In 1976 it was possible to acquire everything coming out at the time. I had subscribed to *The Advocate*, a gay movement newspaper at that point, for a while already. I discovered *Fag Rag* and *Gay Sunshine*, both literary periodicals. I submitted some of my poems and photographs to *GPU News* (Milwaukee) and started a correspondence with one of the editors. Lou Sullivan. *Body Politic* (Canada) had the broadest international news coverage and a progressive bent. *Christopher Street,* a slick looking magazine, published rising gay writers and treated gay writing seriously as literature.

I subscribed to *Schwuchtel* (West Germany) and *Revolt* (Sweden). I started writing for the German-language edition of *Revolt* and soon found myself *writing* nearly the entire content of it. Dennis suggested I ask for a salary, since I was doing all that work. I wrote the editor Joachim S. Hohmann. As soon as Hohmann got my letter he called me on the phone and in a pique of rage started yelling at me. Hohmann never compensated me for my work, and I wrote to the owner in Stockholm, Michael Holmquist, to report my experiences with Hohmann. Michael wrote back apologizing for Hohmann but regretted he could not afford to pay me for my work either.

It seemed like everyone was writing poetry in the 1970s. The new gay small presses were publishing lots of gay poets' works. Even larger publishing houses published openly gay poetry. I read Allen Ginsburg, Harold Norse, Ian Young, Jack Spicer, Thom Gunn, Perry Brass, David Bergman, George Whitmore, Winston Leyland's *Angels of the Lyre*, Andrew Bifrost's *Mouth of the Dragon*, and many others. I was very pleased to be able to publish my transition of poems by Bergman, Young, and Whitmore in *EXEMPLA*. (Rob and I had founded *EXEMPLA: Eine Tübingen Literaturzeitschrift*. We attracted three more to the editorial board and published twice a year.)

Knowing of my reverence for Ian Young's poetry, Joachim Hohmann (who edited *Der unterdrückte Sexus*) asked me to translate his work into German for a book. Of course, I did those translations free of charge, expecting the usual payment of free copies of the book. When my copy of *Schwule Poesie am Beispiel Ian Young* arrived, I was outraged to see that Hohmann had tweaked my translations and taken credit as the translator. I had sent Ian Young a copy of *EXEMPLA* with its section of gay poems.

Young wrote me a letter filled with fury. I was flabbergasted. Dennis asked me, "What the hell did you tell this guy?" I had written Young about the special issue of *EXEMPLA*, which he had somehow misread, perhaps thinking I owned a small press and would publish a book (or a series of books?) of the poets he had steered to me. Considering how all of my work had been done *gratis*, it was a rude shock to see how nasty gay men in the world of gay small press publishing could be.

One of the gay novels I had purchased in the US was John Rechy's *City of Night*. Largely autobiographical, Rechy's hustler protagonist reveals the vast pre-Stonewall gay underground in America. I found my own experiences in the shadowy gay underworld of Albany reflected in *City of Night*. Rechy taught me so much about the gay world that I found personally instructive. I fantasized about becoming a gay hustler. Rechy went back to whatever room he was renting, and each night wrote down that day's experiences. This is how he captured the immediacy of his experiences and translated it into prose. I became an avid reader of Rechy. His term "sexual outlaw" expressed exactly my sense of myself.

Serious nonfiction by and about gay men was being published, many of which I read as "how-to" books. *The Homosexual Matrix* (C.A. Tripp), *The Gay Mystique* (Peter Fisher), and *Society and the Healthy Homosexual* (George Weinberg) explored the post-Stonewall New Gay Man. Jonathan Ned Katz documented our existence from the earliest days in *Gay American History*. Among the how-to books I found instructive were Larry Townsend's *The Leatherman's Handbook*, which deepened my understanding of whom and what I was getting involved with in Munich, and Laud Humphrey's *Tearoom Trade*, which explored sex in public toilets.

I discovered the first gay rights movement, which had begun in Germany, as documented in *The Homosexual Emancipation Movement in Germany* (James Steakley) and *The Early Homosexual Rights Movement* (John Lauritsen and David Thorstad). *Der gewöhnliche Homosexuelle* (Danneker and Reiche), *Der Ledermann spricht mit Hubert Fichte* (Hans Eppendorfer), and *Ins Ghetto gedrängt* (Hans Georg Jaekel) gave me entry points into gay men in West Germany.

Frank Ripploh's autobiographical film *Taxi zum Klo* told the tale of the perils of being any openly gay school teacher. (Even today fifty years later I value this film for capturing the texture of life in 1970s West Germany. I also value *We Were Here*, a documentary of the AIDS epidemic in 1980s San Francisco for the same reason.)

In strong contrast to the American conceptualization of gay men and lesbians as a quasi-ethnic minority deserving of equal protection under the law and participation in consumer capitalist society, I struggled through the arguments of gay West Europeans' theoretical writings. At Osiandersche Buchhandlung I came across *Das homosexuelle Verlangen,* the German translation of Guy Hocquenghem's *Le désire homosexuelle*, arguably the first theoretical gay polemic arising from the spirit of '68. Hocquenghem brought together Marxist and psychoanalytic theories and blended them into his manifesto for readers to join the political struggle. Hocquenghem brought in Deleuze and Guattari's *Anti-Oedipus* (which I read in an English translation, from which I was unable to take much away at that time) and Lacan, whom I would not read until many years later. I read a German translation of their "Rhizome," which made plenty of sense to me. It outlined knowledge as a rhizomic structure—there is no center and knowledge is interconnected in multiple, complex ways. This reflected how I had amassed my knowledge in numerous, rather random ways and which were all interconnected in complex ways. This also reflected how words could have multiple and personal meanings within my own thinking, as opposed to the uninflected neutral dictionary meaning.

I also read parts of Mario Mieli's *Toward a Gay Communism*, which had not been translated from the Italian. He was the first to demonstrate how consumer capitalism bent homosexual desire to the service of middle-class consumption. He seemed to be diametrically opposed to the assimilationist thrust of mainstream gay activism of the 1970s. (In retrospect I appreciate how Hocquenghem and Mieli laid the groundwork for queer theory, which would eventually erase Marxist theory and the grounding of homosexual desire in the body.)

But what did all of this have to do with how it felt to me "being gay" (or "*schwul sein*")? I embraced my gay identity as a quasi-ethnic minority identity. It was obvious to me how Blacks (in the US), Turkish *Gastarbeiter* (in West Germany), and women (in general) were seen as socially inferior groups; gay men and lesbians seemed to be even more marginalized. But I was also aware that all women, Blacks, and Turks all had full, rich individual lives. So did people like me.

I also embraced Foucault's argument of how homosexual acts became a stigmatized social identity. Homosexual acts were a sin, a crime, and thanks to people like Krafft-Ebing, a psychopathology. The physical act became the sole factor in defining us but tainting our entire existence. Many years later, when I struggled for a research topic for my dissertation, I attempted an *Auseinandersetzung* (confrontation) with the ironic process whereby creating a minority social identity meant to exclude, in fact created a group of insiders. For the title I borrowed Eve Kosofsky Sedgwick's term "chiasmic bind."

I struggled to get a clearer understanding of the argument by writers of political ideology that by stigmatizing homosexuals as social outsiders, they in fact were ironically absorbed into the consumer capitalist society by the very thing that made them outsiders. (I would later see how profit-seeking capitalists would enable the mainstreaming of gay people when they discovered the profitability of the "gay dollar.")

There were still two very important aspects that I felt were unaccounted for and left out of all this. One was "gay sensibility," an awareness of myself, my fellow gays, and how we perceived the homophobic society we lived in. We were not like the proverbial fish unaware of the water they swim in. I was very aware of our shared perceptions of seeing the world from a particular outsider's perspective. I was very aware of how those pop songs communicated on an emotional level all the ways love could go wrong. These were usually sung from a straight woman's point of view, which resonated to the bottom of my soul. This interior life could not be reduced to mere physical sexual acts.

I took a *Hauptseminar* on Stefan George at Tübingen. In the German university system course types include *Proseminar* (seminar) and *Hauptseminar* (advanced seminar), among others. In some seminars, the student wrote a research paper by himself; in others, it was a group project (*Gruppenarbeit*). Stefan George was a major German poet little known outside the German-speaking world who wrote in the early part of the twentieth century. He is identified with the Symbolist movement, played a major role in revitalizing German culture, and was a complex and strikingly odd, queer individual. He surrounded himself with a circle of disciples, some gay (known as the *George-Kreis*). He lived the life of an ascetic, usually staying with one of his preferred disciples. George was passionate about his poetry and his young men. His sex life with these men is known, but little studied. His poetry is rife with what I call gay sensibility. He is most noted for his Maximin poems: He fell in love with a youth who died at a tender age. In his Maximin poems George apotheosized his beloved. George's evident homosexuality was largely refuted until the 1970s.

When I began this class, I was very upset that other students in the class sniggered over George's oddities, especially his homosexuality. The professor openly encouraged this homophobia. It continued. Then I spoke up and challenged the professor and his students over their open homophobia, elevating his poetry while denigrating the person. Much to my surprise, the professor invited me to speak as a *Schwulenaktivist* to enlighten them and gave me an entire class period.

At the end of the semester our *Gruppenarbeit* research paper was submitted. I had also written an essay arguing there was such a thing as a gay sensibility. (In retrospect I have to ask myself why I thought this professor would have any light to shed on notions of gay sensibility.) He called me into his office, asked me to point out the parts of the paper I had written, and asked me in an air of suspicion if I had actually done the work myself. He never commented on my gay sensibility paper.

The other aspect of my gay life left out of the writings of these historians, polemicists, psychoanalysts, and theorists was the dimensions of my sexual life beyond the purely physical aspects. I had a life partner (where sex played a very small role in our relationship). I had lots of tricks ("one-night stands") and secondary sexual partners ("fuck buddies," "friends with benefits," and other relationships for which there were then no names). I had an occasional leather master, who initiated me into Munich's BDSM subculture. (My bondage bottom leathersex was distinct from my other sex.) When I pursued potential tricks, I was usually the hunter. I found the pursuit as delectable as the sex itself. I tended to fall a little bit in love with most of my tricks. In particular I fell in love with Helmut. I also fell in love with an East German pilot I picked up at Pub 13 and who had only recently defected to the West. He was very handsome in a Teutonic way and his body was rock hard from keeping himself in proper shape for the East German Air Force. I wanted to introduce him and brought him to an evening gathering to drink and smoke hash with my friends. In short order, he fled the den of our drug-addicted iniquity. I found the anonymity of public sex and bathhouse sex totally unsatisfying.

As with so much about all things gay, there were not yet words or concepts for what I experienced. The richness of my gay sensibility, my interior life, and my sexual life—something that I shared with and bonded me closely with my fellow gay men—did not yet have a word for it. Decades later, Walt Odets would coin the word "homocathexis" for this.

29

Among the gay men that I had struck up a correspondence with were Georg Hallberg and Peter Gethman, who lived in Stockholm. They invited us to come to Stockholm and stay with them. In preparation Dennis and I took a Swedish course at the university. I had also read about the RFSL (*Riksförbundet För Sexuellt Likaberättigande*—National Association for Sexual Equality). The Swedish organization, which was founded in 1950, focused on equal rights and worked with the cooperation of the Swedish government.

On our two-day drive up to Stockholm we had a car accident. We stopped for a red light in Denmark and got rear-ended by the car behind us, who was going through the red light. We were unaware of the unspoken rule in Denmark that a yellow light means, "Hurry up before it turns red." No mechanic in Stockholm would repair the crash damages. When we got back to Tübingen, the car was declared totaled and got impounded.

Aside from the car accident, we spent a wonderful several weeks in Stockholm. George and Peter introduced us to their friends by throwing a party for us all to meet each other. There was a scant commercial gay scene and Swedish gays maintained private social circles. We were very fortunate to have made such good friends. They showed us around *Gamla Stan*, the old town. They owned a summer house on Yxlan, an island in the Stockholm archipelago and brought us there for a weekend. We went blueberry-picking. I heard my first cuckoos in the island's woods. We went sailing.

They took us to an opera at Drottningholm Castle, a seventeenth-century opera house that still had its original wooden stage props and effects, to see a Swedish opera. Dennis and I explored the city on our own as well. We took a day trip to the university town of Uppsala, north of Stockholm. It, too, was very charming. I was struck by how progressive and open Swedish society was to gay people.

Georg accompanied me to my meeting with members of the RFSL. All of the leadership showed up for this unusual opportunity to be interviewed by an American. The guys were very welcoming. The interview went well. I made friends with Lars Lingvall, Kjell Rindar, and Stig Peterson. Between our hosts, Kjell, and Lars, there was plenty of sex to be had, of the sort that I sometimes cemented lifelong friendships with. When I got back to Tübingen, I wrote an article about the RFSL and submitted it to the *Advocate*. Turnaround time was fast, and my manuscript was returned with a boilerplate letter from Mark Thompson stating, "This does not meet our current needs" rejection letter. I was disappointed, and somewhat surprised (though I should not have been) that American readers had no interest in gay politics outside the US. I was doubly upset to find two letters with Tübingen return addresses and the stamps not cancelled enclosed in the sealed envelope from the *Advocate*. Hel reminded me that Dennis and I were no doubt being watched by the West German authorities.

30

We had made no travel plans for the summer of 1978. When Dennis told me he had no savings, I told him, "But I do. Let's go to Britain." We laid out a plan to stop in Canterbury, stay in a gay hotel in Central London, and stay at a condo in York that a colleague of Dennis's owned. We would then stay with Muir, a student from Scotland I had met at Pub 13 in his flat in Edinburgh, and take the car ferry over to Ireland.

We departed from Ostend, Belgium. I drove our car off the ferry when we landed in Ramsgate. After ten minutes of trying to drive on the left-hand side of the road and negotiate the first roundabout, I pulled to the side of the road in total panic and asked Dennis if he would take over all the driving in Britain. He got us safely to our first stop in Canterbury. We went to the cathedral for a tour. Much to our surprise, our tour guide turned out to be the niece of our landlady Frau Frieß.

In London we stayed in a gay hotel called Redfield's. The gay hotel was a novelty for us. It turned out to be very cruisy, especially in the sauna. We were free to have "overnight guests" in our room. The hotel was located in Earls Court, which we quickly discovered was a gay neighborhood, with several gay pubs and a disco. I immediately homed in on the Coleherne. It was a very popular and cruisy leather/Levi pub that was packed afternoons and evenings. There were easily more than a hundred men in the place at any given time.

It had a J-shaped bar in the center of the room. On the left the short end of the J was the leather side. The long bar on the right was where most of the cruising went on. The men's room at the far end of the Levi's bar also saw a lot of action. A narrow space between the men at the bar and the men crowding the rest of the room left little space to move. You had to squeeze your way through the throngs of men, brushing up against all those bodies. There was groping.

On my first visit to the Coleherne on my first day in London I went home with a short, hairy redhead from West Yorkshire. Ken had moved to London the year before in order to have a life as an openly gay man. He was an artist who supported himself as an artist by working as a window dresser at Top Shop on Carnaby Street. At the time I did not know that Ken would become my lifelong best friend. (Forty-five years later Ken is still painting, I am still writing, and we are still best friends.)

The next afternoon I invited Ken to our hotel room. My friend Jonathan Heller from SUNYA, who was working in London that summer, joined us. We went out to dinner and made the rounds of the gay pubs in Earls Court. We met Ken at the Coleherne after lunch every afternoon. Because English pubs closed for dinner every day, patrons drank fast. Leisurely socializing with friends mixed with fast cruising. Ken introduced us to some of his friends, who offered to show us around London.

But the Coleherne was heaven to me. I spent every day tricking with one guy after another. I devised an impromptu cruising strategy. I would identify and target three guys I wanted to go home with. I would exchange glances and then approach them one by one. As closing time approached and guys began picking each other up, I would head for my first choice guy. If he was not interested, I'd move on to the next. Having three guys to work with, I always found someone.

When the Coleherne closed after lunch hour, everyone poured out into the street and continued socializing and cruising on the sidewalk. The landlord of the pub would always remind everyone not to take their beer into the street and to disperse quickly. The police were always looking to arrest patrons for public intoxication and shut the pub down for disturbing the peace.

Of all the other guys I had sex with I made a second friend. John Scobie was a tall, dark, hairy, and bearded man (exactly my type), who looked dashing in his uniform. He was the first guy I let fistfuck me. He was a flight attendant, a not uncommon occupation among the Coleherne patrons.

Our next stop was York. We visited the cathedral and found a gay pub. There we met a young Australian guy. We palled around with him for a while. He had an English lover who supported him. When he learned his boy was spending all his time with us, he flew into a jealous rage, accusing him of sleeping with us, which was not true.

From there we drove up to Edinburgh and stayed with Muir and his flatmates. They were all theology students. We visited the sights. In the gay pub we went to a lunch hour where a fistfight broke out between patrons. Muir told us gay Scotsmen were a rough and tumble sort. I went to a shop to buy a pack of cigarettes. Although I knew the salesclerk was speaking English, I couldn't understand a word. This was when I realized that English was like other European languages with its numerous dialect variations. Muir was not out to his roommates. They found out when Dennis and I stayed with them. Later in Tübingen Muir told us his roommates had kicked him out of the flat as soon as we left.

I was so taken by London (the Coleherne and all that wonderful sex, to be precise) and talked Dennis into foregoing Ireland and returning to London. We booked a room at another gay hotel since Redfield's had no vacancies. Ken showed us around London, mostly other gay pubs. London seemed to have a gay pub or two in every Central London neighborhood.

All too soon it was time to head back to Tübingen. We stayed in Bonn with a friend of Dennis's. We were invited to a formal sit-down dinner. His friend, Eddi, was studying to become a government functionary, as well as all of Eddi's assembled friends. While these guests chatted with Dennis, I was ignored. I felt like Dennis's trophy wife who was there to adore him and not worth acknowledging. The table conversation focused on national politics and the attendees' professional ambitions. I tried to inject myself in the conversation, but no one acknowledged me. I became so frustrated that once I summoned my Dutch courage, I just plowed in. I regaled them with the story of my experiences of being fistfucked on our trip to London. This stopped the conversation cold. Dennis and Eddi jumped up and hustled me out the door. Eddi never spoke to Dennis again, and many years later Dennis still blamed me for destroying this friendship. I once saw Eddi on a TV report about West German politics. Sure enough, there was Eddi, speaking in his role as a senior-ranking minister of some government department. Back then my revenge filled me with an immense sense of satisfaction.

When Dennis and I got back home, we got together with Muriel and Hel. We told them our travel adventures and they caught us up with happenings in Tübingen while we had been away. Hel broke the news to me that my special friend Helmut had committed suicide, which was big news in the *Schwäbisches Tagblatt*. He had driven his car into a brick wall and died instantly. Helmut had done the nearly impossible. He had graduated from *Realschule* (trade school). This was education for those considered not intelligent enough to go to *Gymnasium*. Helmut had gone back and gotten the necessary education so that he could study mathematics at the university. I knew he was a budding alcoholic and had the charming personality of an alcoholic. Helmut had been withdrawing from me emotionally. Shortly before our trip to Britain, I had a long heart-to-heart talk with him at Pub 13. I was very disturbed by whatever was going on with him. He kept saying, "*Du bist nicht schuld*, Les." But I was convinced I was somehow at fault, and I was angry he wouldn't tell me what was going on with him. Helmut's suicide broke my heart.

31

My academic work had always taken a back seat to my social and sexual life and my outside reading in all things gay. There was no time clock on my studies—there was no set number of years in which I had to complete my studies. You simply took courses, wrote papers for courses you wanted a graded *Schein* (course certificate) in. After two years at Tübingen I applied for my *Zwischenprüfung,* for which I was granted an MA. It was granted only for my studies in *Amerikanistik.* In order to qualify for recognition in *Germanistik* and *Slawistik,* I needed to pass the exam in Latin called *das kleine Latinum.* The exam consisted of translating a Latin text into German.

I found it impossible to hang on to the grammar and vocabulary of Latin. I also noticed that I was having a harder and harder time in my Russian classes. I simply was not retaining new vocabulary words. I didn't realize that my alcoholism was progressing and increasingly interfering with my ability to learn. I only ever drove drunk once. Clancy and I went to a party further up the hill from our apartment. When I backed up, I nearly drove into a ditch. Clancy took over and drove me home. I stopped going out to Pub 13. Instead I went with Dennis to Brendan and Linda's apartment, drinking and smoking hash, and listening to Fleetwood Mac's new record *Rumours* every night. I grew steadily more negative, complaining about German people, about being rejected for the jobs I had applied for (which would have kept me in Tübingen), and my fear of going native.

The broadcast of *Shoah* on West German TV was a watershed moment. It was the first time West Germans born after World War II saw what their parents had lived through and what they would not talk about. The nation was stunned. Some 20 million people (one-third of the population) watched it. The film sparked debates in families. The broadcaster got thousands of calls from viewers in shock and shame. It began the process of national soul-searching and working through collective grief. My last trip before I left West Germany was to Dachau, outside of Munich. I had feared how I would be able to continue to live there after experiencing a concentration camp. When I visited the KZ the feeling of it as a place of evil was visceral.

As I geared up mentally for my move to San Francisco, I was stunned by the news I heard over AFN. First was the Jonestown massacre in Guyana. Jim Jones, the charismatic leader of the People's Temple, a religious sect that he started in San Francisco, had persuaded all his followers in their remote community to drink poisoned Kool-Aid and commit mass suicide. Second was the news that Harvey Milk, the first openly gay man elected to public office in San Francisco, and Mayor George Moscone, had been assassinated by Dan White, a disgruntled fellow city supervisor. The last shock was the White Night Riot on May 21, 1979, the eruption of the San Francisco gay community's reaction to White being found guilty of manslaughter, a lesser charge than the original charge of first-degree murder.

32

I often contracted *Tripper* (gonorrhea) and got treatment from a doctor in the *Altstadt*. His office was located on the top floor of an *Altbau*, with a spectacular view over the Neckar River, the Neckar Island, and the hills beyond. While waiting to see the doctor and face a visit with shame, the view filled me with a sense of peace and joy. I felt blessed to live in such a beautiful place.

During one of these periodic visits, the doctor examined my asshole and discovered I had a fistula. Fistulas, which I had never heard of before, were caused by anal sex or an STD. On that visit my "asshole doctor" had that stern look of a German patriarch on his face and warned me, "Herr Wright, *Sie müssen Ihren Lebensstil aufgeben.*" (You must give up your lifestyle.) I was indignant. I didn't care for him passing judgment over how I conducted my life.

Weeks later I had an appointment with him to have the anal wound treated. It was a simple office procedure and I had expected to walk home. The doctor told me that was impossible. I needed to take a taxi home. This caught me unprepared. When the taxi driver brought me to my door, I pulled out my wallet to pay for the ride. I panicked, realizing I didn't have any cash on me. (This was before the time credit cards became widespread in West Germany.) There was no cash in the house. I made profuse apologies to the driver, who really had little recourse, and cursed me out for stiffing him.

That summer while Dennis and I were walking through the hospital complex on our way home from the *Altstadt*, I was suddenly overcome by chills and weakness and started sweating. Dennis walked me to the *Notklinik* (emergency room). The examining doctor could not figure out what was wrong with me, so I was admitted to the hospital and placed in the isolation ward. They left me untreated overnight, unwilling to do anything until they knew what was wrong with me. They suspected polio, but in the morning a doctor told me I had *ausgebreiteter Tripper* (disseminated gonorrhea). I had been infected in the throat from sucking the cock of an infected partner. I would not have noticed any symptoms.

I was kept in the isolation ward for the duration of treatment. My private room had a huge picture window and a sliding glass door to the hospital grounds, a beautifully manicured lawn with several plum trees. I had a sweeping view of the Neckar Valley. My door allowed visitors to come and go without passing through the hospital itself. Dennis brought the portable TV from home, which was my only distraction for the next five days. I was given ample apple juice to keep me regular. I was forbidden alcohol. I secretly panicked over this. I had not gone a single day without alcohol in several years.

On the fifth day I was put on a shuttle bus that took me to a small conference room, where I was met by another doctor and an official from the police department. They explained that it was against the law to engage in sex as long as I had a venereal disease. It was the law that I had to report all the names of my sex partners over the previous six months to the police. If I failed to do all of this, I would be put into jail. I had no idea what the names of all those anonymous tricks had been, I did not want to admit how many men I had had sex with. I refused to give the names of the sex partners whose names I did know. That felt like confessing to a crime and naming names. (It didn't occur to me that they more likely wanted to contact those men to let them know they had been exposed to a venereal disease.) I told them I must have contracted it from a man on my vacation in England. They seemed to be satisfied by my answer and had me sign a document before releasing me.

My departure date was approaching. Dennis arranged a farewell party for me at the Frieß's country house in Strohweiler, out on the Swabian Alb. All our friends came—Muriel and Hel, Greg and Marlene, Brendan and Linda, Michael and Alexander, Clancy Clements, Elsa Lattey, Dennis's friends Jim and Susan Mayer visiting from Boston, even my IHT buddy Bernd Müller and Jackson Jane and several others. Everyone brought food and wine to share. We moved the dining room table out into the garden. People sat on the stone wall, on the grass, or on chairs from the kitchen. Joints were passed around. Clancy played his guitar. It was a bright and warm early summer day. I was surrounded by all my friends, and I felt so much love that day. They all wished me well with the next chapter in my life's journey.

As I took a long look at my gathered friends, "Bliss," a short story by New Zealand writer Katherine Mansfield came to mind. I thought of the character Bertha staring at the pear tree in her garden, at both the beginning and end of the story. At the beginning Bertha sees all her bliss for her wonderful life embodied in that pear tree. At the end, after she realizes she has been betrayed by her husband and her best friend, she looks at the pear tree again, which again fills her with a sense of bliss.

My friends and I were all university folks and, one by one, would all eventually leave Tübingen behind. What for four years had felt like a lifetime to me and had the feel of permanence for me, now revealed itself for the chimera it was. I went indoors and closed the bathroom door. I cried, realizing this life was ending and we would all never be together again.

I had arranged an *MfG* (*Mitfahrgelegenheit*—rideshare) with Tübingen students who were driving to London. On my last night in Tübingen, Dennis took us to a party arranged by some people he knew, but whom I didn't know. I spent the evening getting drunk. Dennis gave another guy a ride home. In the car he accused me of stealing his pack of cigarettes. I had no recollection but apologized profusely. Once home, I passed out.

Early the next morning I was awakened by the doorbell. My *MfG* ride was waiting for me. Exhausted and incredibly hung over, I gave Dennis a long, hard hug. I searched his face but could not read him. He had never said a word about me leaving. I grabbed my suitcase, squeezed into the back seat of the full car, and sank into a fitful sleep.

PART TWO

PART TWO

33

To avoid driving into Central London, my ride dropped me off at the Morden Tube station at the end of the Northern Line. I took it into Central London and transferred to the Circle Line to Earls Court and carried my suitcase to Penywern Road. (I had sent three mail bags full of books to San Francisco and carried a light suitcase with me. This is all I would own when I started over there.) The building Ken lived in was a wide, whitewashed Edwardian row house that had been converted into flats. Ken lived in a tiny bedsitter on the basement level in the back of the building. The tony window looked over the tracks of the Earls Court Tube station.

I rang the bell. After a couple of minutes, Ken appeared at the door, "There you are. Come on. I've just put the kettle on. Care for a cuppa?"

"Sure," I said. I felt grimy and wanted a shower.

"Right then, kid. It's upstairs on the ground floor. Here's a towel and a shilling for the water meter." All the utilities in Ken's room were metered—the electric, the cooker, the electric fire. There was a single phone by the front door that everyone in the building used. I needed a coin if I wanted a hot-water shower.

Ken's bedsitter was a large room. At the far end there was a gas stove and a kitchen sink. Both were metered. A single bed was at the rear end. Ken had a stuffed chair, a TV set, and a radio. Paintings filled the walls. We would share his bed.

We chatted a bit. Then Ken had to go back to work. "Here you go, kid," he said as he gave me a set of keys. "See you this evening."

I put on fresh clothes and headed out. Around the corner by the Tube station there was a currency exchange office, where I exchanged my marks for pounds. I headed down Old Brompton Road and headed to the Coleherne for an early afternoon lager or two. As usual, the pub was packed. Most of the men were wearing jeans. They were on lunch break. Leather would come out in the evening. The air was thick with the smell of beer, cigarette smoke, and men. The smoky air buzzed with masculine voices speaking with a variety of accents—Australian, Scottish, American, several English accents, which I could not yet distinguish. Like German accents, you could identify the region where the speaker came from and even their social class. I sometimes had trouble understanding Ken, who spoke with a working-class Yorkshire accent.

In the 1970s Earls Court had become a gay neighborhood and the Coleherne the legendary leather bar, an international crossroads that drew locals and foreigners alike. It had opened in 1866. For many years, when homosexuality was illegal, the Coleherne was two bars with the crowd segregated, with straights on one side and gay men on the other. In 1979 the crowd segregated themselves between leather and Levi's. In the 1970s its notoriety attracted celebrities like Freddie Mercury, Kenny Everett, Rudolf Nureyev, and Anthony Perkins.

I took my pint of lager, freshly pulled and served at room temperature, and squeezed into a space between two guys. I scanned the crowd slowly and got a good look at everyone brushing by. I spotted a guy about my age (I was 26). He had a thick ginger beard and warm brown eyes. Tufts of light brown fur poked over the collar of his white polo shirt. He saw me staring at him.

He smiled and walked over. "How are you doing, mate?" He smiled at me with a glint in his eye.

I couldn't place his accent, but I was sure he wasn't British. We introduced ourselves.

His name was Derek, a name I had never heard before. "I'm Les," I replied.

"Nice to meet you, Les." He pronounced it "Lez," just as Ken did.

We covered the basics. I told him I had been living in West Germany but was now in the process of moving to San Francisco. He came from Australia and was now working in London. He worked for a travel agency. He gave me his business card. It had a bright red and yellow logo featuring a biplane. His name was printed in raised black letters: DEREK NOAKES.

Derek shared a flat with two other Aussies in Shepherd's Bush. I told him I was staying with a friend around the corner. We each had another pint and chatted on. He had a very interesting life as a world traveler.

I was finding Derek witty, bright, inquisitive—and sweet. And very, very hot. I found him ruggedly handsome and very masculine. What made him even more attractive was that he seemed to be unaware of this. At the least he didn't have that aloof air that some handsome gay men (like Froggy and the Wasserbüffel) had. Derek was the kind of man I found most attractive—hot and sweet, and a little rough around the edges. I found myself falling a little in love with him.

Derek's attraction to me was apparent. We kept on chatting and seemed to click. I couldn't wait to rip his clothes off. I invited him back to Ken's place.

As soon as we got to Ken's place, we took each other's shirts off. We kissed deeply. I felt down the front of his jeans and felt his hard cock. He reached down and found me just as hard. I undid his jeans and pulled his cock out. I got down on my knees and started sucking him.

Derek pulled me back up and undid my jeans. We both took our jeans and briefs off. We pressed our bodies together, rubbing our chests against each other's. Derek squeezed my ass. "Fuck, you're hot," he said. "I want to fuck that ass so bad."

He turned me around and buried his tongue up my crack, licking the sensitive ring of my anus. "Do you have anything I can grease you up with?"

I thought for a moment, but all I had was a jar of Nivea cream. It worked. But it was very messy. Derek worked his cock into me, at first slowly and gently, allowing me to relax and open up. This felt so good. He felt so good.

Derek had me on my back so we could look at each other. We looked into each other's eyes, something I had never done with a partner before, as the waves of pleasure washed over my body. As he continued to fuck me, I felt an intense pleasure I had never known before. I had never experienced an anal orgasm before.

I felt myself falling into Derek's eyes as he devoured me with his. We came together without even trying to time it that way. We hugged as we caught our breaths, and we both started laughing.

This had been good. I felt a sudden, deep connection to this man, who had been a stranger just an hour ago. He kissed me some more. I hugged Derek again. I could tell he had felt the same instant connection.

Derek started putting his clothes back on. "I don't mean to be rude, but they'll be missing me at work by now. When can I see you again?"

I was filled with a rush of excitement and pleasure. "How about tomorrow when you get off work?" I couldn't wait to see him again. "I'll let Ken know. If there's any problem, I'll call you."

Still naked, I hugged Derek. "Save some of that for tomorrow, mate."

I savored this feeling of excitement. The idea of being with Derek again made me feel warm, and safe. There was something unexpectedly promising in this encounter. I couldn't wait to tell Ken about meeting Derek.

The three of us went out for Indian food. It gave Ken the opportunity to check Derek out and for the two of us to get know each other better. After dinner we went to the Coleherne. Ken met up with some friends of his. Ken found a guy he wanted to go home with and gave Derek and me permission to use his flat overnight.

Ken took a week's vacation time to spend with me. He showed me around London, which always included stopping in at the neighborhood gay pub in each district. The West End had as many gay bars as Earls Court. The Salisbury near Leicester Square was one of Ken's favorites. It was a watering hole popular with actors, and Ken pointed out a famous British stage actor I had never heard of—he was fall-down drunk, and a barkeep was loudly asking him to leave.

He also took me to Covent Garden to check out the little shops there. On my own I found my way to the bookstalls at Waterloo Bridge and to Karl Marx's tomb in Highgate Cemetery. Ken showed me the cruisy areas of Hampstead Heath, as well as some of the more popular "cottages"—cruisy public toilets.

When Ken went back to work, I mostly hung out at the Coleherne. I had sex a couple of times. I got together once with John Scobie, who was friends with Ken. A blond photographer took me to his flat. He photographed me before we played. One day I ventured out to the Salisbury on my own. I was approached by an editor at a newspaper on Fleet Street. He brought me back to his office and we spent the rest of the afternoon drinking there. He got drunker than me. He told me he and his lover owned a large house way out in the country in Essex. He tried to convince me to go home with him for dinner and spend the night with him and his partner. Much against my will, which the alcohol was weakening, he managed to coax me as far as the nearest Tube station. He tried to drag me physically through the station gate. But I refused to go any farther. In the middle of the crowd, he started screaming at me. Safely on the other side of the gate, I watched him descend on the escalator, yelling at me all the way down.

Meanwhile, I saw Derek nearly every day after he got off work. Sometimes we went out for dinner. Sometimes we went to his flat. I cooked him dinner a couple of times. Sometimes one of his flatmates, a fellow Aussie, cooked dinner and we all ate together. I can still remember the tacky blue wallpaper and the smell of curry in his flat.

Derek took me to the Pimlico Street Market, a flea market that stretched

LES K. WRIGHT

for a good mile along a city street. We bought each other a little gift. I gave him a dog-eared paperback of poems by Rumi. Derek got me a ceramic tile from an old parlor fireplace—a pair of intertwining blue and green vines in art nouveau style against a white background.

I stretched my stay in London out into a few more weeks, much longer than I had intended to stay. The longer I stayed the more I felt torn between staying on and seeing how things might go with Derek in London and getting back on the road. I had a Greyhound ticket that did not become active until my first bus ride. I was flying standby to the US. In other words, I was under no time constraints. But people were expecting me. After some inner struggling I decided to stick to my original plans.

I told Ken and Derek of the date I had chosen to leave. The three of us went out to dinner on the last evening. I spent my last night with Derek. We got up early since flying standby was tricky. When I was ready to go, we embraced one last time. Derek gave me a wrapped gift.

I took the Tube to Heathrow, went through customs, checked my bag, and got a seat on the first available fight. When I settled in my seat, I pulled Derek's present out and opened it. It was an Indian cookbook with an inscription—"Learn to cook this and I'm yours for life." I cried, realizing it was too late to turn back.

34

I landed at Logan, claimed my suitcase, and passed quickly through customs. I rode the T into Boston proper, sweating profusely in the subway car. I got off at Charles Street and walked to Larry Salmon's apartment on the west slope of Beacon Hill. The sticky, humid Boston summer heat I was walking through was suffocating. It smelled of car exhaust and Dunkin Donuts.

Larry was sharing an apartment with a friend, a woman slightly older than him. Larry was on faculty at the Fashion Institute of Technology in Manhattan. They both had a noticeable fashion sense that showed in their clothes.

Larry led me to his bedroom and let me settle in. We would be sharing his bed. "I'll only be staying a couple of days." I got on the phone to Jack Powers to arrange to get together. (Jack had visited us in Tübingen. There was a lot of discussion of poetry and Jack cooked us breakfasts in beer.)

I also got a hold of Jim Mayer, who planned to take me up to Marblehead on the North Shore. His wife Susan was still in West Germany interviewing for positions in Munich. She had just completed her MBA at Harvard. Jim was nearly done writing his dissertation on American naval history. I could only vaguely imagine their lives as Harvard grads.

Jack founded a poetry store called Stone Soup Poetry. He published a literary magazine with the same name and promoted local authors and poets. He was already becoming recognized as a Boston original "bohemian." Jack invited me to breakfast at a diner in the Combat Zone.

Once a smart shopping district in the heart of Boston, as in home to the original Filene's, Downtown Crossing was now a sleazy and dangerous neighborhood.

Jack told me about Glad Day, a gay bookstore, on Boylston Street in the Back Bay. After we ate, I walked to Glad Day Bookshop to peruse. I picked up a copy of the current issues of *Fag Rag* and *Gay Community News*, and *Dancer from the Dance*, a novel by Andrew Holleran. I would read both on the bus cross-country. The Boston Ramrod was in walkable distance, so I dropped in for a few beers.

The next morning, I boarded a Greyhound for Port Authority. This started the 30-day clock on my bus pass. In New York I stayed with Peter Leigh on the Upper West Side. Peer had been a guy Denis had tricked with at the Coleherne and then offloaded on to me. He had straight black hair, smoked fiendishly, and was quite rotund. He took me down to the West Village for my first time. Thereafter I went to Christopher Street every day. I found men for sex in the bars and on the street.

John Scobie invited me to a matinee of the new hit musical *Sweeney Todd,* starring Angela Lansbury and Len Cariou. Whenever on a layover in New York, John stayed at the apartment of a close friend of his. Our theater tickets were by compliments of him—Stephen Sondheim. John apparently always stayed at Sondheim's apartment on lay-overs in New York.

That night Peter took me to the Mineshaft, a hard-core leather bar and sex club. They had a strict dress code—no sneakers, no tennis shirts, no cologne. Most guys wore jeans and a white T-shirt. The entrance was up a flight of stairs. The playrooms were downstairs. There was a room with bathtubs where guys let other patrons piss on them. This was the first time I had participated in watersports.

Late that evening I was on the roof talking to a guy when I looked down into the street and saw Peter about to get into a taxi. I called out to him and asked him to wait for me. He told me to take the subway home. I turned to the guy next to me and accepted his offer to go home with him. He hailed a taxi. As we rode across the city in my drunkenness, I blurted out I was going with him because my ride had left. He shouted at the drive to stop the taxi and screamed at me to get out. He pushed me out the door, and the taxi took off. I had no idea where I was. It was three in the morning. When I came across a couple sitting on a door stoop, I asked them where the nearest subway station was.

Next morning, I caught the Greyhound to Chicago to stay with Bruce Broerman, who had been in a graduate seminar with me at SUNYA and who had been our neighbor in Würzburg. My cross-country trip began to blur by this point. I went to Bruce's house in Oak Park, dropped my suitcase off and took a train into the city.

I had arranged a blind date with a guy Richard Gampert had referred me to. We were to meet at the Chicago Eagle. I got there, ordered a drink, and waited at the bar. I surveyed the crowd. Ten minutes later a very hot leather number came up to me. He asked me if my name was Les. He then introduced himself as Steve. "If I didn't like your looks, I was not going to introduce myself. Richard has sent some trolls my way in the past."

After a couple more drinks, we went back to Steve's apartment. We smoked some grass and he gave me an MDMA—the "love drug" induced an incredible sense of well-being and heightened the senses during sex. A later generation would call it "ecstasy" for good reason.

The weekend with Steve blurred by. I remember Steve cooking breakfast. I remember more sex. More drugs. A threewway at Steve's where we took turns fucking the guy. Lying in bed with Steve, talking about nothing in particular. On Monday morning, still coming down from all the drugs and sex, I went back to Bruce's house. When he asked me how my weekend went, I didn't know how to tell him about it. I just said I had a very good time.

The next stop of my cross-country trip was Denver, where I stayed with Hel Bredigkeit's old roommate from Ann Arbor, Don Weekes. Don was very short, almost petite. He had stayed overnight in Tübingen once. I had tried to have sex with him at that time, but he wouldn't because he was in a monogamous relationship. He took me out to the Triangle, a gay bar. We got drunk, of course. When we got back to his apartment, we had sex. I made the mistake of mentioning this to his lover afterwards. The boyfriend's response was to tell me I drank too much.

It was at this point in my cross-country trip that my drinking and drugging ceased to be fun. It was as if a switch had been flipped. No matter how much I drank to recapture that feeling of delight and well-being that drugs and alcohol usually took me to, it eluded me from that point onward.

I finally finished Andrew Holleran's novel on the last leg of my bus ride to San Francisco. The book's title *Dancer from the Dance* was taken from the last line of W. B. Yeats's poem "Among School Children." The conventional interpretation of this line is that we are defined by what we do. Who we are and what we do are inseparable. If we stop doing what gives our lives vitality, we cease to have meaning. (As one guy quipped on Facebook, "If there are no leather bars, am I still a leatherman?") Gay men, Holleran observed, were "the last romantics." In the flush of the gay liberation years, we celebrated our freedom through limitless sex. If we didn't engage in gay sex, we would cease to be gay men.

35

People often moved to California to reinvent themselves. I moved to San Francisco to be a professional full-time gay man. As the Greyhound crossed the Oakland Bay Bridge in the mid-morning sun into San Francisco, the scene of Buck arriving in Manhattan in the film *Midnight Cowboy* came to my mind. The bus went through an industrial district and pulled into an open bay at the bus station. I couldn't put my finger on it, but there was something that did not look like an East Coast city. Was it palm trees?

Tad Baugh met me at the station. He greeted me with a hug and a big smile and launched into a Welcome to Gay San Francisco tour. The bus station, on Sixth Street at Market Street, bordered on the South of Market Street neighborhood. Tad drove us along Folsom Street, pointing out leather bars, sex clubs, and sex shops. We went into one, selling magazines, paperback jackoff books, and sex toys. Booths in the back of the store played gay porn, but they were actually used as private sex spaces. A few leather bars were already open. We sat outdoors and had lunch at Hamburger Mary's.

Tad then took me around "The City"—down Montgomery Street, a pass through North Beach and Chinatown, up to Coit Tower, past Fisherman's Wharf, and out to Aquatic Park. From there we went to a small parking lot at the foot of the Golden Gate Bridge, where Tad took a classic tourist photo of me with the bridge behind me. We went through some suburban-looking neighborhoods and through Golden Gate Park. We stopped at the windmills and Tad pointed out the cruising areas there.

We headed back into the center of The City to Polk Street. This was a gay neighborhood at that time. We strolled along Polk. I went into Paperback Traffic, the gay bookstore in the neighborhood. We poked our heads into a few other gay shops.

Tad took me out for dinner at the Giraffe, a popular gay restaurant on Polk Street. After dinner Tad drove us to his apartment in the Castro. He had a corner apartment on the top floor at 700 Castro Street. The kitchen window faced west, overlooking Castro Street and Yerba Buena Park. After nightfall, the Castro Theatre marquee stood out as a beacon of welcome. After I took a shower, Tad pulled me naked out of the bathroom and we had sex. Soon after we both fell asleep.

When I woke up in the morning, Tad had already left for work. I found a note and keys on the kitchen table. "Here's your set of keys to the apartment. Help yourself to breakfast." Besides our leathersex connection, we shared a passion for German and Russian. He taught these two languages at a private high school in Marin County.

I showered, made myself some breakfast, and checked my wallet. I still had $400 in travelers checks. I would have to find work. I had never been in this position of knowing no one who could lead me to a job opening.

I stepped out onto Castro Street into the morning sun. I was overtaken by a wave of terror. As I looked down the street, the thought of walking down Castro Street and being seen by other people filled me with fear.

I saw a sign over a liquor store half a block down. I headed to the liquor store, bought a quart of vodka, and went back to Tad's apartment. After a couple of glasses of the tasteless liquid, my heart stopped pounding and I stopped feeling shaky. I was ready to face being on open streets.

I walked around the Castro neighborhood. The businesses—bars, restaurants, stores—buzzed with activity. The street was full of young men. Herb Caen, the popular San Francisco columnist, described the Castro at the time as being filled with 29-year-olds all with a 29" waist. I quickly discovered that Castro Street was full of gay men hanging out every day and every night. I had arrived at the height of the sexual celebration of gay liberation.

There were lots of gay men, mostly in their 20s and 30s, dressed in jeans and a short-sleeved shirt of some sort, and sporting a moustache, everywhere. Several of them smiled at me. I walked up and down Castro Street, up and down 17th Street, where I came across the Jaguar Bookstore, where guys were having sex. I walked down Market Street to Church Street. Then I headed back to Castro Street.

I found a gay bookstore on Castro Street. It was also called Paperback Traffic. It carried all the gay magazines and journals I had subscribed to in West Germany. There was a shelf of new titles, which I perused. I selected two books to buy—*States of Desire* by Edmund White and *Faggots* by Larry Kramer. I got a burger and fries at Without Reservation and started reading *States of Desire*. It was an account of White's experiences of gay life across the US. What he encountered was very different from the urban gay landscapes I had just visited on my Greyhound odyssey. As with Maupin's "Tales of the City" representations of gay San Francisco, I had never encountered the gay worlds these men described.

36

Living in the Castro was like living in a gay small town. Still officially called Eureka Valley in 1979, the Castro District was in the geographic center of San Francisco, bordered by the Mission District, the Haight-Ashbury, Noe Valley, and Twin Peaks, the highest point in the City. Castro Street intersected with 17th Street and Market Street, which ran for three miles to the Embarcadero and is the main commercial thoroughfare of historic San Francisco. It ran down to Powell and Market, the shopping district, and on past it to the Financial District. The center of the Castro neighborhood, the intersection of Castro and 18th Streets, was referred to as the "navel of the gay universe," after Umbilicus Urbis Romae, the "navel of the city of Rome."

The Castro had several landmarks. Above all, it was home to the Castro Theatre, a neighborhood movie palace built in the 1910s and relocated to its current location in the 1920s. In 1979 it screened both new releases and revival films. (Prior to the invention of VHS tapes, the only way to see old films was at special revival screenings.) By 1979 the Castro Theatre was also becoming the public auditorium for a variety of live gay community events.

Down the street was Cliff's Variety Store. As the neighborhood became predominantly gay, the store sold nearly everything anyone in the neighborhood could want, from chandelier moldings to dishware, from electrical supplies to tools, toys, and souvenirs. Once upon a time, a streetcar line ran along Castro Street over the hill from Market Street to Noe Valley but was now long gone.

On the corner of Castro and 18th Street was Star Pharmacy, a place that stayed open until midnight and later opened 24 hours a day. Between Star Pharmacy and Cliff's, you could get whatever you needed. The corner became very cruisy. There was a pay phone just outside Star Pharmacy. The phone would ring, and someone on the street would answer. The anonymous caller would then invite the person who answered the phone to get together for sex, right then and there.

A couple doors up the street, next to Dino's Liquors, was a bench and a wall next to the parking lot behind the store. Guys sat on the bench to cruise for sex and stepped behind the wall to carry out the action. All you had to do was smile at a man passing by and that would be enough for the two of you to stop and chat and follow through for sex. A local photographer published a book of the bench taken every hour for twenty-four hours. Further up 18th Street, a man would stand naked in his bay window and motion to a passerby he found attractive to come up for sex.

All three main commercial streets in the Castro—Castro, 18th Street, and Market Street—were filled with gay bars catering to varying sorts of crowds. In 1979 the Badlands was a cruising bar, the Midnight Sun was the neighborhood's first video bar, the Pendulum was a Black bar, the Nothing Special seemed to be a home for alcoholics, the Twin Peaks catered to the older crowd, and Patsy's was a country-and-western bar.

Some of what I miss most about that time and place was going out on errands, or even just for a walk, through the neighborhood and running into one friend after another and spending hours just standing on a street corner talking, talking, *talking*.

In my first days in San Francisco, I never ventured outside the neighborhood. I could buy food, do my banking, go to the post office, and recreate right there. My first trip outside the Castro was to the DMV for a California driver's license.

I started asking the men I met in the bars or went home with how I might find a job. Tad was of no help. After three weeks of living with him, he informed me that I had to move out. Tad was turning out to be more of a character than I could handle. On Castro Street he would flirt with me in Russian, pretending to be a Russian teenager. In his apartment he played me recordings of Hitler giving speeches. His best friend was a Jewish man he called "Mutzi" and whom he teased mercilessly. Tad also filled me in on what had happened to him when he moved from Munich to West Berlin. He dressed in his Nazi uniform when he went out to the Berlin leather bars. (This was illegal.) He was consuming more and more drugs, which he blamed on the psychotic break he had one night in the Prinzknecht, which landed him in a *Nervenklinik* (mental hospital).

I was now looking for a place to live as well as a job. A guy I had tricked with gave me the name and number of a recent trick of his who was looking for a roommate.

37

Billy Komasa was very friendly. When he interviewed me as a potential roommate, he also told me to go downtown and register at a temp agency. He said that was how many gay newcomers got work. He rented his spare bedroom to me, which had a mattress on the floor. I moved my bags of books by taxi. (Later, when I was the one looking for a roommate to move into my place, I was warned to beware of anyone who moved via taxi.) I went down to the Financial District and signed up with an agency. All the clients as well as all the job counselors were gay. My counselor advised me on how to dress and how to act on a job interview, and to be mindful that any temp job could lead to a full-time job. The temp agency took a huge cut (usually one month's wages), which is why they were in the business.

I started getting office jobs, filing, typing, and answering phones. These jobs lasted from a day to a couple of weeks. The work was mindless, mostly what no one else wanted to do. But my employment was steady enough for me to get by. In those days it was still possible to afford to live in San Francisco on the income from survival jobs. The few "nice" clothes I had were five years out of date. I had a pair of dress pants with flaring bell bottoms, a pair of leather "elevator" shoes, and a couple of paisley shirts— the Elton John look, then in fashion when I left SUNYA.

I met a guy in the Badlands. His name was Richard Miller. He had a slender build, blond hair and blue eyes, a bushy moustache, and a bubble butt. When we got naked later that day, I saw he had a huge cock and no body hair. We quickly became lovers.

While dating Richard, we drank in the bars all up and down Castro Street. We ate a lot of Chinese takeout. Richard lived on upper Market Street (halfway between Billy's house and Castro Street) in a railroad flat. He lived with three other roommates. The guy he rented from and who was one of the four living there was an older alcoholic queen. The revolving door of tricks went on every day. Richard and I also brought tricks back to the apartment.

One night we picked up an Australian. We took MDMA. Then Richard and the Aussie decided to give me a red wine douche. They fucked me at the same time.

Richard and I were taking whatever drugs we could get our hands on— cocaine, MDMA, speed, acid, even angel dust at one point. We both stayed away from heroin—only drug addicts shot drugs. We roughhoused in the apartment, and at one point we broke a dining room chair. His roommate exploded over this and evicted Richard.

In any event I did not last long living with Billy either. Billy detested Richard. I had made the mistake of having sex with Billy once, and that was the end of my residence at 18 Henry Street. (Billy claimed that Harvey Milk had once lived there.) Billy evicted me.

Richard and I found an in-law apartment on Belcher Street around the corner from the Balcony bar, possibly the sleaziest gay bar in San Francisco. While we moved from Market Street to Belcher Street, we hand-carried our possessions from one place to the other. A stranger stopped me on the street and offered me five dollars to let him give me a blowjob, so I brought him to the Belcher Street apartment. Richard was pissed off when I arrived late back at the Market Street flat. He was even madder that I did it for a measly $5. (Richard had once been a go-go dancer at a Polk Street bar and went home with customers if they offered him enough money.)

George Applegate, our prospective new landlord, invited us for drinks on his back porch and told us all about his friend Rod McKuen. Then he showed us the apartment. It was dark, and, as we discovered through that winter, the heating unit blew black smoke into the apartment, which stained the walls and ceiling. George lived upstairs, so he heard the loud parties Richard threw for his theater friends. Our drinking was notorious. Richard's theater friends referred to the two of us as Scott and Zelda.

Our drinking took up more and more of our paychecks. We saw to it that our rent and utilities were covered. But we sometimes went for a week eating macaroni and cheese because we had no money for food. Richard had bartender friends who would cash his checks. He taught me how to kite our checks. Jug's Liquors, a block from Belcher Street, accepted my checks on the weekend when I needed to buy booze.

Richard's involvement as an actor in his theater troupe had him away at rehearsal a lot. I was jealous of Richard's outside commitment. At first, I stayed home and fumed. When he got home, we headed out to the bars together. After a while, I started hanging out at the Deluxe, a gay bar in the Haight (Richard's rehearsals were in the Haight-Ashbury), and waited for him. They were rehearsing a gay-themed play by Richard's best friend Charlie. It was called *Blue Moon* and Charlie called it his "dinosaur play." To make ends meet, Charlie worked at the bed-and-breakfast his lover owned. He hoped to become able to support himself as a full-time playwright. Charlie published under the name C. D. Arnold. (Charlie saw some success when Theater Rhinoceros staged his *King of the Crystal Palace* and won an award for it in 1983.)

Shortly before Christmas I finally landed my first full-time job. I answered a wanted ad from Cogswell College. The interviewer asked me if I was willing to commit to staying in the job for a year. I of course answered yes, never considering why they would ask me this. I was hired as the office assistant to the registrar. Cogswell College was a very small technical college up on Nob Hill on Stockton Street. Two cable car lines crossed at the intersection one block further up the hill. The nicest part of my job was commuting by cable car.

My first Christmas in San Francisco found me living with Richard in our first place together. I invited Derek to come and visit us. Dennis also let me know he was planning to spend Christmas in San Francisco and visiting an old college friend. (I suspected he was also planning to check on my progress.) Dennis visited once for an hour. He had apparently seen all he wanted to see. Derek joined us on our rounds of the bars, and we had threeways.

I became angry and violent when I drank. One night Richard and I had an argument, and he went out to the baths by himself. That evening I downed a fifth of vodka by myself and flung the empty bottle out the back door. It smashed on the cement. I spent much of the night talking to someone in the apartment. I came into a moment of lucidity and realized I was actually alone. I became enraged and put my fist through the picture window in the front room.

The next morning George evicted us.

By this point I was blacking out every night. I often woke up still drunk. I always went to work and sober up by about noon and have the worst imaginable hangover all afternoon. I felt my soul was disintegrating. My emotional range included anger and despair. The only release was through drugs and alcohol. There was no joy in my life. My days seemed gray, endlessly gray, one after another. I lived without hope. I had no friends, no plans for my future. I felt no love in my relationship with Richard. I had no outside activities. I had no friends. My life extended from my apartment to Cogswell College to the bars on Castro, Polk, and Folsom Streets.

When we got evicted from Belcher Street, we found an apartment in the Hayes Valley, less than ten blocks from Belcher Street, but a world apart. In 1979 it was a sketchy neighborhood, a very poor Black ghetto. Our place in Hayes Valley on Ivy Street was half a block from the Lower Haight housing projects. We were the first wave of urban gentrification.

Bands of teenaged boys from the neighborhood were known to follow gay men down these streets, calling them names and threatening them with violence. Those were no empty threats. Community United Against Violence (CUAV) advised all gay men to carry a whistle and blow it if they found themselves being attacked. Richard carried one, I did not.

Coming home from work one afternoon, a gang of five teenagers followed me for several blocks. When I wanted to step up to my apartment, the stairway was a problem; it was a wooden structure tacked onto the building but completely exposed, offering no safety. They cornered me. I was terrified. I got halfway up the stairs. They were gaining on me. I turned around and screamed. Obscenities flew out of my mouth. I threatened to kill them if they got any closer. A stream of racist obscenities followed. They stopped dead in their tracks. Then they slowly backed down the stairs.

Richard and I went to midnight showings of *The Rocky Horror Picture Show* every Saturday at the Strand Theater on Market Street. I was so stoned and drugged that it took me a dozen viewings before I could figure out the movie's plot. (I have now seen this film more times than any other film except *The Wizard of Oz*. Much has been written about Oz as a metaphor for gay men, and all queer people. Looking back I understand a central message of *Rocky Horror*—"Don't dream it, be it" to be a message of the Stonewall generation to come and be your whole, authentic self.)

One night we were both loaded to the tits. While standing in line, with my hands burrowed into my jacket pockets, I suddenly fell flat on my face, landing on my chin and chipping one of my upper front teeth, breaking it nearly in half. I bloodied up from the chin cut and internal mouth lacerations. Richard got very upset at all the blood and insisted he take me to the ER. I had no idea that I was cut up as I was feeling no pain. I had my mind set on another wild *Rocky Horror* event. I demanded we go in, and he gave up battling me. We went in.

The next morning, I woke up to find myself covered in blood and missing half of my tooth.

I had stopped reading altogether by now. One day I opened a novel and started to read it. I read the first paragraph five times and could never remember what I had just read. My alcoholism was destroying my mind. I knew. I was aware of how drinking turned my Dr. Jekyll into Mr. Hyde. My alcohol and drug consumption really frightened me. I didn't dare admit it to anyone.

38

Somehow, I was hanging on to my day job at Cogswell College. I came in to work drunk or horribly hung over every day. My body reeked of booze. I sat at my desk and typed student transcripts all day.

When I was hired, the registrar was a young Chinese woman, who was sleeping with the vice president of the college. When he broke off their relationship, he fired her. With no registrar around, I oversaw the daily operations of the registrar's office for months while a job search went on. The college did not give me a pay increase to cover my extensive new duties. I managed to hold the fort down as a functional drunk.

Eventually they found a replacement, a middle-aged, overweight woman named JoAnn Vandenberg, who lived out in the Avenues. She always wore a dress and a brown pageboy cut wig that she never stopped fussing with. She was constantly poking her own hair with a rat tail comb under the wig. She was all business with me and the student workers and ruled the registrar's office with an iron fist.

JoAnn knew I had a drinking problem, though she never said a word. I sometimes came in to work still in my green fatigues with an athletic shirt and black work boots and dog tags around my neck. I had often not been home the night before. I didn't care what people at Cogswell thought of me.

I started missing work and covering for my absences. I told JoAnn I was going to see a therapist. I made an appointment with Tom Moon and met with him once. While he was asking me open-ended questions, circling around what was bothering me, he noticed huge holes in the cuff of my jeans. They were cigarette burns I had never noticed. I recognized this was another sign of my alcoholism. I never went back to the therapist again, but I continued to take one day a week off from work and drank.

I started riding the California Street cable car over Nob Hill to drink my lunch at Kimo's Bar on Polk Street. I usually got too drunk to go back to work. I'd call JoAnn from a pay phone and tell her I was going home sick with a stomach bug. I'd spend the rest of the day drinking in the Castro.

On the days I actually worked a full day, I walked down the hill to Montgomery Street and stopped by Sutter's Mill, a popular gay bar in the Financial District, for half a dozen drinks on the way home.

Richard and I were fighting more than ever. This soon escalated to the level of physical violence. One evening when Richard went out to the baths to get away from me, I waited for him to come home. When he showed up around 4:00 AM I jumped him in the front hallway, murder in my heart. I broke his right arm and a few ribs, and I gave him a black eye. I passed out, and he went to the ER at San Francisco General Hospital. Richard never pressed charges. He moved out immediately, leaving me with an empty apartment. All I had was a bare mattress. I didn't understand why I had felt such deep rage.

On top of my drinking, I was taking a lot of speed. I also snorted a lot of cocaine. I was now drinking scotch and gin and taking speed to keep from passing out. I did speed bourbon once—I didn't black out, but rather watched myself, as if watching a movie, do crazy and dangerous things, unable to control my behavior. No matter how I resolved to cut back, I always ended up getting more and more fucked up.

After Richard left me, I could not afford the rent for the Ivy Street apartment. Ken just happened to be visiting me from London, arriving in the wake of my breakup with Richard. I was looking for a new apartment. Ken introduced me to a guy he had met at the Bear Hollow. Jim Maguire joined me in the apartment search. Several places had been rented by the time we got ahold of the landlord. One landlord was fixing a building up and we pestered him three days in a row until he exploded.

We ended up landing a three-bedroom house at 3036 Market Street, a few blocks above Castro Street. The rent was steep for the time, and we needed to find a third roommate. We asked the salesclerk at Dino's Liquors on 18th Street at Castro to put the word out. He told us he was looking for a new place. With little effort I now had two roommates. Since they were both named Jim, I called Jim Maguire "Little Jim," because he was shorter than Jim Peck, who I called "Big Jim."

We set up house together and started partying. Little Jim became my new main drug connection. He also took me around to his favorite sex clubs—the Trench and the Caldron. We threw large parties at the house.

The house at 3036 Market Street was at the bottom of a long, steep, and winding curve. The steady sound of traffic made hearing someone talk in the front rooms difficult. Tires often squealed as a speeding driver slammed on the brakes to avoid crashing into the cement barrier that divided the lanes. The last bend could not be negotiated over 35 mph. (Drivers typically came down the hill at 50 mph.) We occasionally heard a car scrape along the side of the barrier. One guy ran into the light pole outside our house and snapped it off at its base. He came to our door and asked to use our phone to call for help.

I tricked with a guy named Chuck Eames. We looked like twins. He was the dishwasher at an upscale restaurant on Polk Street. He became my drinking companion and kept up with my drinking. We picked guys up and had threeways. My world was continuing to get smaller.

One night when the Badlands closed, I started walking up 18th Street to go home. I stopped to piss in the shrubbery in front of a house. There was no one on the street. Out of nowhere a cop showed up and asked me what I thought I was doing. "Go fuck yourself," I told him.

He wrote me up for public urination and indecent exposure. I showed up in court, and the judge mercifully dropped the indecency charge and fined me for urination. I had called Richard and asked him if he could help me out financially. He told me to go fuck myself.

By then I was wallowing in self-pity and crying a lot. Everything I touched seemed to turn to shit in my hands. Chuck left me because of my drinking. Despite taking speed I was now passing out and waking up later still speeding. Sometimes I pissed the bed. Once I lost control of my bowels in Badlands and walked home with my pants full of shit.

On a three-day drinking and drugging binge, I called Suicide Prevention. I was now drinking two quarts of vodka. I called several days in a row. I gave voice to my despair. The speed made me talk nonstop. I must have been fairly incoherent.

Every time I called, I got the same woman. On the third day she asked me, "Do you think you have a drinking problem?"

I answered yes.

"Do you want to do something about your problem?"

Again, my answer was yes.

"If you don't pick up the first drink, you won't get drunk," she said. The thought had never occurred to me.

She referred me to a place called Eighteenth Street Services, an outpatient program in the Castro for gay men struggling with alcoholism.

When I got off the phone, I got down on my knees at the kitchen table and prayed to a God I did not believe in to release me from my obsession with drink. I cried very hard, aching to be released from the nightmare I had been caught up in. But I put down my last drink and crawled back into bed where I slept for 18 hours. The next morning, I woke up and drew my first sober breath.

The date was May 3, 1981.

39

I had vivid nightmares for several nights. They were violent battle scenes from *War and Peace*. They woke me up, and I would feel relief at finding myself sober and in my own bed. Suddenly I stopped waking up in a state of dread and impending doom. I was no longer dehydrated and acutely hungover. I was suddenly aware of the sunlight streaming in my window. I was soothed by the sound of traffic coming down Market Street past my front window.

As I walked down 18th Street and up Castro Street to catch the MUNI Metro to go to work, I noticed the strong, sweet smell of jasmine in the air, the fresh breeze off the ocean, the banana tree on 18th Street and the enormous poinsettia bush in bloom next to the post office. I smiled hello to the guys I passed on the sidewalk.

I was filled with an overwhelming joy. I became hopeful. I was seeing my way out of the never-ending nightmare my life had become. My sense of taste returned. Colors were vivid. I became attuned to the sights and sounds around me. My desire for sex came roaring back. I started having feelings again, lots of feelings, strong feelings.

Now that I had stopped drinking, my mental faculties started returning. I could read again and retain what I had read. What had taken me a full day to do at work, I now finished by 9:00 AM. I craved sugar and would run out to the nearest corner store for a handful of candy bars on my coffee breaks. I went back to the YMCA and spent my lunch hours swimming laps at the Chinatown Y. Swimming gave me endorphin highs again. I slimmed down and beefed up to my swimmer's build again. I turned heads on the street again. Bored with nothing to do in the office, I would disappear. I would watch Chinese women from Chinatown practicing tai chi in the park below Cogswell College. I would watch the tourists on Union Square. I would go for longer and longer walks all over Nob Hill, through the Financial District, down to Union Square, and as far as Portsmouth Square in Chinatown.

I started formally dating men, a whole new experience for me. I dated a Jewish guy from Chicago who liked to go to the opera. I dated a manic-depressive concert pianist who enjoyed playing for me and with whom I developed a master/slave bondage relationship.

And then I met Bill Hartman. He was exactly my physical type—hairy, beefy, facial hair, and blond. I was especially attracted to that rarity, the hairy blonds. He was very warm and nurturing. He had an inquisitive mind, good politics, lived a bohemian lifestyle. He had founded the *Bay Times* and was long a gay activist. He had grown up in rural Mississippi and fled to San Francisco to escape Christian homophobia and the narrow minds of the local folks. Bill looked after me when I got sick—alcoholics in early recovery get sick a lot as their bodies try to adjust to not having alcohol in their systems. We laughed a lot together.

Bill was also a recovering alcoholic who had rejected AA because he continued to use recreational drugs. This was the one factor that held me back from a full commitment to him.

Another factor in seeking to give up drinking was my desire to return to graduate school. I knew I wasn't up to the rigor of the intellectual work if I wasn't sober. In the depth of my alcoholic despair, I had sought a way out by applying to UC Berkeley. My acceptance letter arrived after I had gotten sober. It was a godsend that I was accepted. I BARTed over from the Castro to Berkeley for my first visit to campus. It was a one-block walk from the downtown BART station on Shattuck Avenue to the west entrance. I walked through a grove of eucalyptus trees to the campus itself, kneeled, and kissed the ground. My eyes filled with tears of gratitude, thankful for being readmitted into the Sanctuary of Higher Education. I approached the eucalyptus grove, which from a distance appeared to be one enormous tree. As I got closer, I could discern individual trees. I had an epiphany. All those individual efforts on my part suddenly added up to a greater whole. It seemed it all had been a path leading me to this gate of reentry. Suddenly, all was clarity and light.

I went to my intake appointment with Eighteenth Street Services. They were located on the second floor above the Badlands. I was both scared and relieved to be finding a way out from my drinking. They diagnosed me as cross-addicted to alcohol and speed. They handed me a contract with a list of all the things I had to do to be accepted into their program. I was comfortable with everything on the list—with one exception. They required me to attend three AA meetings a week. I had never attended an AA meeting, but I thought, "I may be an alcoholic, but I'm not as bad as those people." I knew nothing about the recovery process, but I resisted the thought of having to go to such a meeting. Nevertheless, I went.

The first meeting I attended was the Wednesday Night Castro Discussion group, informally known as the "Show of Shows." It was a very large meeting of maybe a hundred gay men. They were all in their 20s and 30s and happy and laughing and attractive. I thought there had to be some sort of a catch. These people could not possibly be real alcoholics. They were in no shape near my own demoralized and pathetic condition. I was wearing tattered clothes, as I had no money to buy new ones, and I was barely eating a diet to sustain my health. My face was still bloated, and I had a beer paunch. Many were gym-toned. They were the picture of health and serenity. I could not figure them out.

I drank gallons of water over the first couple of weeks. I had an unstoppable craving to drink and met it by filling my system with tap water. I managed to white-knuckle those first couple of weeks before my support group started.

At first it was very scary being in a room with a bunch of strangers. A couple of them dropped out quickly, but those of us who stayed bonded. We did all the sorts of things that have become commonplace for present-day rehab centers. We got medical and psychological education; we learned relaxation techniques; we discussed our drinking and our character defects. We were sworn not to have sex or become romantically involved with each other.

My Phase One group lasted three months, and I was so proud to graduate from it that I signed up immediately for the Phase Two group. This small band of men and counselors became my lifeline.

In those days, gay men visited the venereal disease (VD) clinic on a regular basis. Contracting gonorrhea or syphilis was treated like catching a cold or coming down with the flu. There was a lot of pressure from the medical community on gay men to change their sexual ways. The San Francisco Health Department accepted the high rate of VD among gay men as a given. The City maintained a free VD clinic in an office south of Market. It was a very cruisy place. Gay men knew any guy picked up there would be disease-free in a few days.

At the suggestion of my counselor John Beeman at 18th Street Services

I went to the clinic out of an abundance of precaution to get tested. The doctor I saw asked me if I recognized him. I told him no and thought maybe he might be an old trick I didn't remember. My past was beginning to catch up with me. Things I had done, people I had interacted with (for better or worse) when drunk, were now showing up, forcing me to deal with them in sobriety.

The doctor then asked me if I remembered passing out at the Balcony several weeks ago. I remembered coming out of blackouts and finding myself at the Balcony, but not ever passing out.

"You were really loaded," the doctor said. "When I saw you fall down in the middle of the crowd, I picked you up and offered to take you home. I ended up driving you to five different addresses where you thought you lived. I left you at your doorstep in Hayes Valley." I had moved so many times during my first two years in San Francisco I could barely keep track of everywhere I had lived. To this day I still have no idea which building Richard was living in where we broke that dining room chair. The doctor's final words were, "I'm glad to see you're sober now."

When I started Phase Two of my rehab program I fell for a guy in my new group. I was increasingly ambivalent about Bill Hartman's drug use and so was open to looking around again. Violating 18th Street's rule against sex and romantic involvement with another group member, I started dating David Perry.

David was handsome in a Hollywood matinee idol sort of way. He had an enormous cock which he kept on public display by wearing tight jeans. I invited him to a threeway with Bill. Before I knew what was going on, David was manipulating me into a relationship, what folks in AA called "taking someone hostage." David chased Bill away. David complained to me that Bill had accosted him on the street, screaming, "How dare you steal my boyfriend." David clearly saw himself as the victim. He then reported that his roommate was about to evict him, and he was desperate for a place to live. I moved him in with me. Only later did I learn that his "roommate" was his lover, and he was being kicked out because the lover broke up with him. He moved in via a taxi.

David lied about not drinking. Once he blamed his prescribed Xanax for his slip. Another time he blamed my friend Ken, who was visiting from London, for bringing a bottle of mouthwash containing alcohol for his slip. Everything was always someone else's fault. David painted himself as a hapless victim.

He was unemployed, so I supported him on my meager grad student teaching wages. He got occasional work from Peter Evans, my first gay best friend in AA, painting houses. Peter was infatuated with David and gave him work in the hopes of getting into his pants. David once wore my favorite jacket to work without my permission and painted in it. He spilled paint all over the jacket, ruining it. I blew up when I found my jacket. David, of course, turned the situation around so that he emerged as the hapless victim once again.

John Beeman recommended I read M. Scott Peck's *The Road Less Traveled*. He suggested I would find reading Peck useful in rethinking my life as I began a new life in sobriety. People in AA told me that AA was a spiritual program. I didn't read any of their materials. But I learned more by observing and listening to what people said at meetings.

Peck asserted that spiritual evolution required discipline for emotional and psychological health as well as spiritual health. He stated that life is difficult, and we all suffer. People needed to face and work through their problems to grow. (David put it this way: "The only way around a problem is through it. Let all the shit wash over you and move forward." He was fond of quoting things he had been told in recovery, but I wasn't sure how much he actually practiced any of it.)

I gradually realized that David was a psychopath. The people at 18th Street Services called this antisocial personality disorder. Such people sometimes became alcoholics and the prognosis to recover for such people was infinitesimally small.

This piece of knowledge led me to Peck's book *People of the Lie*, which had just been published. He recounted some case histories of psychopathic and sociopathic patients, resistant to any form of help. Peck cast such psychologically disordered people as evil. Such people were consistently self-deceptive, deceiving other people, accusing other people of what they themselves are doing, and maintaining a front of social respectability. They were completely self-centered and unable to see from the perspective of another person, incapable of feeling empathy, as well as lacking introspection.

I saw all this in David. I also saw that he was almost charismatically charming to get what he wanted. He was incapable of love but professed it to manipulate me. He clearly believed his own lies and said whatever would get him off the hook, claiming it was the truth. He valued other people only to the extent that they were useful to him. He complained that other men were only interested in him because he had a huge cock. (This never stopped him from keeping it on public display.) When I broke up with David, a couple dozen guys in gay AA came to me in the name of "making amends" and told me they had had sex with him behind my back. This widespread deception among fellow AAs shook my faith in the integrity of people in AA and made me mistrustful of people in general. AA literature suggests that when making amends it was recommended to not reveal past infidelities to a spouse who knew nothing about them. There was no point in creating pain where none had existed. The amend was to stop doing that.

Peck also asserted that "love is an action, not a feeling." Sexual attraction is not love, but a path to cathecting to someone. That romantic connection is the starting point for love to take root and grow in. Love is an investment in the spiritual growth of the other person and yourself. John Beeman stressed to us that relationships are not a business investment, we should not be expecting a return from our investment. We needed to do our best and then "let go."

When I was near the emotional bottom of my enervating entanglement with David, I went alone to the Living Sober New Year's Dance. San Francisco's Living Sober Western Round Up was one of the first and by far the largest annual convention of gay AA. The dance was one of several fundraising events Living Sober held each year. The remarkable fact of these dances was that they were the only one at that time where not a single man would be high or drinking.

At the dance a strikingly handsome asked me to dance. Gary Prutsman was a furry, blond bodybuilder. I was smitten. The longer we danced, the more I lusted after him, the more I anticipated going home with him. As with many of my tricks, I fell a little bit in love with him.

He took me home that night. Gary and I explored each other's bodies intensely and lovingly. I found his body fur lush. We caressed and kissed and rubbed fur. Gary fucked me slowly, and for a long time. We were up until dawn (dare I say) making love. I wanted Gary to be my lover. I wanted that so badly. But I was still involved with David.

I told Gary about David and how horrid my relationship was. Gary shared at an AA meeting my story anonymously, and the fact that he didn't know what he could do to help. David happened to be at that meeting. He knew Gary was talking about me. David was furious with me and accused me of badmouthing him around AA.

Within six months of my involvement with David, I could no longer tolerate him. I felt that all the energy I had been putting into him had been stunting my own spiritual growth. One day he came home drunk and passed out on the living room sofa. I called the police to have them remove him from my house. They asked me if David was threatening me with violence. He was not. They asked me if he lived there. I explained that he did, but I had been paying his rent. The police told me that they had no authority to get involved.

I talked about this with other guys in AA. I spoke to another guy's sponsor, a guy named Kenny. He offered himself to me as my temporary sponsor. He advised me as to how to deal with this situation. He invited me to stay with him and not divulge to anyone where I was staying. This way David could not find me. Kenny told me to have all the utilities turned off temporarily. This flushed David out of the house. Then I changed the locks so he couldn't get back in. This did the trick.

40

With four months of sobriety under my belt, I started graduate school at UC Berkeley. I resumed my study of Comparative Literature, focusing on German, Russian, and English literatures. Berkeley did not credit any of my coursework in West Germany toward their program. I had to start as a first-year graduate student and do a second MA as part of my PhD program.

I was hired as a Graduate Student Instructor (GSI) to teach first-year German. Along with wages I was expected to support myself on this income. My tuition was waived.

I took mostly German literature courses and backtracked on my Russian language studies. I found the work rough going. My memory was taxed in ways it was not ready to function yet—memorizing Russian vocabulary and grammar, and doing deep textual analysis.

Being accepted by Berkeley took some work. My application was initially denied. I appealed and Ken Weisinger, one of the professors who taught Comp Lit and German literature courses, made a case for reconsideration. I had met privately with Ken at his house where we discussed my academic intentions more closely. He owned a restored Victorian on 19th Street overlooking the Castro and downtown San Francisco. He told me one of my recommenders had written about my drinking problem. I assured Ken I was no longer drinking and was in AA. He also said my undergraduate GPA was a little below what Berkeley required, and there was concern that

I might not be able to do the work. I told him those grades reflected my drinking career more than my intellectual ability.

After the semester started, Ken invited me to his house for dinner, and a night of sex. I later observed he had a pattern in having affairs with grad students.

This was when I experienced the onset of hepatitis B. One day I could barely finish swimming the first lap. I was exhausted and didn't have the strength to keep from drowning. When I was diagnosed with hepatitis B, my doctor consulted with the doctors of the two men I had had sex with in the previous six months. Both tested positive for hepatitis A, but negative for B. The doctors were at a loss to understand how I had been infected. Years later this proved to be "seroconversion syndrome," resulting from my being infected with HIV.

Ken was one of the two men I had had sex with when I came down with hepatitis. He was quite distraught that he might have been the person who infected me. I had to stay home for weeks to recuperate from the hepatitis. Another GSI was asked to fill in for me. The university graciously continued to pay me. (Graduate teaching was legally ruled as "student aid," not employment. I had no legal option to apply for short-term disability.)

Ken became my mentor and defender. When Klaus Müller, the professor in charge of the German GSIs, mounted a campaign to have me fired for being gay, Ken let me know about it. Ken found Müller's treachery absurd. Ken pointed out that he himself was an openly gay man. No one else could see how my sexual orientation was a detriment to my ability to teach. Müller's campaign went nowhere. But Ken did alert me that I had enemies in the department.

One day Big Jim came home from clerking at Dino's Liquors and said he had heard the oddest neighborhood gossip that day. More than one customer told him that some kind of gay disease was spreading in the Castro. Guys were getting sick and dying very quickly. There were rumors that this was a government plot to kill gay men.

No one understood what was going on. But one gay man after another was dying. The longer this went on, the more numerous the deaths became. There was no name for what this was. But word spread. No one knew how it spread. Some thought it came from too much sex. Some thought poppers caused it. Men stopped having sex. Some thought kissing might spread it. Gay AA grew very rapidly as more and more guys quit drinking, thinking that might keep them safe. More guys started working out and eating healthier, thinking that might save them. One week a man looked healthy. A week later they'd look like an 80-year-old man. Businesses in the Castro shut down as the owners died. The ongoing party of sex, drugs, and rock and roll stopped as Castro Street became a literal ghost town.

The disease finally got a name—gay-related immune deficiency (GRID). We were baffled how a disease could differentiate sexual orientation. Then came the "four H's." GRID seemed concentrated among homosexuals, hemophiliacs, Haitians, and heroin addicts. It was assumed that all gay men in San Francisco had been infected. I assumed from the start that I had been infected. It also became assumed that all of the infected would die of this disease. There was genuine alarm that this would be the end of our gay community. A full-scale epidemic was decimating urban gay communities across the country. But no one outside the gay community seemed to be aware that something was happening.

A guy I had gone out on a date with who appeared perfectly healthy was dead a week later. My fuck buddy Larry Salmon died. My downstairs neighbor died. Little Jim moved to Fort Lauderdale, and he soon died. Gary Prutsman died. More and more friends and acquaintances died. I started keeping a list. I made a shrine putting photographs of my dead friends on my bedroom wall. The *Bay Area Reporter* obituaries grew longer and longer every week, eventually taking up three pages each week. This was how I was able to keep track of so many men I knew. When the number of dead of the men I knew reached 100, I quit counting. If someone was not seen for a couple of weeks, we assumed he had died.

Some of what followed has become a matter of public knowledge and history. While these years remain as fresh in my memory now as when they were happening, AIDS has become largely forgotten. In the wake of the emergence of the Covid pandemic, no one in a position of power thought to confer with us survivors of the AIDS epidemic for how to cope with the Covid pandemic.

Year after year of mounting deaths led to survivor fatigue. I reached a point where I could no longer attend funerals. ACT-UP was formed, and much of our despair and rage was channeled into this political response. For my part, I got involved with AIDS education and support groups. I found myself the sole survivor of each support group I joined. At the depth of despair, I volunteered at San Francisco Suicide Prevention, hoping to be of help to the most desperate. I found this emotionally exhausting work. I listened to gay men describe situations that made mine seem insignificant. A firm rule in suicide prevention work is that you can never tell someone that suicide is okay. But suicide seemed like the merciful way out for some of my callers' lives. I quit because I couldn't tell them that was okay. Like so many of us who lived through that period, I experienced complex trauma without being aware of it. I just grew numb.

41

I completed my Berkeley MA in 1983. I was exhausted from doing grad school and coping with the AIDS epidemic. I really needed a break. I survived, just barely, on occasional temp jobs. The best of these was running a summer ESL program for the Pacific American Institute (PAI) on the CSU Northridge campus. I found it impossible to live in the San Fernando Valley without a car. PAI agreed to split the cost of a rental from Rent-a-Wreck. The car broke down every day. I ended up renting a car from Alamo and paying for it out of my own pocket. I ate lunch by myself in the campus cafeteria. This is where I discovered Valley Girls really did speak like Valley Girls. I also discovered how homophobic they were. Their hostile name-calling did not place them in a positive light.

The most exciting part of the summer session was when all the students went on strike. They stayed in their dorm rooms and refused to go to class. They were on the phone to their fathers back in Japan complaining that PAI had refused to arrange a day at Disneyland, as spelled out in their agreement. In the end PAI caved in, and I took them all to Disneyland. As soon as they got in the gate, they all disappeared.

At the end of the day, I would drive down to Hollywood for dinner and gay AA meetings. I found Los Angeles gay AA to be as warm and welcoming as it was in San Francisco. I quickly made friends and became part of the gay fellowship there.

Later that summer I submitted a proposal to UC Berkeley Extension to organize a not-for-credit course on Weimar German culture. I never heard

LES K. WRIGHT

back from them. Six months later I got a flyer in the mail announcing a seminar on Weimar German culture. When I complained about this bit of treachery to Ken Weisinger, he pointed out that I did not hold any copyright for my idea—that's the way it goes in academe.

I returned to San Francisco where I was still in the middle of my endlessly rotating roommate situation, and really tired of running my "halfway house." I was going to lots and lots of AA and other twelve-step program meetings. I began doing volunteer work for 18th Street Services. The most challenging one was the group for cross-addicted men living with AIDS.

I applied for job after job and got a steady stream of rejection letters. One day I saw a job ad for someone to run the stamp and coin department at the Emporium-Capwell department store. Along with my skills and job history, I included my knowledge of stamps as a lifelong collector. It seemed unlikely to me that anyone else with my familiarity would apply for a retail job.

The interview went well. I would be the department sales manager and have one employee under me. I would not be employed by the Emporium since this was a franchise owned by Jacques Minkus. I recognized his name immediately. He was noted for publishing stamp albums for every country and for including countries the Scott Stamp Catalog refused to list. I was impressed to be working for one of the giants in the philatelic world.

Day to day, the job was boring. I rarely had a customer. My assistant Mike Tobin, an ex-Navy man and a very old-school queen, was the coin expert. Nearly every day someone would stop by to ask him to identify or appraise a coin. Most of my business was filling standing orders for new issues for mail-order customers. My ability to do this grew difficult over time. Jacques would short me on these standing orders (guaranteed sales) and recommend I offer the gypped customers other stamps. My customers dwindled as a result. I began to understand that the Minkus Stamp Company had entered a downward spiral into bankruptcy. Jacques was unable to pay the stamp-issuing agencies and they were refusing to send him stamps on credit.

There were other limitations. Mike and I were not permitted to buy from customers. Stamp companies operate like used bookstores, which do sell to and buy from customers. Another problem for me was that my salary was substantially less that the unionized retail salespeople. As a DSM, my pay should have been at least nominally higher. When they went on strike for higher wages, I was forced to cross their picket line. I had no union behind me. I didn't even work for the same employer. This led to poor relations between them and me after the strike ended.

My salary of $17,000 was not enough to cover my living expenses and I began to rely on credit cards to help make ends meet. I got one offer for a credit card after another in the mail. I took every offer, maxing out every single card. I must have had a dozen credit cards.

I was very stressed out over my debt. I developed acute insomnia. I was constantly on the edge of panic. I was afraid of losing my house. I was worried that I'd end up in a debtors' prison. I went to a credit counselor for help. My counselor went over my paperwork and said, "There is nothing I can do. You simply don't make enough money to arrange any repayment plan with your creditors."

An ex-Army sergeant came up to my stamp counter one day. "You're a very handsome man," he said. "I'd like to take you out for dinner and get to know you." I was flattered. I savored being the pursued instead of the pursuer for a change. I couldn't recall ever being offered dinner before jumping in the sack with a guy. I was intrigued.

Milton and I dated a bit. But I didn't find any common ground. I was uncomfortable by how one-sided the relationship was becoming. Milt brought me flowers, gave me a painting, and started pleading with me to love him. I became scared of his obsessive behavior.

Then I met Mike Keating. He was a new face at the Castro Country Club, a sober coffeehouse my friend Steve Hayes had opened to give all us sober gay men a safe social space to take the place of bars. To operate as a club, Steve had to charge a membership fee. This was a dollar a day. If you wanted, he took a Polaroid picture of you and posted it on the wall. You could include your name. One consequence of this was that we all got to know each other better outside of meetings because we knew each other's name, and this grew into a very large circle of friends. In the early 1980s gay AA became known as "the largest private gay social club in San Francisco." There were always other men to go out dancing with, go on day trips together, go to the movies. During these years members would open their house for potlucks on Thanksgiving and Christmas. Most of us came from elsewhere and such open houses were very welcome to those of us who felt like holiday orphans.

I was taken by Mike's good looks. He was a hairy, mustachioed black Irishman, with salt-and-pepper hair. He was slightly shorter than me. He was a fifth-generation San Franciscan (it was rare to meet a San Francisco native). He was the third generation in his family to be a firefighter. He was recently divorced and newly out of the closet. His ex-wife and their three teenaged children lived in Novato, up in Marin County. Mike was now living in an in-law apartment he rented from a fellow fireman out in the Avenues.

We started dating and Mike always stayed overnight at my place. We went to a lot of AA meetings together. Mike got to know most of the gay Fellowship. We went to Golden Gate Park a lot. We went on an occasional ride out of The City. Mike owned an old beat-up metallic blue 1967 Mustang. Mike was a good cook. When the men were staying in the firehouse, they had to take turns cooking for the crew. Mike was also overly fond of TV. I found myself keeping Mike company while he watched TV.

San Francisco and the Bay Area was a hotbed for New Age spirituality and attracted both truth-seekers and flim-flam artists. Jim Jones's People's Temple had begun in San Francisco. The Esalen Institute, located just down the coast in Big Sur, had given birth to New Age philosophy. Some AAs were forming study circles to read *A Course in Miracles* and put its teachings into practice, which I understood was to achieve love and the peace of god by changing one's thinking. The text sums its belief as "Nothing real can be threatened. Nothing unreal exists." Erhard Seminars Training (EST) struck me as the scariest of these New Age trends. EST had its San Francisco offices in the same building Cogswell College was housed in. We occasionally encountered ESTians in the elevators, and we all agreed every one of them was a total asshole.

Buddhism was also popular. This I looked into. Buddhism was not a religion and did not seem to conflict with religious beliefs. I began going to meditation sessions at the San Francisco Zen Center. I found the discipline allowed me to empty my mind of my constant ruminating and gave me a peace of mind as I got glimpses of "living in the present," something AA had suggested I do. (Years later Eckhart Tolle's *The Power of Now* gave me clear instruction on how to live in the now.)

When I came into gay AA, Terry Cole-Whittaker and her New Age brand of the "prosperity gospel" were growing in popularity. The title of her book *What You Think of Me Is None of My Business* became an oft-repeated truism among AAs. *How to Have More in a Have Not World* had just been published, and she was touring with a revival-style "share and declare" seminar. Peter Evans was very much taken in by this idea that strong spiritual faith could be translated into material wealth. He paid the steep admission price for me to join him at a San Francisco seminar. I was taken aback at watching followers in the audience stand up, share their stories of financial disaster, and pledge their material resources to Dr. Terry. This included maxing out their credit cards for her.

After exploring and dabbling in all these spiritual paths, I decided to let spirituality find me. I found truth in the story of how the Buddha became the Buddha in Herman Hesse's *Siddhartha*. I found truth in the mystics' practice of looking inward for the spirit to emerge from within.

***

I spent my first year in AA paying far more attention to the social dynamics. I picked up on AA's program, its philosophy, and the Twelve Steps through AA speakers and other peoples' "sharing."

After a meeting in the house on Castro Street owned by the Episcopal Church, a guy came up to me and asked me if I had a sponsor. I said no. He replied, "Honey, I could tell. You're a mess and you need a sponsor. I am now your sponsor. My name is Doug."

Doug set me straight. Anyone who saw themselves as their own sponsor was a fool. I needed direction. I needed to work the Twelve Steps, thoroughly and in the order written. Doug nudged me gently through the Steps. He was very patient and loving with me. He became my trusted confidante and friend. He listened to my complaints, my fears and worries, my struggles with each Step as he took me through them. They boiled down to "clean house, trust God, and help others."

I wrestled a great deal with the "God question." I spoke to many other AAs about their experience with finding their "Higher Power, whom we choose to call God."

Everyone had a different answer. I was told not to worry too much about this. I could think of god as Good orderly Direction or Group of drunks or appoint a door knob as my Higher Power. Gradually I learned that this spiritual source had to come from outside of me and that it was the act of having faith in something—anything—that was paramount.

I cleaned house—I reviewed my life with an eye to people I had wronged and what I had done to them and to myself. I forgave myself; I made amends to those I had hurt or otherwise wronged. I learned to look for what my part had been in creating the problems in my life. I began to practice prayer and meditation. I learned to "let go." I learned to take responsibility, and curb being selfish and self-obsessed. I learned to help others. I learned much, much more. While I continued to be confused by the god problem, I gradually recognized a change in my outlook and my behavior. I was becoming more like my fellow recovering alcoholics, learning to be more accepting of life and all its problems, facing life with a hopeful outlook. Looking back over my early days in recovery, I realize I had undergone a gradual spiritual awakening, so gradual I was not aware of it as it was happening. That prayer the day I put my last drink down was where I had begun to walk a spiritual path. This was all too subtle and mysterious for me to grasp until I was able to see it by looking back and seeing how far I had come from where I had started.

Doug Moorman was my first sponsor, exactly the kind of sponsor

I needed to get me started. After a while, Doug started getting sick and ending up in the hospital. He never talked about it. I was shocked when his mother called me to tell me Doug was in the hospital and had asked to see me. I showed up and discovered he was dying of AIDS and wanted to say good-bye.

It took some time before I was ready to find another sponsor. The first three men I asked died within a short time after we started working together. For a long time after that I stopped asking.

As I became conscious of having a spiritual life, I started going to Trinity Episcopal Church services. Many gay AA meetings were held there. Father Robert Cromey was a long-time proponent of gay rights. He had written *In God's Image: Christian Witness to the Need for Gay/Lesbian Equality In the Eyes of the Church.* Given that he was straight, I found his commitment all the more admirable. I took comfort in the familiarity of the elaborate Episcopal rites. I was disturbed by much of the dogma, and focused on the actual teachings of Jesus, seeing him as a great spiritual leader and not one-third of the trinitarian god of dogma. As AA had suggested, "Take what you like and leave the rest."

42

While working at the Emporium, I was invited to join a group called the San Francisco Gay and Lesbian History Project. Allan Bérubé had heard of my interest in gay history. He and Jeffrey Escoffier had founded the informal salon in the late 1970s. Members shared their research in gay and lesbian history, networked, and studied texts together. I brought Foucault's texts for discussion. Many now-notable academic historians were regular attendees, and for historians visiting the Bay Area, our group was a must-visit. I met Gayle Rubin, Estelle Friedman, John D'Emilio, Esther Newton, Nan Boyd, Lillian Fadermann, and many others there. I was included in a social circle that included Eric Garber, Willie Walker, Tom Holt, and Allan.

Allan was working on a huge history project in those days, which he eventually published as *Coming Out Under Fire: The History of Gay Men and Women in World War II*. His book would become a seminal text, win him international acclaim and a MacArthur genius fellowship.

Allan freely shared his work with us. He modelled how to do "grassroots history," which I found highly instructive, as I was not formally trained as a historian but rather as a literary scholar. Allan's instruction would prove invaluable when I founded the Bear History Project (BHP) and wrote the first history of gay Bears.

In 1985 amidst the justifiable fear that artifacts of San Francisco gay history were being irretrievably lost, the Gay and Lesbian Historical Society of Northern California was founded. As more and more gay men succumbed to AIDS, more and more of their biological families were

LES K. WRIGHT

showing up and throwing away the dead sons' personal papers, having no idea of their historical significance and often as a deliberate effort to erase any sign of their son's gayness.

An open call was sent out to all interested parties to discuss founding a historical society in this crucial time for gay history, deciding its geographical scope, structuring the organization, and other matters. We pooled our own holdings of gay and lesbian books and periodicals and ephemera. Soon the volunteer board of directors was replaced with an elected board. I was appointed to the first board *ex officio* as newsletter editor. Willie Walker made his home available for the temporary storage of archival holdings. I was the first editor of the newsletter and collaborated with Eric Garber, Paula Lichtenberg, and Lou Sullivan. Lou, whom I had known from when he worked with *GPU News* in Milwaukee, did the typesetting.

When I met Mike Keating, I was still working for Minkus. After much soul-searching and making no headway in casting about for a new career direction, I decided to recommit to becoming an academic. I returned to UC Berkley to complete my PhD program.

I was back to surviving on my GSI teaching. I taught Freshman Composition in the Comparative Literature Department. I had some latitude in the books I chose for my students to read, discuss, and write papers about. I was able to practice integrating traditional critical analysis with some of the newly arising literary theory approaches. I had students read some Roland Barthes and Foucault. When Larry Kramer's play *The Normal Heart*, about the early years of AIDS in New York City, was published, I had students read it. I found it incomprehensible that Berkeley students seemed to be unaware that the AIDS epidemic was raging only 15 miles away. Much to my surprise, a reporter and a photographer from *Time* magazine showed up one day to do a report on my class and me.

One semester David Shengold was assigned to me for training in classroom teaching. I had a reputation for my classroom teaching skills. Having a GSI under me also freed me up from having to grade 36 student essays every three weeks. David eventually switched his major to Russian. He ended up having a very successful career as an opera expert in Manhattan. When I knew him, I had no idea his father was the world famous psychiatrist whom Oliver Sacks saw to help him overcome his speed addiction and who wrote *Soul Murder*, which later helped me deal with my childhood trauma.

Freshman composition was a required course for all students. Because there were so many more students than sections of this course, my classes were top-heavy with graduating seniors who had first right to enroll in this requisite course. Often there was a student who knew at least as much as I did about an author or text we were reading. This kept me on my scholarly toes. I learned never to lie to students, but simply admit when I did not know something.

The years that I was completing my doctoral coursework were a pivotal moment in my fields of study. I was among the last Comparativists who studied Eurocentric literature. The discipline would soon shift to a global perspective and unique blends, such as Korean, Serbian, and Nigerian literatures. My primary field was German literature, and I had read through the German canon from the Middle Ages to the 1970s in courses and outside reading. I would need to write my dissertation on German literature to be viable on the job market. I studied a good deal of the Russian canon from Pushkin to the Futurists and émigré authors. I had no pretensions of a career as a Slavicist. The only English-language literature courses I'd taken were at West German universities. I had done most of my reading outside of courses. I had taken two courses on Commonwealth literature (Anglo-Indian and New Zealand). This became post-colonial studies in English departments. I had read French literature in Comp Lit classes and on my own. Near the end of my coursework I studied Dutch. This was encouraged with a fellowship in Netherlandic Studies. My hope was that this might help me land a job teaching Gay and Lesbian Studies at a Dutch university. Ironically, colleagues in the Netherlands started turning to me to help them find the same position at an American university.

The Comparative Literature Department was home to a dizzying number of schools of literary theories. In the formalist camp Saussure, Russian Formalism, and structuralism were old news. Semiotics and narratology had currency. But Derrida and deconstruction, thanks to faculty member Avital Ronell, was especially valued. In the historicist camp, "New Historicism" was the approach of the day. This is where Foucault fit in. Stephen Greenblatt reframed how to read literary texts in their original context. In the political camp the Frankfurt School was falling from pride of place. I read Mikhail Bakhtin's examinations of social and economic class and language, and who invented the terms "heteroglossia" and "carnivalesque." Post-colonialism, arising within British literary studies, was burgeoning. Edward Said's *Orientalism* was a seminal text. In the feminist camp, Elaine Showalter's *The Madwoman in the Attic* demonstrated how women's identity was constructed as a minority "other." Anthropologist Gayle Rubin coined the term "sex/gender" in her seminal essay "The Traffic in Women." Queer Theory was just beginning to colonize the English Department as I was wrapping up my coursework. After Derrida, the other standout theorist among Berkeley academics was the Neo-Freudian theorist Jacques Lacan. Lacan's complicated theories couched in equally complicated neologisms baffled many of us. Penetrating his writing was akin to attempting to decipher Marx.

Throughout my graduate work, I persisted in my focus on gay and lesbian literature. Comp Lit faculty continuously warned me against doing this, predicting that would destroy my academic career before it even started. In particular, Simon Karlinsky held up to me how the publication of his *Sexual Labyrinth of Nikolai Gogol* had ruined his reputation among Russian scholars. Ken Weisinger told me I was unlikely to ever get hired, but I should consider my doctoral education an enhancement to my personal life.

I spent a very long time, a year, perhaps two, exploring a meaningful topic for my dissertation. Because of the immediacy of the AIDS epidemic and my own fear of dying from AIDS before completing it, I began to focus on "AIDS as a Social Construction." I thought this would be a fitting final act in my life. I submitted my paper to the "Essentialism versus Social Construction" conference in Amsterdam. When I arrived at the conference, I was informed I had been moved to a different panel, as I had originally been included on a panel with Simon Watney, who had recently published *Policing Desire: Pornography, AIDS and the Media.* I was disheartened to learn my proposed work was now redundant, but relieved to find this out before putting any significant effort into it.

I came away from this conference feeling underwhelmed. A number of us were invited by an organizer of the conference to join him for dinner at a restaurant. This meant an opportunity to meet each other in a more relaxed situation and network. When I joined the party, I found a chair vacant at the far corner of the table. A very famous gay intellectual sat to my immediate right. He never spoke to me and instead kept his back turned to me the entire evening. With this subtle slight he succeeded in blocking me from participation. I was unable to see anyone or hear any conversation. I was outraged by this, but the message was very clear. Thereafter I joined my friends in the German-speaking circle.

On a happy note, I had sex with a very famous gay intellectual, who informed me I had become a member of a secret society of gay men. He traced a "gay genealogy" back to Walt Whitman. He had had sex with Allen Ginsburg, who was his link to a chain of gay men who had had sex with another gay man who could trace this "daisy chain" back to Whitman himself. My having sex with him and swallowing his cum linked me to this chain. Any man I had sex with after that point also became a gay descendent of Whitman.

I moved on to exploring writing about post-World War II gay male literature. It would be a comparative study of American, German, and Dutch gay literature. In a nod to Eve Kosofsky Sedgwick's work I titled it *The Chiasmic Bind*. The scope of the project proved much too ambitious. I narrowed the scope of my project to small press novels by gay male authors describing and contributing to the construction of gay community. At first, I tried to apply Derrida's deconstruction to these gay texts. I quickly abandoned that. My project was to place these texts in their historical and cultural contexts. My focus was extrinsic. I saw no value in the intrinsic project of destabilizing these texts and engaging in a "play of words."

Avital Ronell agreed to be my dissertation director. I had originally wanted to ask David Miller, since he was the only person in the department doing gay-related work. But I had had only bad experiences with him. Once he left me waiting outside his office door when I had an appointment with him. I could clearly hear him having a social visit with someone inside. Another time and coming completely out of left field, he attacked me for being a "San Francisco gay." (Only later would I learn about this presumed hostility between "San Francisco gays" and "Berkeley queers.") Earlier when I had proposed David be on my doctoral exam committee, Ken Weisinger took me aside and warned me to disinvite Miller since Miller would use the opportunity to stop me from passing my orals.

I took one of David's classes. This was the only time I ever encountered queer theory in the classroom. David had invited his friend Eve Kosofsky Sedgwick to come in and discuss her recently published book *Between Men: English Literature and Male Homosocial Desire*. I found Eve's study puzzling. She identified in 18th and 19th century British novels homosocial "triangulation" system, whereby two men could express their homosocial desire for each other through a common female sexual interest, without it being mistaken for homosexuality. The only thing I could figure from this was that homophobia played a major role in how straight men expressed their friendships with each other. I didn't see what this had to do with actual homosexuals. At one point, Eve made a comment about gay men (which I no longer clearly remember), which I, as a gay man, knew wasn't true. In response I raised my hand and asked about Walt Whitman's famous repudiation that he had made late in his life declaring that he was not homosexual. She ignored my question and took another question from someone else. Not willing to be brushed off, I stayed after class to speak with her privately. David grabbed her, and the two hustled down the hall and disappeared around a corner, successfully avoiding me altogether.

During the time I was writing my dissertation, the English Department offered an informal discussion meeting for those writing on gay-related topics to present their work and discuss it. My request to join the group was denied. I found this inexplicable at the time, but later wondered if that had been David's doing. All the while my Comp Lit professors were advising me against my gay-related dissertation, queer theory was colonizing the English Department. I was also unaware that David Halperin and Leo Bersani were publishing gay work at Berkeley.

In the end Avital signed off on my dissertation. We never met to discuss my ongoing writing. Her only feedback was to direct me to a French book on the invention of heterosexuality. There was no Derrida present in my work. At that point I only wanted to finish my PhD. I requested a confidential letter of recommendation for my portfolio. (Years later I saw her letter when a German university had rejected my application and returned the entire dossier, including those confidential letters of recommendation. Avital's letter was two sentences, proclaiming my work was "promising.") I had sought Avital's support in my job search, but never heard anything from her. When I complained to Ken, he shrugged off my distress, telling me she was very involved with helping one of her Derrida disciples negotiate a position with Princeton.

As I entered the end stage of my academic training, I started attending the mandatory Modern Language Association (MLA) convention, held annually the week between Christmas and New Year. This was a double heavy burden for us ABDs ("all but dissertation"). I had to book a flight and a room at a nearby hotel and pay for it out of my own pocket. This was done in anticipation of job interviews at the conference, which might or might not be granted. When I started at SUNYA, I had intended to teach German and Russian at a small liberal arts college. By the time I was ready to apply for those positions, the Cold War had ended, the Berlin Wall had fallen, and the Soviet Union had imploded. Colleges and universities stopped teaching Russian or German. I graduated into a non-existent job market. My backup Plan B to teach gay and lesbian literature had suddenly been rendered irrelevant, having been usurped by queer theory and Queer Studies. I hustled to reformat myself as an English scholar. I attended three MLA conventions and was not invited to a single interview.

43

The AIDS epidemic raged on. By 1986 a test had been developed to detect exposure. I went to the University of California-San Francisco's medical clinic to take the test and got my first formal diagnosis. It said I tested positive for exposure to the HTLV-III virus. (There was a battle going on between France and the United States at the time as to who had discovered the AIDS virus, hence the HTLV-III name; the French claimed the HIV name.) I was not surprised. I had assumed that since the epidemic had begun, I had been infected. The doctor I met with at UCSF told me I was in the "highest at-risk" group. He expressed surprise that I was still alive.

I had thought knowing for sure I was infected would bring me a sense of relief. But it gave me no relief. Anything I found (or thought I found) irregular in my body made me think I was getting sick. I noticed I sweated whenever I walked outdoors. I thought it was HIV-related. (San Francisco is surrounded on three sides by water, so the air is always humid. The temperature is usually cool, so you wouldn't think you could sweat. But now I was becoming paranoid.)

I did not know how long I had to live. None of us did. In 1986, AIDS was a death sentence. I believed that I would live a maximum of two years after the onset of the first opportunistic disease. I based all my life decisions on that timeline. I had to weigh between my long- and short-term goals. What would prove my most disastrous judgment was never to plan for retirement. I was 32 at the time. I certainly never expected to see 35, let alone 40 or 50. By 50, it was a little too late to start planning for retirement.

I got involved in the community-based Stop AIDS Project. We signed up gay men on the street to attend informal discussions about AIDS. We organized small discussion groups and asked for someone to volunteer their homes for the meeting. It was a first effort to disseminate information and discuss concerns. The concept of safe sex had not yet been developed. I hosted several meetings in my own home.

I also joined an organization that organized support groups for people living with AIDS. Eight guys were in a support group. We rotated meetings in members' homes. The groups were peer-led. One by one, the other members of my group died. I was the sole survivor. I went through four such groups and always ended up outliving everyone else in my group. Maybe I should have felt fear and loss. Mostly, I felt guilt (for surviving) and anger (for being abandoned).

Meanwhile, things were deteriorating between Mike and me. When I wanted to go to an AA meeting, Mike declined. When I wanted to go hang out in the Castro, he declined. He wanted me to stay home and watch TV with him. Over time, this pissed me off more and more. Once I lectured him that we lived just blocks from the gayest place in the world, but all he wanted to do was stay home and watch TV.

We had our biggest blow-up over a trip to Europe I had planned to make in the summer of 1986. I took out a $5,000 student loan to pay for my "Farewell to Europe" trip. I conceived of it, in part, as a research trip to conduct interviews with gay men there on "the social construction of AIDS as a gay disease." I was accepted into a summer French language program at the Sorbonne. They arranged a summer sublet for me in Paris. (This program helped improve my competency in French to pass my written exam in it.) I arranged to visit all my friends in Europe. I believed this would be the last time I would ever see these people. I also believed I was gathering material for my dissertation. (I had no idea my work would prove too little too late, unaware that Simon Watney was already working on this topic and would publish it a year later.)

My flight from San Francisco to Stockholm included two changes— one at JFK and one at Frankfurt. I remember the Frankfurt terminal having jury-rigged barricades. The Chernobyl disaster had just happened, and fears of terrorism were on the rise.

My friends George Hallberg and Peter Gethmann met me at the airport. I stayed with them in their two-floor condo in a high-rise on the outskirts of Stockholm. The summer weather was bracingly cool and invigorating. Sweden is primarily a rural country. The views from their high-rise were over unbroken countryside. The guestroom was like a cubbyhole with no windows. The sun dips below the horizon for a very short time, but it never gets dark in the summer. My cubbyhole afforded me the darkness I needed to sleep.

I set about making my rounds immediately once I got to Stockholm. I tried to interview a gay doctor working with AIDS patients. At his apartment, he offered me a drink, but I politely declined. He then refused to be interviewed, saying he was tired of giving interviews, and insisted on taking me out to dinner with some of his friends instead. As this was my first day in Stockholm, the jet lag was hitting me very hard. I could not stay awake through dinner and begged off from staying for dessert. He was angry and dismissive, but finally granted me permission to be rude, leaving before the end of the meal.

I set up an interview with another friend, RFSL gay activist Kjell Rindar, to talk about AIDS in Sweden. We conducted the interview in German. (After the interview ended, Kjell switched to English.) After the interview, we got naked and Kjell fucked me.

I also met with the fellow RFSL activist Lars Lingvall for an interview. Lars took me for a walk in Wasa Park. We had lunch in the Gamla Stan and then went to his apartment for the interview and sex.

By the time I had overcome my jetlag I was on a night train to West Berlin. I got a sleeper car, and I slept for most of the train ride. I was awakened in the middle of the night when the train reached the mainland and was unloaded from the ferry onto tracks in Rostock. Berlin was another two hours away.

I stayed with Cornelia Walter and her boyfriend Joel. I knew Cornelia as a fellow German GSI at Berkeley. Joel had started a company selling collectible movie posters and Cornelia worked at an art gallery. They were very involved with the Berlin night culture, and they took me to a midnight art gallery opening, a cabaret, and a 3:00 AM dinner.

I had made an appointment with Michael Bochow, a sociologist and a founder of *Deutsche AIDS-Hilfe* in West Berlin. Michael had visited San Francisco and was familiar with what had become known as the "San Francisco model" for dealing with AIDS. (This model treated patients with compassion and respect. Health and social services were provided in one facility. The medical community cooperated with local community groups and the government public health department.) Michael and I used the informal "*du*" form of address. I found it awkward that all the other employees spoke to me in the formal "*Sie*."

I spent time walking aimlessly through the neighborhoods of Berlin, remembering my previous visits and my vision of the gay Mecca it had been in the 1920s. The gay commercial scene was thriving. I browsed in Prinz Eisenherz, the gay bookstore, and other gay shops. There was no

American-style gay neighborhood. I remembered how I had promised myself to move to Berlin if the Berlin Wall ever came down. In 1986 that seemed like a distant dream I'd never see in my lifetime.

So far, my AIDS interviews were not turning up a lot of AIDS as a gay disease. It was not nearly as widespread in Europe as in the US. Sweden had not yet come up with their proposal to quarantine all AIDS-infected people by placing them on an island in the Stockholm archipelago.

After Berlin, I took the train to Amsterdam. I stayed with my old AA sponsee Henk, who had moved back home to the Netherlands with his American partner Jay. They had bought and remodeled a condo in a converted warehouse on the harbor behind the Centraal Station. Jay was working full-time as a middle manager at an American corporation and supporting both of them. Henk was quite upset at being unable to find full-time work. He was over forty, which made him *persona non grata* in the Dutch job market. He was working as a doorman for an upscale hotel and was required to wear historical garb from the 18th century.

Through the GLBT Historical Society in San Francisco I had met the gay Dutch historian Schuyler Kaas. We struck up a personal friendship through our mutual interest in gay history. He taught me a great deal about Dutch gay history and the gay lay of the land in Amsterdam. Mostly I remember drinking *koffie* together. I invited Schuyler to come and visit me when I was living in Paris.

From Amsterdam, I took the train south to Bonn. I stayed with my Tübingen friend Muriel, who was now Muriel Piel, divorced from Hel and married to Peter Piel. Muriel later related to me that she had fallen in love with Peter at first sight. (She had also recounted to me that Dennis Anderson's new partner, a guy named Klaus, had appeared a little too quickly after my departure, hinting that Dennis had likely been seeing Klaus behind my back.) Muriel had left her sociology studies to become a full-time wife and mother. I spent a wonderful, if brief, visit with Muriel and Peter.

From Bonn, I took the train south to Tübingen and stayed with Brendan Donnellan. Brendan was still teaching English composition and reading German philosophers. I had no AIDS-related agenda but spent my time visiting old friends. It had been eight years since I had moved away, and the town was exactly the same. The Tengelmann supermarket had the same cashiers working there and the shelves were stocked exactly as I remembered. I found Tübingen to be much smaller than I'd remembered it. My life there had been very full. The *Altstadt* restoration was now complete. With an entirely intact medieval *Altstadt*, Tübingen was now a picture-perfect tourist destination.

Michael Schmidt took me up to his *Schrebergarten* situated on a former vineyard. I found the sun too intense. Michael was surprised because I always spent a lot of time in the sun getting a deep tan in my Tübingen days. I explained that my time living in cool, foggy San Francisco had lowered my tolerance.

From Tübingen, I headed to Paris for my French language course at the Sorbonne. My apartment was a fourth-floor walk-up on a side street in the Marais District. My apartment faced the street, giving me a view of the wall of 19th century apartment buildings. I could see into many of the front rooms. There was a kosher pizzeria at street level directly below my apartment. Early in the morning before people were out, the street water hydrants flooded the streets, washing the cobblestone lanes clean.

Just down the street was *Les Halles*, which had been the huge and grimy fresh food market when I explored it with my German classmates in 1971. Now it was a massive, and mostly underground, shopping center. Also down the street was the new Centre Pompidou, a postmodern art museum.

The Marais had formerly been a Jewish ghetto. Exploring the neighborhood, I quickly realized it was now gay. Several gay bars were just round the corner. The first time I walked past the bars a couple of the guys called out to me and beckoned me to join them for a drink. As much as I wanted to join them, I kept away. I was worried I might be pressured into an alcoholic drink.

The Marais became a gay neighborhood much the way San Francisco's Castro District had. Both were run-down neighborhoods with low rents and real estate prices. Both were centrally located and had good public transportation along with the emergence of gay businessmen eager to establish commercial venues. Two things differed, however. North American gays came to see themselves as a minority group, much like African Americans. French gay men, like other gay Europeans, never developed as deep a sense of themselves as a minority group. Hence the lack of a perceived need for gay neighborhoods. In fact, many in France in opposition to the formation of a distinct gay social identity denounced it as "communitarianism," i.e., rejecting the idea that gay identity arose from membership in a community.

I had dinner at outdoor restaurants in the neighborhood. The first time out my waitress asked me if I wanted dessert and recommended *gâteau à la chantilly*. I didn't know what chantilly was and worried it might contain alcohol. As she explained how to make it, I realized it was whipped cream. I felt like an idiot.

I met up with recovery friends from San Francisco, a gay couple who were vacationing in Paris and staying in a five-star hotel. I invited them to my apartment for coffee, but they were unwilling to come into my neighborhood. I met them at their hotel near the Place de la Concorde. They spoke no French and seemed to be alarmed at the idea of having to mix with the locals.

For my AIDS in Europe project, I had arranged to interview Daniel Defert, an important AIDS activist in France and the partner of Michel Foucault. In 1986 Foucault had already been dead for two years. Daniel invited me to his apartment for the interview, which I conducted over coffee and cake. He was very friendly and forthcoming and was happy to see an American taking serious interest in his work. As always, I was tape-recording the interview. But Defert shifted between professional and personal modes making it difficult to know when to stop recording. What still sticks out in my memory was Defert telling me that his partner had denied having AIDS and so dismissed the idea, saying he couldn't die from a social construction. Defert seemed to still be upset at Foucault's denial of a reality that was not socially constructed. At the time of the interview I was unaware of the fact that Defert had always been very vague about how Foucault had died. (As of this writing, I have not listened to my recording of that interview and do not know if Defert did indeed say this.)

The SFSU liaison office with the Sorbonne offered cheap tourist day trips for us American students. I went to Versailles, Giverny, Mont Saint Michel, and Chartres. The Chartres Cathedral caught me completely by surprise. Its modest appearance from a distance disguises the remarkable richness of its interior design and detail. Most Americans are familiar with it for its stained-glass windows. Partly built starting in 1145, and reconstructed over a 26-year period after the fire of 1194, Chartres Cathedral marks the high point of French Gothic art. The vast nave, in pure ogival style, the porches adorned with fine sculptures from the middle of the 12th century, and the magnificent 12th- and 13th-century stained-glass windows, all in remarkable condition, combine to make it a masterpiece.

As I walked into the nave, I felt a sense of being overwhelmed by what artists call "the sublime." This feeling became one of immense calm and comfort. I felt embraced by something transcendent. I went up to an altar with a bank of burning candles. I dropped a franc in the donation box and took a candle. I lit it in memory of all those young gay men who had died from AIDS. Then I prayed.

My official justification for taking out that student loan was to come to Paris to study French. Soon enough classes started. I spent the morning in class. I was the only non-female student in a class of 35. Our instructor sat at a desk elevated on a podium and taught in a schoolmarmish manner that reminded me of my teachers in Mülheim. One morning he showed up with a black eye. I did well in class, though the instructor had told me I needed to speak more often in class.

I discovered English-language AA meetings and began attending a daily noon meeting on Avenue George V. It was an international mix of mostly younger people. The spirit was very open and comradely. Everyone was welcome to join the group for lunch at a nearby restaurant. I met a German gay man about my age. We went out for coffee after lunch one day. We conversed entirely in German. Our coffee led to an unexpected affair.

I spent my afternoons visiting museums and wandering around various neighborhoods. I had already made the rounds of the tourist attractions with my German class back in 1971. But I did repeat two things. I went up the Eiffel Tower and I visited the Père Lachaise cemetery. Schuyler had come to visit me so we went to the cemetery together. I visited the graves of Jim Morrison and Edith Piaf, and left flowers at Oscar Wilde's tomb. We had coffee at a nearby café. I recalled how Rastignac at the end of *Père Goriot* walked to the highest point overlooking Père Lachaise and contemplated his future.

At this point in my "field research" of interviews with my European "cultural informants," it was becoming clear that, at best, my project to trace the rise of "AIDS as a 'gay' disease" was premature. My thesis had been presumptuous. I would need to find another topic to write about.

44

One day I got a letter from Mike writing to me say he was joining me in Paris and had booked a flight to the de Gaulle airport. He gave me his arrival information and asked me to meet him at the airport. I was royally pissed off. Mike had fought me tooth and nail not to go to Europe.

Halfway through my stay in Paris, Mike joined me for the rest of my trip. On Mike's second day in Paris we crossed paths with the German guy I was having an affair with. He opened up to me about personal issues as the AAs often do with each other; Schuyler was taken aback by the guy's openness. Mike immediately picked up that I was sleeping with this guy. When we got back to my apartment, Mike flew into a rage and started an argument that went on for hours and went nowhere. This eventually exhausted me, and I stopped arguing. I told Mike I did not want to waste my time arguing with him and waste the opportunity of being in Europe.

The work part of my trip was over. So I retraced my route, introducing Mike to some of my friends.

Our first stop was Amsterdam. We stayed with Schuyler. I showed Mike around the tourist Amsterdam. The most memorable event of that stop occurred when I was attacked in the middle of the street. I was photographing some old buildings when two guys grabbed my backpack and tried to pull me to the ground. I yelled for help. Mike managed to chase them off. I dashed into a coffeehouse where the customers there simply watched the whole thing without reacting in any way.

I thought it was an attempted gay bashing, but Schuyler assured me it was not. They must have been Italian squatters who were angry I was photographing their squat. Schuyler advised me to write a letter to the Queen.

We went to Baden Baden to visit Hel Bredigkeit and his new wife Dorothea. It was a quiet visit, catching up on each other's lives. Hel and Dorothea drank and smoked hash. Hel congratulated me on getting sober and turning my life around. He gave me a print of medieval Tübingen as a memento of our visit. This was the last time I ever saw Hel. From Baden-Baden he moved to Zimbabwe for a job and dropped out of touch.

After a short visit to Tübingen, we went to London and stayed with Ken. I took Mike to the Coleherne, but I found it boring. Mike and I did not drink, and I was not free to trick with anyone. We visited some of the tourist sites. I was growing tired of the trip and wanted to go home and deal with ending my relationship with Mike.

Mike and I stayed together for another year, but the arguing got worse. We had another blow-out argument on Thanksgiving morning. I stormed out of the house and spent the day walking around San Francisco. My Thanksgiving dinner was a burger and fries at Burger King on Powell at Market at the cable car turnaround. It was an eatery I found open. The food tasted like cardboard. When I returned home, I found that Mike had left the Thanksgiving feast he had prepared for us sitting cold and untouched on the kitchen table.

By this time I had had 44 roommates at 3036 Market Street. I was tired of my ever-changing roommates, of Mike, and of that house. I set about finding a place in Berkeley. Word of mouth through the Comparative Literature Department led me to a small one-bedroom apartment on Virginia Street in the "gourmet ghetto" of North Berkeley, half a block from Chez Panisse and a half-hour walk to Dwinelle Hall, where all my classes were.

I moved into my new digs across the Bay in the summer of 1987. It was my first time ever living alone. Other than going to campus to teach, I spent the semester at home reading in preparation for my oral doctoral exams. I had a tight schedule to get through every book on my exam list. I never did get all the way through it. When I knocked off for the day, it was too late at night to take BART to San Francisco.

I loved my new apartment, though. It had a long hallway in the middle of the fourplex with rooms off it like a railroad flat. It was easily comfortable for one person. I lined the hallway with bookcases. I put my desk in the front window, which overlooked an elementary school. I bought a single sofa bed in the Haight-Ashbury in case I had company. (I had always had overnight guests everywhere else I lived.) The apartment had a full bath and a sunroom off the narrow kitchen. I put my file cabinets in the sunroom along with my orchids, which got indirect sun from every direction. They thrived in that space. The walls were paper-thin—the apartment's only drawback. I had neighbors below me and next to me.

I walked to the nearby Safeway for groceries. The French Connection, a coffeehouse, sat opposite Chez Panisse. I rented a PO box at the post office across the street from the Connection. The original Peet's Coffee House was a block away. Next door to Peet's was the Live Oak Bookstore. It had a great humanities book selection. Despite all these distractions, I found it very lonely living in Berkeley. I had no time to make friends in Berkeley and didn't know where I would meet people. All my friends lived in San Francisco, and I could not get to AA meetings there.

In 1987 Surgeon General C. Everett Koop sent out an AIDS mailing to every household in America, a first step by the federal government to start dealing with AIDS. I had two reactions to getting this in the mail. One was to laugh at how pathetic this was—too little too late to mean anything to me personally. It rubbed salt in a wound, deepening my sense of being all alone in Berkeley with my AIDS secret.

While living in Berkeley, I was surprised that my parents wanted to visit me. It was the only time they'd ever offered to visit me in all my years since I had moved away. They had never expressed interest in visiting me in West Germany or San Francisco. They planned to come the very week of my doctoral exams. They were inflexible. They wouldn't come a week before or after, but *exactly* during the week I'd be sitting for my exams. I had no choice except to say no.

At the start of the spring semester, I came across a brand-new zine called *BEAR*. It was a local production, photocopied on 8½" x 11" paper folded in half and stapled together. The publisher Richard Bulger had an office over the old firehouse on 16th Street in the Mission where guys came in off the street to pose naked for the magazine. The zine was filled with pictures of masculine-looking men of varying builds and in a range from handsome to average-looking.

An early issue of *BEAR* had a personal ad, which I answered. I spoke on the phone with the guy. It turned out that David White was also in recovery and HIV+. He came over to Berkeley to meet me. A bearded blond, he was a couple of years older, and he had very thickly muscled thighs from being an ice skater as a kid. He had no body hair. This became a problem over time. I was in the process of developing a fetish for furry men, which became a rigid requirement for sexual attraction.

After a long talk, we had sex. An office worker, David had worried that he felt people found him "strange" and seemed to feel guilty about being a "pervert." As a fellow leathersex practitioner, as someone who also felt "different," I relieved him of those fears. Later, David would turn out to be the most loving and intuitive bondage master I ever had.

In the evenings I walked up to the campus of the Pacific School of Religion (PSR) to a vantage point overlooking San Francisco and the Bay. I fantasized about attending the PSR because the campus was so romantic. But I was so lonesome for my City by the Bay that I often cried while staring at the City.

I submitted a paper on my revamped proposed study of "AIDS as a 'gay' disease" to a conference in Amsterdam organized around the debate of "essentialism versus social construction." My paper was accepted. To raise funds for this trip, I mailed out an appeal to all my friends. The response was lukewarm—it had cost me more to do my mailing than what it brought in.

I ended that year at Berkeley having exhausted all my sources of income. I had no idea how I would keep a roof over my head, let alone write my dissertation.

45

I spent that summer housesitting for Ken Weisinger, who was traveling in Italy with his ex Richard Lee. Ken's house was a Victorian up on 19th Street overlooking the Castro and downtown. Billie Aul and her husband Tim Smith were staying at my place in Berkeley. I hosted dinner parties at Ken's that summer.

The Comp Lit Department contacted me to let me know that a college on the East Coast was interested in interviewing me for a one-year teaching position. It was a joint appointment in the German and Russian departments. They needed a temporary replacement for the faculty member who had quit on very short notice well past the hiring season for another job. Hamilton College had called around to all the major universities trying to find a graduate student who could do the job. I was one of only three people they could locate. Did I want to interview? Was I willing to move to upstate New York?

My interview was conducted over the phone. Part of it was in German, part in Russian, and part in English. It went very well. The Russian faculty member mentioned that if it was a good fit, I could be kept on as a tenure-track hire. I leapt at the opportunity. I looked forward to trying out living in the region I had grown up in. (McGraw was a 90-minute drive from Clinton.)

I talked it over with David, who was willing to move to Clinton, New York. I described to him what snowbelt winters were like. He only ever lived in the country in Sonoma County. I assured him this would be very different. There was no way I could prepare him for what country living in the snowbelt was like. He looked forward to the change of scenery. I then went into accelerated moving mode. My landlord refused to let me sublet, so I had a moving sale. It broke my heart to dismantle my home library.

Teaching German and Russian at a small liberal arts college had been my academic dream. I was very excited by the opportunity to do so. Such positions had become extremely rare. I read David's willingness to move to Clinton with me as a very positive omen for him becoming my life partner. I was also keen to return to my upstate roots as an openly gay and partnered man. I hoped to establish a new relationship with my family. But I kept silent about my HIV status. It was important to me to see how I was treated by my family without them being influenced, one way or the other, by the knowledge that my days were limited. I perversely felt like the prodigal son. I was aware that I was coming home to say goodbye.

The year at Hamilton proved very challenging. Both of my colleagues, Sydna Weiss who taught German and Frank Sciacca, who taught Russian, turned out to be closeted. Our social life with fellow faculty was nonexistent. Sydna pointed out that I had a one-year contract and no one wanted to invest in someone so temporary.

David and I sought out gay life. We went to the sole gay bar in Utica a few times. The other patrons kept their distance. We went to local AA meetings. We made friends with two gay men there. Brian also had AIDS and was on a similar mission to mine. He had left Los Angeles to move back home in pursuit of his lifelong dream to be a pilot. He was flying puddle-jumpers for a regional airline. Angelo was a closeted Catholic priest. His dream was to move to New York City and work with gay men with AIDS. At about the same time Angelo discovered David and I were a leathersex couple, he also learned he was about to be removed from the priesthood for being a "practicing homosexual." Angelo believed people into BDSM were "sick," and he dropped us as friends.

David got work through a local employment agency as a clerk-typist for General Electric. He reported that his fellow employees called him Tinkerbell. He became aware that he was being watched by management. He felt very uncomfortable at work.

I enjoyed teaching. I enjoyed switching between German and Russian and English in the classroom. I found the students bright, but not very motivated. I learned what it was like to teach highly privileged students. I learned about the unwritten rule of the "gentleman's C's." (At elite universities, the legacy students' fathers are donating lots of money, so it's understood the student will never get a grade below C—unless the university wants the big donations to stop. This is part of the old boys' network.) I learned about a culture of alcohol abuse kept under wraps by the administration. Only after David and I returned to San Francisco did Sydna inform me that the Hamilton faculty and administration had been scandalized by my bringing my same-sex partner and living as an openly gay couple. I was chagrined to learned they had found out we both had AIDS and believed that I had infected David.

We both felt very isolated that year. We survived by traveling. We visited my friends in Albany, a two-hour drive away, on the occasional weekend. We made a trip back to San Francisco. David joined me on my trip to the MLA convention in New Orleans over the winter break.

David felt trapped. We fell to arguing with each other.

My parents came to our place for Sunday dinner once. (This was the only time they had ever traveled to visit me.) When they arrived, Mom went straight upstairs to our bedroom and went through our closets and dresser drawers. I couldn't guess what she was looking for and I was outraged at her obvious lack of boundaries or respect for my privacy. The last thing I remember Mom saying to me was, "No matter what kind of trouble you get yourself into, you always come out smelling like roses."

I deliberately said nothing to Mom and Dad about my having AIDS. I wanted to be clear about how they actually felt about me. When I got back to San Francisco, I told Mom. Her response was, "I thought so. And, frankly, I expected you'd be dead by now."

I wondered about my effectiveness as a teacher. My student evaluations were positive. But I was surprised by two unanticipated things. My German students wrote and performed a skit satirizing me. In it I was interviewed by David Letterman. Another student for whom I had written a letter of recommendation for a study abroad program in West Germany wrote me a letter of thanks when he returned saying he believed my recommendation had gotten him accepted.

Toward the end of the year, I asked about my chances for staying on at Hamilton. I was informed that they never hired an ABD. I was angry to discover I had been lied to. But I was also relieved, as was David, that we were going back to San Francisco.

David and I took several weeks for our drive back home to San Francisco, staying with friends along the way. We visited Jonathan Heller in Washington, D.C., Larry Tate, our nudist bodybuilder buddy in New Orleans, and David's sister in Tucson. We were supposed to stay with my high school best friend Tom in Houston. We stopped in when we got to Houston. But Tom was now deep in the closet, living with his wife and children (and having sex with men in dirty bookstores). Coming face to face with him living this lie made me so uncomfortable I could hardly tolerate being in his and his wife's presence. I extemporized that we needed to get back on the road. David and I drove to El Paso and checked into a fleabag motel that night.

When we got back to San Francisco, Sander Gilman invited me to participate as a Fulbright/DAAD post doc fellow in his program at Cornell on "Sex and Disease in German Literature and Culture." The seminar was fascinating and a lot of work. I ran into my high school sweetheart Julia Jenkins, who was managing a Ben & Jerry's in downtown Ithaca. Several times she invited me to get together with her friends. I had no free time because of the amount of work the seminar required. But Julia didn't seem to understand that.

Mom persisted in getting me to come for Sunday dinner. My visit was a waste of time. As soon as the meal was over, Mom and Dad jumped up from their chairs and went to busy themselves. Sylvia called them on that and said, "You wanted Les here to come for dinner. Stay and talk to him." They also wanted me to stay the rest of the summer and paint their house. I turned them down, remembering all the times doing projects for them netted me a steady stream of criticism with no thanks for my help.

During that time Brian was in the hospital for AIDS-related illnesses. I visited him several times in Syracuse, and he lent me his car. I was grateful both for his generosity and the opportunity to see him in his last days.

When the Cornell program ended, I went right back to San Francisco.

46

When we moved back to San Francisco, David was able to rent another apartment in the building he had been living in before. I sold our car. I saw a doctor at the university to get retested for HIV. Of course it came back positive, but I also got plugged into the healthcare system and started taking AZT. (It was now 1989 and AZT, the first treatment for AIDS, had come on the market.)

David found a job. I was now ABD and only needed to write my dissertation. I had run out of income options to continue with my degree. Within weeks I fell into a very deep depression and spent all my time holed up in the living room. I became desperate. I went to a psychiatrist who diagnosed me with clinical depression. He told me I had probably been depressed all my life. (I was aware that debilitating depression ran through Mom's family.) I was prescribed an antidepressant. (This was shortly before the emergence of Prozac.) It's hard to say how much good it did me. While it elevated my mood, it also left me unable to sleep at night and more or less sleepwalking through the day. I often felt like a zombie.

One day while having lunch at Without Reservation, my regular waiter John Musselman, knowing my taste in men, told me about Bear Hug parties. He let me know where the next party would be. Private sex parties had sprung up as a response to the Public Heath Department's order shutting down the gay bathhouses in San Francisco to stop the spread of AIDS.

The next party was held in Jim Birch's home in Berkeley. Guests paid $1 for membership and signed their fake names on the attendance list.

The 1989 earthquake had recently happened, and the Bay Bridge was shut down. We took BART to get there. David and I went together but went our separate ways when we got there. We stripped naked inside the front door and put our clothes in a paper bag. Men socialized in the kitchen. All the other rooms were devoted to sex. I found myself a furry, bearded somewhat older guy and we played in a bedroom. Afterwards we cuddled and talked. Sam Ganzarcuk would become a very close friend, and to this day, still a confidante.

Along with the Bear Hug parties were Leather Bear parties. I soon became John Musselman's fistfucking buddy. The Bear Hug and Leather Bear parties were now held at The 14th Street House, famous in the sexual underground as the site of many different groups' sex parties. It was managed by Steve Damback and later by Bill Brent.

The guys who organized the Bear Hug parties also established Bear Expo, what became an annual weekend gathering of bears. Each year it grew larger. It was the precursor to the International Bear Rendezvous (IBR), which became the premier worldwide gathering of Bears.

I started holding "What is a Bear?" discussions groups at Bear Expo. In those early years, the term "Bear" was rather vague, and there was no consensus yet.

In the months that followed I realized that this Bear phenomenon was something much bigger than just the next passing obsession in the gay community. I explored the various expressions of "bearness," participated and kept mental notes, guided by Laud Humphrey's example in his *Tearoom Trade*, where I learned how to cruise public toilets. In 1990 I wrote up my findings in an article I submitted to *Drummer* magazine. Jack Fritscher published my "Sociology of the Urban Bear" as a cover article. It was the first time "Bear" appeared in print. Jack Fritscher holds the distinction of being the first person to published "bear" on the cover of *California Action Guide* in November 1982 and on the cover of *Drummer* (Issue 44). *BEAR* also proceeded my article, which might be better cited as the first quasi-academic treatment of gay bears. (Later the publication of my first *Bear Book* would make the Library of Congress create the category of "(gay) bear.")

My depression ended my relationship with David. After the breakup, I moved back in with Mike at 3036 Market Street. During this time I developed an AIDS-related condition called Immune Thrombocytopenic Purpura (ITP), and my T-cell count was 55. I went to Ward 86, the AIDS outpatient ward, at San Francisco General Hospital for experimental treatments in the afternoons and ran around doing footwork for the welfare office in the mornings. (I was without income and Mike demanded that I go on welfare.)

The name of Ward 86 came from being located in Building 8 and on Floor 6. (I thought it was a bad pun—I had been "86'd" from bars for being too drunk and was now "86'd" for having AIDS. I was thankful every time I went to Ward 86—AIDS patients in Ward 5B died there. I visited several friends there.)

Ward 86 was always crowded, overflowing with people in the waiting room and in the corridor. I sometimes waited for hours to be seen because an emergency patient was rushed in. By 1990 I was now seeing African-Americans showing up at Ward 86. We all watched TV in the waiting room. One day we saw a new commercial: an obviously affluent straight white man goes to the doctor in a panic saying he thought he was dying. "The doctor told me it's just heartburn. Boy, was I relieved." We all looked at each other and burst out laughing.

I was a regular reader of *BEAR* magazine. I met Richard Bulger who tried to convince me—and Mike—to pose nude for the magazine. Mike had no interest. My interest lay in writing a column for the magazine. Bulger already had one full-time staff member, Luke Mauerman, penning a regular column. But he agreed to my proposal for a film review column.

I was excited to see my first column appear in *BEAR*. I submitted a second review.

When the magazine came out without my review, I asked Richard what had happened. He told me my column was eating up advertising space and that he was dropping it.

A few years later *American Bear* began publishing. By then my *Bear Book* had appeared and I was known as "the Bear historian." I wrote Tim Martin, the editor, and asked if I could write a column. He turned me down, telling me that he thought Ron Suresha would object, and he didn't want to offend Mr. Suresha. When that magazine folded and *A Bear's Life* appeared, I offered once again to write about Bear history. They accepted three brief columns from me. Then they went under. When *BEAR* magazine was resurrected with ownership passing on to a new publisher in Las Vegas, I offered to write a column about "Bear icons." They enthusiastically agreed. After no further word from them, I got in touch again six months later. This time they told me that my writing was not appropriate for their magazine.

47

I felt well enough to try dating again. I placed an ad in *The Bay Times*. I decided to "dream big" and ask for what I believed I was looking for. I was specific about looking for a hairy bearded man over 30 and of a romantic bent. I got a single reply from a man who described himself as being who I was looking for. I was thunderstruck at first sight of this man.

His name was Adam Jones. We agreed to meet for coffee at Sweet Inspiration on Market Street in the Castro. I was living with Mike rent-free and I had just gotten my cock pierced. (Looking back now I wonder how I could have afforded a body piercing when I didn't have the money to buy food.)

I came a bit early, got my coffee and cake, and sat at a table near the door. A few minutes later a strikingly handsome, red-bearded man walked through the door. He was beefy and on the short side. He looked like the twin brother of Timothy Busfield in *Thirtysomething*, a popular TV drama at the time.

My heart leapt at the thought this might be the man who answered my ad. "Are you Adam?" I asked him, standing up to greet him.

"I am. And you must be Les." He had a deep, resonant, baritone voice.

While he was at the counter getting coffee and a pastry, I stared at him, scarcely believing my luck in meeting someone who embodied my physical ideal and was interested in meeting me.

Adam and I began telling each other about ourselves, our interests and passions. He was a classically trained singer working as a technical writer in

Sausalito. He had recently moved from Windsor in Sonoma County back to The City. We shared an interest in a wide range of music, movies, and northern California. The longer we talked the more enchanted I became. I felt a deep connection taking root. I eagerly wanted to take him to bed, despite my rule against having sex on the first meeting with a guy I wanted to date. I had found that such a rush into sex altered the dynamic into a one-time-only trick.

Adam appeared to be responding to me as I was to him. It became a dance in which we coordinated our moves to mirror back to the other. I found myself beginning to fall in love with this near-stranger. I felt a deep soul connection. I did not hold these feelings back but told Adam I felt a deep connection and was already falling for him. Adam told me he felt the same way. He had to be the soulmate I had been looking for. He also had AIDS, which deepened my connection to him. I let my guard down and made myself completely vulnerable to Adam. I had never believed in love at first sight. And here it was happening to me.

I wanted Adam badly. I wanted his body, I wanted his sex, I wanted to dive into his soul. Against my rule, I invited Adam back to my place. My Prince Albert piercing was only a few days old, and I was supposed to refrain from sex until my cock had healed. I went against the medical advice. Naked, Adam was magnificent. I savored his stocky torso, his hairy chest, his massive cock. He had the body of a less-muscled Jack Radcliffe, the *BEAR* magazine's cover Bear, who had became the icon of ideal Bear beauty. I preferred Adam's natural body to the body muscles from obvious gym training. Our first sexual encounter left me truly, deeply, madly in love.

Mike was suddenly diagnosed with terminal-stage cancer. The last time he had seen his doctor a year before, his lungs were fine. He started chemotherapy, which made him feel worse. He threw up constantly. When his ex-wife learned about his prognosis, she was suddenly back in the picture. His friends in the Fire Department also started showing up again. All these people rallied around Mike, now that he was dying of a respectably heterosexual disease.

My anxiety at the prospect of becoming homeless grew almost unbearable. I reached out to friends in gay AA and my gay history circle, and to members of my parish at Trinity Episcopal Church. I realized that people were becoming seriously burned out by the ongoing AIDS epidemic, financial and economic resources stretched to the breaking point. No one had anything to suggest to me. I found myself completely on my own and living in a social vacuum.

One day I ran into Willie Walker on Castro Street. I had not heard from him in months. Walker said, "Your friends are avoiding you because they are afraid of being infected with your 'bad luck.'" A wave of pure terror and a sense of feeling deeply betrayed flooded over me. That moment of watching Walker's face as he said this, the Castro Theatre beside us, has remained frozen like a photograph in my mind ever since. It is impossible for me to think about Walker without that image and those feelings.

Mike's ex-wife had Mike kick me out of my own house. I was headed for homelessness when my friend Ken found out what was happening. He got in touch with a friend of his who had a spare room in San Francisco. That friend, Tom Libby, had an architecture student staying in the room. As soon as the student moved out, I could move in. I appraised Tom of my situation, and he was fine with letting me live with him rent-free.

This was the moment when I began to believe in angels. I had learned in AA the belief that God works through other people. This was the moment I began to believe in angels. Somehow, when the future looked hopeless, some unanticipated person or circumstance would show up and prevent an inevitable catastrophe.

My new roommate Tom owned a two-flat Victorian in Bernal Heights and lived in the upper flat. Tom had left a college position teaching urban studies and art history in Chicago to move to San Francisco with his partner Cliff, a professional chef. Cliff had died of AIDS two years before I moved in. Tom was still helping friends dying of AIDS, and he was willing to let me live with him, knowing I'd probably die on his watch too.

Adam lived alone in an apartment on Balboa Street out in the Richmond District. It was in the back of the building and the living room picture window faced the golden onion domes of the Holy Virgin Orthodox Cathedral on Geary Street. He was recently out of a relationship and had moved back to The City to start fresh. His former partner was a psychotherapist in Sonoma County. When the partner found out Adam had contracted AIDS, he kicked Adam out. Adam had violated their monogamy agreement.

Because Adam lived alone, I soon spent all my free time at his place. We easily fell into a daily routine. In the morning we would wake up together, take a shower, take our AZT, and have morning coffee. Adam would drop me off at Sweet Inspiration, where I would have more coffee, and Adam would drive to work in Sausalito. I would take the bus back to Bernal Heights and spend the day writing my dissertation. At the end of the day Adam would pick me up and we'd head to the Richmond. We'd stop at the Safeway and buy fixings for dinner. (Adam's specialty was chicken Alfredo.) My contribution was my food stamps and helping out in the kitchen. We usually listened to light jazz on KKSF or the Nylons or Toots

Thielemanns. His version of "Old Friends" became "our song." (Recently I heard this recording for the first time in decades, and it devastated me. It brought back a rush of happy memories of these years and the belief that Adam and I would be best friends for the rest of our lives.) After dinner we'd watch a movie rented from the neighborhood video store. We usually made love before going to bed.

On the weekends, we would go for drives through the countryside of coastal Northern California to destination spots—the coastal towns of Sonoma County, the vineyard towns of the Sonoma and Napa Valleys, and as far as the coastal towns of Mendocino County. (Little did I realize at the time that Adam was revisiting places filled with his memories of his life with his ex. Nor did I realize I was Adam's rebound relationship. He would turn out to be one of those people, like me, who are so terrified of being alone they will latch on to anyone coming along first.

We also went on two weekend stays up the coast. The first was a day's drive through the coastal redwoods and a hotel stay in Eureka, in Humboldt County, part of the Emerald Triangle. Adam sprang our second trip—to Mendocino—on me as our informal honeymoon. We stayed at a bed-and-breakfast where we had our own one-room cottage. Mendocino is perched directly on the shoreline of the Pacific. A spit of land extends parallel to Mendocino, offering a famous view of the town. This view, reversed, is the establishing shot of the fictional Cabot Cove, where the TV show *Murder, She Wrote* is set. There is a small downtown that stretches a couple of blocks, with several shops catering to the tourists, who overrun the place on weekends.

Our first evening there we drove to a little harbor below the town for dinner. The restaurant had tiers of tables, arranged as in an auditorium, which overlooked the harbor. We went back to our cabin and listened to a couple of 1930s radio dramas on tape.

We headed back home on Sunday. Along the way we stopped in Marin County for a walk across one of the hills facing the Pacific. Finding no one else on the hills, we walked a bit down the ocean-facing side and took our clothes off. We made love under the California sun. I felt our lovemaking had brought us into a transcendent space. I got glimpses of Tristan and Isolde's tryst in the medieval love cave. Looking back today, I remember this as the peak moment of our love, a blending of the flesh and the spirit, for lack of better words, where I first became aware of how physical love is inseparable from emotional love. I never once had the slightest sexual interest in another man while I was with Adam. It was the first time I was monogamous, and this was out of desire and not formal agreement.

***

After I moved in with Tom, the chaos of my life continued. While trying to write my dissertation, I had had to cope with being evicted from my home, scrambling to find another place to live, coping with AIDS—and being diagnosed with full-blown AIDS. My new relationship with Adam was my emotional anchor. More angels appeared in my life at this time.

When I got my diagnosis of "Disabling ARC" ("AIDS-related condition," which was later absorbed into the "full-blown AIDS" category), I applied for SSI permanent disability. My application was quickly accepted, and I began to receive the pittance of $200 a month payment. At the time Social Security was approving AIDS-related applications, timing them to coincide with the projected life expectancy. The strategy was meant to save the government money by deferring payment long enough for the AIDS patient to die before they had to pay out.

During this time my friend Hubert Kennedy, the Karl-Heinrich Ulrichs scholar, had retired to San Francisco. We met for lunch every week. I tried to coax him out of his atheism. We discussed political philosophy, mostly nineteenth century theories—Hubert was a practicing anarchist, and I embraced socialism, more in theory than in practice. Some of his unease with socialism seemed to have stemmed from his discovery and exploration of Karl Marx's homophobia.

I was much taken by Edward Carpenter, the British socialist utopian and early gay activist. Carpenter knew many of the most important left-leaning intellectuals and activists of his day. He was friends with Walt Whitman and D. H. Lawrence, among many others. He met the working-class George Merrill, who became his lifelong partner. They moved to Sheffield, where they lived as openly gay men. Carpenter was a generation older than Merrill and celebrated the social and sexual democracy of gay men. He came from the upper echelons of English society, while Merrill was working-class. E. M. Forster, another friend of Carpenter's, modeled his novel *Maurice* on their relationship. The socialist and anti-war activist Fenner Brockway called Carpenter "the gay godfather of the British left."

Anarcho-syndicalism seemed to be the sweet spot for us. I pointed to the anarcho-syndicalist societies portrayed by Heinlein in *The Moon Is a Harsh Mistress* and Ursula K. Leguin's *The Dispossessed*. I think of Noam Chomsky, the anarcho-syndicalist political activist intellectual and I recall seeing the film of his *Manufacturing Consent* at the Castro Theatre. Years before Greg Benzow had turned me on to a book by Colin Turnbull called *The Forest People*, an ethnographic study of a central African tribe he lived with for several years. To me it sounded like a non-capitalist paradise. (At the time I did not know that Turnbull was gay and had a lifelong partner.)

Although now remembered for his writings and translations of Ulrichs and the German anarchist and man-boy lover John Henry Mackay, Hubert was an accomplished mathematician. Hubert had been a mathematics professor at Providence College in Rhode Island. After he came out, the college's administration and his colleagues froze him out, treating him as a *persona non grata*. Retiring and moving to San Francisco allowed him to escape professional hostility and devote himself full-time to his research in early German gay history.

We discussed my progress on my dissertation. My dissertation director Avital was never available to meet with me to discuss it. I had submitted a request to join a lunch-time discussion group organized in the English Department for students writing on queer topics. My request was turned down. At the time I did not know why.

Hubert's mantra to me as I struggled with my dissertation was, "Don't get it right; get it written."

I found out about Mike's death when Tom saw his obituary in the *Chronicle*. Mike had been cremated and his ashes released into the Bay. I had been excluded from his memorial service. I wrote his daughter to ask for the return of my possessions which held sentimental value. I also asked her about Mike's will. She informed me that all of the contents of the house on Market Street had already been disposed of, and I had been written out of his will three days before he died.

I was furious over all of this. Tom said, "There's nothing you can do about it legally. Just let it go."

Around this time *The Chronicle* published an article in its Sunday edition about the challenges for gay people at UC Berkeley. My name and the example of my experiences as an out grad student were singled out for praise. I had no idea who would have spoken to the *Chronicle* about my experience or even that being out in Berkeley in itself would be noteworthy.

One night Adam did not come home from work. I stayed up waiting for him to come home. The longer I waited, the more worried I became. Adam showed in the morning still in his work clothes. Literally, he jumped in his shoes when he saw me waiting for him. I was very angry. I confronted him. "Where have you been all night?!"

At first, Adam deflected, saying, "What I do and where I go is none of your business."

"But where were you? Why didn't you come home? I was worried something had happened to you."

"I went home with a guy I met at the Lone Star," Adam said. He never drank, at least not in front of me. We had never gone out to a bar together.

"Was last night the first time you met this guy?" I smelled a rat.

"Well, no. I've been seeing him for a while now."

"What's going on with this guy? How long were you going to wait before telling me about this guy?"

"I don't know," he said. "I was going to wait until I knew where things were going with him." I eventually learned the guy's name was Tom Fontaine. Adam told me he had fallen out of love with me. "How does one 'fall out of love'?" I asked him.

Over the next couple of days Adam told me he couldn't take any more of my negativity. When I first told him about my situation, he felt sorry for me; his former partner had taken pity on him and taken care of him when he needed help the most. Adam said he wanted to pay it forward and "help" me. I was outraged. Adam had taken pity on me and disguised it by pretending to be in love with me. I realized he was a supreme actor in the role of the "perfect lover." Why had I never suspected anything?

"I hold my cards close to my chest," Adam said.

As the Germans say, "*Ich war zum Boden zerstört.*" ("I am destroyed to my very foundations," i.e., utterly devastated). I had been lied to, deliberately misled, and utterly betrayed. I now understood why Adam had seemed to grow a bit distant from me, was stand-offish at my graduation party, was reluctant to be included in my graduation photographs. He was already involved with Fontaine and planning to leave me. He said he held off saying anything until I had finished my PhD to avoid disrupting that.

I went crazy. By one of those ironic flukes, a guy on the bus tried to pick me up. I was emotionally raw and did not want to be touched by another man at that point. I told him he'd have to wait until I was ready for sex again. He told me he was seeing a man who was in the process of breaking up with another guy. To make a long story short, I realized this was the guy Adam had dumped me for: Tom Fontaine.

I found out where Fontaine lived and walked to his house with Adam's car parked on the street, and stood outside the house for an hour or so. I fantasized vandalizing Adam's car. I couldn't sleep and I stayed up all night walking the streets of San Francisco. In three months I lost 50 pounds. I was consumed with rage and hurt and frustration and sadness. Most of all, I was filled with unbearable heartache. I put on my Patsy Cline audio cassettes as I drove between Bernal Heights and the Castro along Dolores Street. It seemed fitting I was driving on the Street of Pains. Patsy's sad, mournful pleading and false front bravery touched my very soul. I cried and cried and cried, almost nonstop. I thought I would never stop crying.

I didn't know one person could hurt another person this badly. I finally understood all those songs and romantic movies. I grasped what it felt to fall in love and be betrayed and abandoned by a lover, to be jilted, to know unrequited love.

As my crying and grieving grew deeper, I realized that there was more than just heartbreak. I had begun to grieve the loss of the hundreds of men I'd known who had died of AIDS. I had been numbed completely to the AIDS epidemic up until then. Now emotionally unfrozen, old, long buried memories of childhood sex abuse and incest surfaced, unleashing the emotional blunt of that childhood trauma.

I found a psychotherapist who specialized in working with incest survivors. I worked through Mike Lew's *Victims No Longer*, a guide for male incest survivors to recover and heal from their trauma. I began attending ISA (Incest Survivors Anonymous) meetings. These meetings were emotionally delicate—incest survivors have particularly difficult trust issues. I was relieved to find a safe group of people who understood what I was talking about and whom I could trust. I spoke on a panel of incest survivors at that summer's Western Round Up. I read Leonard Shengold's *Soul Murder*, his study of the traumatizing effects of sexual (and other) abuse and deprivation on children. This explained the emotional bottom I had come to—I felt that soul murder within me and why I now felt socially dead.

Then something very strange started happening in the ISA meetings. New people were suddenly showing up, claiming they suffered from multiple personality disorder due to childhood sexual abuse. They told bizarre stories of being forced into sexual slavery in childhood. These events all happened in odd places. Multiple personality disorder had become a popular malady in those days. It was hard to trust the plausibility of many of these stories. After a while it became clear that, whatever mental problems these people were dealing with, they were infiltrating the ISA meetings, trying to take control of the meetings for unclear purposes. Their violation of the group members' trust undermined the meetings, and eventually these meetings collapsed.

And yet, after two years living on welfare, the kindness of angels, and the generosity of Tom Libby, I was still not dead. I had networked to make a career transition into technical writing. Hubert lent me the money to buy a car so I could get to interviews (and eventually, a job in the Silicon Valley). A friend snagged me an interview at his software company. But his boss rejected me, fearing I was really there to get her manager job. I dated a few guys briefly after my breakup with Adam. One of them was a Mexican American who had grown up in El Paso and majored in German, and he was working as a technical writer so he arranged an interview for me with his software company. I really liked the guy. He was very handsome and sexy. We had so much in common. He also had AIDS but I found it strange that I could never get a read on him. He seemed impenetrable. He broke off with me. A couple of weeks later I got a phone call from his mother saying he had committed suicide. He had driven up into the Sierra Nevada and walked out into the snow where he froze to death. She wanted to talk with me because I was the last person known to see him alive.

I renewed my habit of daily prayer and meditation. Tom took me on drives up the coast. We sometimes had lunch in Stinson Beach. Sometimes I just cried, and Tom bore silent witness. I clearly saw that my life was over, but I needed to keep on keeping on as long as I could go.

During this period of my life, my friend Sofia Light reached out to me. We spoke on the phone nearly every evening. She was a solid comfort. She kept me appraised of her work life at Mount Ida College outside Boston. Mount Ida was a small private proprietary college with an open-admissions policy. Most of the students were unprepared to do college-level work, which made them very challenging to teach. They needed skilled and caring classroom instructors. Sofia constantly complained about the administration, which she said was hostile to faculty, controlled everything, leaving the faculty with no autonomy. The salary was way below the national average. (When I was granted tenure in 2000, Mount Ida was paying me $30,000. All the other universities and colleges in the Boston area were paying $80,000 for the same rank, years of teaching experience, and the same academic discipline.)

When Mount Ida launched a search for a tenure-track position to teach English and Humanities, Sofia let me know she would recommend me if I decided to apply. She said I had a good idea of what I was getting myself into, a very bad work environment, but encouraged me to apply if I thought I could stomach that. I needed to pay for my own airfare to the on-campus interview.

Two weeks later I was on a plane to Logan Airport. It was July 1993.

PART THREE

48

Eager to start a new life in Boston, I drove cross-country in five days.

I stayed with Sofia and Beryl on David Square in Somerville for several weeks. In 1993, Davis Square was still very much a student neighborhood for Tufts University, so rents were relatively cheap. The neighborhood would become very trendy. They were hoarders and their apartment was a disaster. They had piles of junk everywhere with lots of clothing on linoleum floors and wood floors, but with no rugs. Beryl moved a large pile of clothes off her bed so I could use it. (She slept with Sofia in Sofia's bedroom.) Sofia pestered me to help her declutter. But I knew I would never persuade her to let go of a single possession, so I always declined.

Ruth invited me to live in her apartment in Brookline. She was living with her boyfriend Steve in his condo in Cambridge. I appreciated having a place to myself. Marlene's apparent was very sunny and cheerful, with a Scandinavian modern minimalist flair.

My first semester of teaching was my first full-time job in several years. At the end of my work day I would come home to Brookline, put a Mozart CD on, and nap in the living room floor for an hour or two. The work was physically exhausting, and I had concerns I might not be well enough to work full-time.

In my first six months in Boston I found my way to (mostly gay) AA meetings. I joined an AIDS support group run by the AIDS Action Committee. I started going to New England Bear events. I met a couple of guys I was interested in dating. I explored various neighborhoods.

After a year and a half of attending AA meetings, I was making no friends and I was never once called on to share. In Boston, the custom was for attendees to raise their hand if they wanted to share and wait for the speaker to choose them. At one meeting a man had a heart attack. We watched him lurch out of his seat and lie on the floor clutching his chest, trembling, and die. I was shaken by this. Someone called for an ambulance and the speaker ended the meeting ordering us all out of the building. At that point I was so disgusted with Boston AA that I never went to another meeting there.

I attended two AIDS support meetings. Then it was cancelled due to a lack of interest. That was the end of my ties to any AIDS community.

I attended New England Bear (NEB) bar nights at the Boston Ramrod. I was invited to a couple of Bear parties. I had sex a few times—and I came away from every sexual encounter with crabs. I put out an invitation over the BML for a post-Gay Pride parade Bear party at my house. In part, I intended this as a welcoming gesture to NEB. Lots of men from the BML showed up, but I didn't see a single NEB face.

I asked a couple of NEB guys to join me for a meal and to talk to them about my issue with making no friends among the NEB. They told me that they were all exhausted from the steady loss of friends to AIDS. None of them were interested in investing in a friendship with me, knowing I would end up dying as well. This collective rejection made its deepest impression on me later when my next partner and I once went to a NEB Sunday brunch at the Chandler Inn. When we showed up there was no room at the table. (Several tables had been pushed together to accommodate the large party.) We were left to sit by ourselves at another table across the room.

Years later a friend told me that I was a "big deal" in the NEB since I was an actual "Bear star." I had no idea. I do remember the NEB honoring me, unexpectedly, with a trophy at a bar night.

I did not do any serious dating in my first year in Boston as I needed to focus my attention on getting started in my first career position. I went out on few dates with guys I had met through the Bears Mailing List (BML). I got together with Steve Dyer, the founder of the BML. He introduced me to Michael Bronski, whom I met over coffee in Harvard Square once. After that, I never heard from either one of them.

An acquaintance from San Francisco gay AA invited me to be his roommate. John W. was a lawyer with two practices—one in San Francisco and the other in Boston. I moved into his massive house in the Jamaica Plain neighborhood of Boston. I could not afford the rent John was asking. In order to make up the difference in rent, I ended up becoming his house-cleaner and dog walker when he was in San Francisco. When I moved in, John had another roommate, a very young lesbian woman who had significant mental issues. I never saw her. At one point, she was admitted to a mental hospital and John asked me to find another roommate.

I advertised on the BML and got one reply. The guy was moving down from Maine for a job in high tech and was looking for a permanent situation. We communicated by email. We learned a good deal about each other. I told him that I would not date a roommate. He ended up looking for a living situation elsewhere. I stopped hearing from him. Then, at an NEB bar night, he had someone there introduce him to me. His name was Bob Black. For the next hour we conversed in German.

Bob was a furry, bearded blond. He was slightly built with dull blue eyes and bore a resemblance to Albrecht Dürer, the German painter. He had also studied to be a German teacher and had taught for a while in Bar Harbor where he lived with his first partner. He ended up working as the liaison for a company in Maine. He also had AIDS. He had decided to change careers into the high-tech field. He had just moved down to Boston to start his first job as a software developer.

We decided to date. I was still not completely over John and cautioned Bob that I might make the mistake of calling him Adam. I was very protective of my heart as Bob and I dated. I chose to steer clear of any guy I was immediately infatuated with. At the time I wondered if I wasn't being totally fair to Bob. Eventually I would be very thankful of my early caution.

Bob and I moved in together after six months of dating. This was precipitated by John W. kicking me out of his house. One day I was doing the weekly vacuuming for John. As usual, I was naked. John was in San Francisco and the young lesbian had moved out weeks before. As I was vacuuming the grand staircase leading to the front receiving room, the young lesbian walked in the front door with her parents. I was very upset by this, in part because John had never told me she was moving back in, and in part because I felt my privacy had been invaded.

My San Francisco fuck buddy Bud Vadon came to visit us soon after we moved to the South End. When he was diagnosed with full-blown AIDS, he sold his company life insurance and was using it to travel while his health held out. He wanted to visit Provincetown. I had also never been there. So we went together.

I was underwhelmed by P'town. It felt like the Castro, with the ocean instead of San Francisco surrounding the gay enclave. Bud and I stayed at a bed and breakfast in the West End. We both got crabs from the sheets. One morning I came out to find a rock had been thrown the windshield of my car. A note tucked under a wiper said, "Get out of my parking space." Bud and I went to the Vault, P'town's leather bar. When we kissed each other in the bar, a bartender 86'd us for kissing.

Despite this somehow typically Boston-style welcome, I continued to visit P'town. Over time P'town and its desolate Cape Cod landscape also grew on me. I stayed with Dave and Tom whenever I visited P'town. Bob had no interest in either my friends or P'town, so I always went alone. I appreciated P'town more in the off season when the crowds were gone. Nowadays, I miss the Cape Cod light, the windswept beaches, and Commercial Street on a sunny day.

At first, Mount Ida College was a joyful experience. I was very happy to be teaching. I was getting to know my new colleagues. Sofia knew I was emotionally shaky, leaving the recant years of emotional and financial instability in San Francisco behind me, and was always nearby for me to reach out to her.

However, Mount Ida was an extremely conservative college. It was a family-owned proprietary college, owned by the Carlson family. Bryan Carlson was the president, and several of the senior administrators were friends of Bryan's. The board of trustees consisted of other relatives and family friends. The family kept tight control of the faculty. Someone from the family was always present at Faculty Assembly meetings, ostensibly to observe, but effectively keeping us in line. Whenever a faculty committee was tasked with something that affected the college as a whole, the administration or the board would put into place whatever they wanted, regardless of a committee's recommendations.

Salaries were always an issue. Mount Ida faculty were paid very poorly. Complaints were always ignored. When some of us sought to form a union, this activity was banned from taking place on campus. We were threatened with being fired. An end was put to this attempt to organize when the administration presented us with "the Yeshiva ruling." An attempt for faculty to unionize at Yeshiva University ended with a court ruling that faculty at private colleges were "managers," and therefore ineligible to unionize. The maddening irony was that Mount Ida faculty had, in practice, no say in our working conditions, no self-governance.

When the ten-year New England Association of Schools and Colleges (NEASC) review was undertaken to renew the college's accreditation, NEASC found Mount Ida in violation of several standards and gave the college a grace period to bring the college's practices up to minimum acceptable standards. One of these was salary. (My $30,000 salary reflected two small raises by the college demonstrating its effort to make our salaries competitive.)

When I was hired, it was a 2+2 college. Some programs culminated in an AA degree. Other programs were just the junior and senior years, culminating in a BA or BS. Most of the programs were career-specific, such as Fashion Design, Vet Tech, or Funeral Direction. I taught in the School of Liberal Arts as a professor of English and Humanities. A student could earn a BLS degree (Bachelor of Liberal Studies). There was no program in English. Most of what I taught were general education and college-wide required courses, such as Freshman Composition, or mandatory electives—courses open to all students but required for a particular major. For example, I taught the Literature of Death and Dying, required of (and taken exclusively by) funeral direction majors or Aesthetics for Fashion design majors.

I had interviewed for my job as an openly gay man who would continue to pursue gay-related research and publishing. The hiring committee was composed of faculty members (no administrators). They had no problem with any of that and saw me as a good fit because I was committed to classroom teaching. In the first flush of my unexpected good fortune in landing a tenure-track job at Mount Ida, I contributed a chapter to an anthology called *Out in the Workplace: The Pleasures and Perils of Coming Out on the Job*. I gave a copy to Bryan Carlson as a token of my gratitude. (He never acknowledged my book.)

When the college computerized and all faculty had a personal computer installed in their offices, the college also issued rules on what we were permitted to do. The rule against pornography put my research in violation of this rule. It forced me to conduct all of my Bear and gay history work, including emailing with colleagues, from home on my own computer and private email.

The administrators' homophobia soon became apparent. They seemed to have no idea that discrimination on grounds of sexual orientation was illegal in Massachusetts. They were naïve in this matter that they did not even try to disguise it. I felt myself being watched. I found my efforts sometimes being sabotaged. I never saw a single student evaluation. I was told I was spending too much time presenting papers at conferences. I discovered, and a couple of times witnessed, that the administration got rid of faculty members they considered a problem. (One common practice was for negative student evaluations to suddenly be found to justify non-renewal.) While in the beginning I had been targeted for being openly gay, I still found this odd because there were at least four other queer professors on the faculty. This elided into a general category of "undesirable." I found myself at the receiving end of hostility from both the administration and my colleagues. Snarky remarks were made about my including gay material in all of my classes. I was criticized by fashion design faculty for including postmodern theory in my Aesthetics class. I was derided for teaching *The*

Social Construction of Disease by Kiheung Kim as an insult to medical doctors. The colleague who oversaw the Social Services program snarked at me with, "So, now that you're no longer dying of AIDS, we're not good enough for you?"

Perhaps the most eye-opening experience I had at Mount Ida was at a summer professional development conference held for the college faculty. There was an exercise intended for us to gain insight into the role which invisible privilege played in our lives. All of us were asked to stand in a row. We were asked a series of questions which began with obvious factors, such as gender, race, socioeconomic background, and religious affiliation to other circumstances and conditions growing up. After each question we were asked to take a step forward or a step backward to indicate our answer. The further you moved forward the more privileged you were, and vice versa. I was quite surprised to find by the end of the exercise I was standing at the point of least privilege.

Gradually I became the victim of mobbing. Cultural anthropologist Janice Harper wrote a book about "workplace mobbing" ('You're not paranoid, they really are out to get you"). It is typically found in organizations, such as universities, where the employee has slight chance of finding equivalent work elsewhere or where contracts, such as academic tenure, make it difficult for the employer to fire the employee. Both circumstances applied to me.

I found myself targeted by a concerted, covert effort by the administration to force me to quit on my own in the face of ever-increasing sabotage, shunning, poor reviews, and constant surveillance. The chair of my department once confronted me in private, demanding to know if the rumors that I had AIDS were true. He had no legal right to ask me. But it became common knowledge. As I suffered the onset of what I suspected was chronic fatigue syndrome, I asked for reasonable accommodation as guaranteed by the Americans with Disabilities Act (ADA). I was given the use of an empty dorm room to take naps in. A week later I found a note slipped under the door calling me a "faggot" and threatening me with violence if I used the room. I reported this to the administration and surrendered the note to them. Nothing further happened. (Through the faculty grapevine I learned another faculty member had received a series of antisemitic notes, and nothing had even been done about that.)

The way I was received professionally at Mount Ida was a confusing mixed bag. When *The Bear Book* was published, the librarian set up a display of all my published works in the front of the library. I held a book signing in the campus bookstore, but no one came. This did not surprise me. When I started teaching my How to Read a Film course, faculty persuaded me to post a weekly notice of the film I was screening that week. I had already announced that my film screenings were open to everyone. I also included a short background essay each week to help set the viewer up for the film. No one from the campus community ever showed up.

When I organized an art exhibition called *Bear Icons*, I approached the college. I was surprised when they agreed to let me mount the exhibit in the new art gallery in the campus center building. As it turned out (of course), they sabotaged me in the process. The only time they would allow the exhibition to run was the week of spring break. None of the students would see it. I asked them about access to the building when the college was closed. I was assured the building would be open. Both gay newspapers in Boston ran my announcement of the exhibition. One paper sent a writer to review the exhibition. A week after the exhibition closed, I got an email from the writer telling me that the campus center was closed and there was no one on campus when he came. This was a classic example of how the administration sabotaged me.

Another faculty member, who taught biology and happened to be gay, informed the administration he was going to Viet Nam for two weeks. This was a very important event, as he was a Viet Nam vet. He was warned that if he went, he would not have a job when he got back. He went, and when he got back, he no longer had a job.

Mount Ida was an open admissions college. Many of our students were first generation, came from poor families, and were not prepared to perform at the college level. The majority of freshmen flunked out or withdrew after their first year. Student turnover was a constant problem. The college was always on the verge of bankruptcy. The Carlsons ran the college as a family cash machine. At one point Bryan celebrated having Mount Ida listed and promoted as an up-and-coming small business. (He apparently did not understand that educational institutions are by law nonprofit.) At another point, Bryan was absent from a meeting called by NEASC requiring all faculty and administrators to participate. That day he was in court serving as a character witness for the college's CFO who was on trial for embezzlement. (The faculty grapevine was kept busy talking about how Bryan gave his friends college credit cards to use for personal purposes. He also created a Naples Institute, a satellite campus in southwest Florida. Tongues wagged among the faculty, ridiculing it as a free hotel for his golf buddies. Bryan even had a campus center building, easily the nicest building on campus, as a place to hold his daughter's wedding reception party.) *The Boston Globe* published the pieces of this complex scandal that had come to light. It didn't enhance Mount Ida's already poor reputation. It made me even more embarrassed to admit that I worked there. I took to mentioning only that I taught at a small college in the Boston area whenever my writing was published.

49

After the publication of *The Bear Book*, it became apparent that the visuals of Bear qualities needed to be explored as well. I organized *Bear Icons* and curated the exhibition with TJ Norris. Following the initial show at Mount Ida, I took it to P'town during their Bear Week, Washington, D.C., and the LGBT Community Center in Manhattan. In conjunction with the NYC show, a panel discussion was organized. It drew an overflow crowd, with many more not allowed into the building.

As the Bear History Project (BHP) continued to expand, I put together *The Bear Book II*. Trying to keep up with everything became too much for me to do the work alone, so I formed a 501(c)3 nonprofit, which I named the Nashoba Institute of Non-Hegemonic Masculinities, and sought to create a board of directors. I recruited Ric Kasini Kadour as a grant writer. I was unsuccessful in persuading anyone to join the board. Ric discovered that Bears were perceived as a "(gay) white male" organization. While it is true self-identifying Bears have been predominantly gay white males, there have always been Bears of color ("black Bears," "brown Bears," and "panda Bears") as well as transbears and ursulinas (female Bears). By that time, grant money was no longer made available to what was considered a "privileged" class of queers. (Never mind the fact that far more white gay men are lower middle-class or poor than the stereotype of the well-heeled gay male consumer.) I also launched an online publication for the BHP called *Verisimilitude*, with a great deal of help from the webmaster Bob McDiarmid. The journal ran for three years.

When John W. evicted me from his house, Bob and I got our first apartment together. It was a fourth-floor walk-up in a typical South End brick building on Massachusetts Avenue at the corner of Shawmut Street. We were on the edge of the South End with the rear of our building facing Dorchester, a poor African American neighborhood. When we moved in, we were the rich gay urban pioneers. A drug dealer lived in the apartment above us, and a prostitute worked out of her apartment at street level. Within the first few weeks of living there, Bob came downstairs to find that someone had broadsided his car and pushed it completely off the street into a neighbor's yard. One day I found a brick thrown through my car's windshield.

I learned that I needed to meet my students at their level and then move forward together. Teaching over their heads accomplished nothing. I altered my teaching method to what I call the "teaching Shakespeare" approach. While addressing the complexity of thought of the brighter students, I also allowed for the students who had difficulty with that. I always gave take-home tests. I allowed students one rewrite of every paper for a better grade. I was dismayed by their resistance to reading literature. They all refused to read more than three books per course. The one time I taught an Introduction to the Novel course was a disaster because of this. (I remain baffled why a student would take a heavy reading course if they wouldn't read.) I gradually relied more and more on films, which students liked. They could read a film much better than a novel, and this provided me with texts to read and discuss with my class.

I developed three "signature" courses, which I enjoyed teaching immensely—the Literature of Death and Dying (taught to NEI students), Aesthetics for Visual Artists (taught to Chamberlayne students), and Foucault for Beginners (taught to the liberal arts majors). The Foucault seminar focused on subaltern voices. We studied narratives from the perspective of "otherized" subordinated social minorities. Texts included Audre Lorde's ZAMI, Antigone, the film version of One Flew Over the Cuckoo's Nest, and Kasper Hauser, and Maus.

In the Literature of Death and Dying course, I began with philosophical definitions of death, looking at the death of the individual, and moved into things like suicide, epidemics, and nuclear holocaust. It became a crescendo that built small and grew into a horror, building dramatically. What I was actually doing was processing the AIDS epidemic and my own seemingly inevitable demise. The three-drug cocktail miracle happened in my third year at Mount Ida. Living in anticipation of my own impending death had deeply traumatized me. This course helped me deal with processing that. I taught this course for ten years.

In 1996, Bob and I started on the new protease inhibitors. For Bob, it was just in the nick of time. He had been starting down the spiral of deteriorating health. I had battled with ITP in which my spleen attacked my white blood cells. The end result was that I had a condition like hemophilia. I would bruise and bleed internally very easily. If I bled at all, it would not stop, and I bruised up quite a bit. Left untreated, I'd have bled internally to death. The experimental treatments I got at Ward 86 had done nothing. The ITP grew worse and worse until I had to have a splenectomy.

Massachusetts voted out rent control (only Boston, Brookline, and Cambridge had rent control). The end of rent control made renting in Boston prohibitively expensive. While not as bad as San Francisco, real estate prices were much too high for us to buy a condo anywhere in Boston or its adjacent suburbs.

We spent months and months looking at other neighborhoods, the inner Boston suburbs, and past the I-495 ring. We went as far as Athol, which was a couple hours away from Boston. We seriously thought we could make a daily commute from such distances. One of my colleagues suggested that we look into Fitchburg.

Fitchburg was an important industrial and rail junction in the nineteenth century. The nice part now was that the city had been too poor to pull down all the grand old buildings of downtown, so its Main Street was historically preserved. Many of the businesses were boarded up, though.

In 1997 we ended up moving into a flat in one of its two slum neighborhoods.

It took us three years to save up for a deposit to buy a house. We commuted 50 miles, an hour each way, into Boston for work. Our first home in Fitchburg was on High Street at the edge of the street's poorest neighborhood. We had the entire second floor, twice our space back in Boston. We filled that up to the rafters within three years as well. I bought my first piece of genuine Gustav Stickley furniture, a Morris spindle chair.

We became friends with the neighbors downstairs in the front. They were in a common-law marriage, and they chain-smoked. The woman baked us cookies at Christmastime, but we never ate them because they tasted like cigarette ash. It was disgusting.

One night around midnight, soon after we had settled in our apartment, I woke up to a fireman rushing into our back bedroom. "There's a fire. You need to get out." I could smell the smoke I saw coming in the back door. Bob and I threw on our clothes and went out and stood in the street.

Three engines were parked on the street behind the house, and the fire was put out quickly.

A week before someone had left a message on our answering machine, saying, "You faggots are going to die."

50

Another factor in our decision to move so far out from Boston was out of disappointment of not having made friends there in the four years we had lived in Boston. The hour drive meant we were giving up an essentially non-existent night life. I would miss being able to go to the Kendall Theater, the art house cinema in Cambridge.

As for connections with the Bear community, we joined the Northeast Ursabears in Connecticut and the Berkshire Bears in Northampton. I decided to form a Bear club in Fitchburg. To find local Bears, I placed an announcement in the local newspaper. In response, the paper sent a reporter and a photographer to interview me. This was printed as a full front page story in the *Sentinel-Enterprise*'s Sunday newspaper.

I was overwhelmed with the response the coverage garnered. Our initial meeting got a huge turnout. We had 40 or 50 gay guys in our apartment, their cars filling up the neighborhood. We decided to form the Montachusett Area Bears, shortened to Monty Bears (*The Full Monty* had been a recent hit movie). We decided to meet monthly at the local gay center on Main Street.

Most of the men who showed up for that first meeting never came back. I wondered how many of them were Boston-oriented suburbanites. Some may have come looking for someone to hook up with. Some, most likely, were just curious to find out who else was gay. The guys who stuck around were all very local, rarely venturing into Boston and occasionally going to the gay bar in Worcester.

The group started off small and dwindled over time into a core group of eight regulars. I ended up organizing everything. The Monty Bears held a few evening potlucks at the gay center downtown. Bob and I hosted a couple of open houses at our place. Two other active members, Michael Seale and Donovan Miller, whom Bob and I knew through NEB, had a house in nearby Lancaster and held potlucks in the summer.

For the club's second year anniversary, we organized a Fall Festival. We rented a meeting room at the local Motel 6 in Leominster. I organized activities, a visit to a local apple orchard, Sunday brunch at the Old Mill, a converted mill with a duck-filled mill pond, and a visit to the grave of John Palmer. (Palmer's fame rested on his being "persecuted for wearing the beard.")

After two years of being in charge of everything for the club, I stepped down. I had asked members what they wanted to do. One guy requested that the Monty Bears do a weekend in P'town. I followed through, but no one signed up. The day before the scheduled trip, the guy who suggested it called me and asked me if I could take his niece to P'town.

That was the last straw for me. Michael and Donovan took over running the club. They kept the club going for another two years. But then Donovan was hired by a company in Wisconsin and they left Massachusetts. The group petered out after that.

I discovered the Men's Resource Center in Amherst. I started going to the Friday night peer support group for survivors of childhood trauma and neglect. I soon became a peer facilitator after doing the training. This was in lieu of going to AA meetings or having a psychotherapist. I even made a couple of friends there.

I now found myself stretched across the entire state of Massachusetts. I lived in the middle of the state so I had to drive east for work (an hour's drive) and go west for support and socializing (closer to an hour and a half). Provincetown was a three-and-a-half-hour drive. (I had remained friends with Dave Thompson, who I had met in San Francisco gay AA and who had moved back to P'town. Together with John Burrows we founded the Provincetown Bears. It had no formal membership. John later founded Provincetown Bear Week.)

As an invited guest at Texas Bear Round-Up (TBRU) in Dallas, I gave a slide show talk about Bear history. While I was there, I got a phone call that Mom had died. I withdrew to my hotel room. I felt horrid. She had been suffering from Alzheimer's for years before her physical death, so her passing was a shock but not a terrible loss.

I went to Syracuse for the funeral. I was surprised by the number of people who showed up. Most I had not seen since my childhood. So many people remembered her with fondness. Several old neighbors from Preble turned up, as well as some of Mom's best friend's kids. (Her best friend, Pat Jenny, had died years earlier.) Uncle Mike showed up with his girlfriend; his ex-wife Geraldine (Mom's sister), did not. Uncle Dick and Aunt Mona came. I gave Mona a hug, but she didn't recognize me and my hug frightened her. She was also suffering from Alzheimer's.

The last time I had seen her was at Thanksgiving at Mom and Dad's. The last thing she said to me was, "How could you write all those awful letters?" I had written to Mona and Mom for years, keeping them abreast of my life. I had no idea they were horrified by my "gay lifestyle." Years later, Sylvia told me that Mom had found my letters so upsetting that she had Sylvia read the letters and only report on what Mom could bear to hear without getting upset.

In September 2002, Bob and I got a civil union in Vermont. It was a "destination wedding," held at a mountain lodge in Stowe. Dad, Sylvia, and Uncle Marty came. Bob's parents came. My friends Marlene Kirsch and Steve Klein came. Dave Thompson and John Burrows also came. A couple of the Monty Bears came. After dinner we held a hot tub party. As often happened, I was so exhausted that I went straight to bed and skipped the party.

Our life in Fitchburg settled into a pattern. We both went to work. At home I worked on BHP and Bob hung out on his computer. Sometimes we went on a long drive on the weekend or drove to a shopping mall. After Bob bought a motorcycle, he spent the weekends riding by himself. I found myself increasingly left alone. I took trips to destination spots around central New England on my own, like Nashua, New Hampshire; Brattleboro, Vermont; and Northampton and Shelburne Falls, Massachusetts. I visited Dave Thompson and his partner Tom a lot in P'town. Tom and I had especially bonded because we were both very shy and suffered from social anxiety. But he was suffering from paranoid schizophrenia. When Tom's mental illness reached the point where he needed to be committed to a mental asylum, he hung himself in the Pilgrim Monument in P'town one Thanksgiving.

I answered a call from the Committee on Lesbian and Gay History. The CLGH was the caucus of gay and lesbian historians, mostly academics and a few independent scholars. Several of the people I had met through the San Francisco Gay and Lesbian History Project were members. I volunteered to take on duties of the chairperson. I also found myself with the duties of newsletter editor, including overseeing book reviews, and membership secretary. It was a lot more work than I had expected.

As the homophobic mobbing at Mount Ida progressively worsened, I reached out to the CLGH membership for support. The CLGH had published a guide suggesting ways to address homophobia in the workplace. I didn't know what I could do about my situation on my own. I never heard a word back from any of my fellow academics. Imagine my chagrin when, a few months later, I got an email informing me that members had decided they wanted me to step down from my duties. I had never gotten any feedback, no helpful suggestions, no friendly warning, no hint of any dissatisfaction. I felt blindsided and sabotaged, utterly humiliated by the whole guild of gay and lesbian academics.

The situation at Mount Ida deteriorated at a faster pace. Sofia's health problems worsened. Because of diabetes and congenital disorders, she was now using a wheelchair. (She was the product of a brother-sister rape incest union. She was a Druze Arab and the incest had been kept secret. As a baby, she had been adopted by an Anglo-American Christian missionary couple in Jerusalem.)

Sofia suffered from increasingly worsening mental illness as well. She was often in a state of barely contained rage. She cried a lot. She would show up in her wheelchair to teach, reeking of urine and drooling, and nodding off in mid-sentence. Mount Ida faculty avoided her. I ended up her only friend among the faculty.

I eventually reached my limit as well. I agreed to meet Sofia for lunch at a Friendly's. When I got there, she was screaming at the wait staff. They were trying to quiet her down and clearly wanted her to leave. I ate lunch while she ranted at me.

Sofia ended up being wheeled out of a class she was teaching, out cold, drooling and reeking of piss. I took over teaching her Senior seminar on ancient and classical literature until the end of the semester. We had one last phone call. I was the last of her Mount Ida peers still on speaking terms with her. We had one last phone call in which I told her I couldn't have contact with her anymore.

The last I heard of her was that her wife Beryl had left her, she had lost her condo, and she was living in Section 8 housing.

51

Bob and I went to Germany in January 2003. It was bitterly cold the whole time we were there. I don't remember Germany ever being that cold—damp cold—when I lived there. We stayed with Brendan Donnellan in Tübingen. The *Altsadtsanierung* was now complete and the city was like a Hollywood movie set. The city was now encircled by a system of freeways making it easier and faster to move around. We drove to nearby Altensteig where Bob had spent a year as an exchange student. We stayed with Simon Goodman, Marlene's ex-partner, and visited Frankfurt and drove around the region visiting museums and historical sites. This was my last trip to Germany.

Soon after our return from Germany, I developed a bad case of shingles and had a nervous breakdown. I didn't have the energy to teach. It was clear the toxic work environment was taking its toll on me physically. I don't know why, but it never occurred to me to go on short-term disability.

The fall of 2004 I had come to campus on the first day of classes only to discover my work laptop stolen. It took the college an entire semester to get me a replacement. Meanwhile they had gone paperless, so all official notices were sent out via email. Since I didn't receive any emails, I didn't know when anything, including faculty meetings, were taking place. I became very paranoid and avoided all contact with my colleagues. I showed up and taught my classes. I ate all my meals off-campus. At home, I stayed indoors, fearing my neighbors might be watching me.

Bob and I decided to relocate to San Francisco. Bob went on the job market and soon found a job at Apple in the Silicon Valley. This left me alone with only my three cats for company.

That winter, the furnace broke in the middle of a frigid February. I had to refill it with water every twelve hours because of the leak. It took several days before I was able to arrange for a furnace replacement.

I spent the next six months closing the house down and teaching out my contract, which ended in May 2005. It was the only way to avoid any legal problem if I had simply walked away in the middle of the semester.

In my search for a teaching position in San Francisco I replied to the two positions I found. One was for the position of chair of the Gay and Lesbian Studies program at CCSF. The other was for the Dean of Humanities at New College of California. I flew to San Francisco for the interview at CCSF. NCC interviewed me by phone. I didn't hear about either college's decision until I arrived in California. In both cases, they informed me they had chosen their inside candidate, faculty already in their employ. I was disappointed but by no means surprised. It is a common practice in the humanities for a hiring committee to interview a series of candidates, knowing from the start they were going to hire an inside candidate, but needing to appear transparent and nonjudgmental and hiring the most qualified candidate.

Leaving Massachusetts was traumatic. My last act was to deal with our three cats Mischa, Theo, and Schuyler. I had tried to find someone to take them. My sister, who currently has twelve cats, refused to take them. I called around to the no-kill shelters and found out they would require me to cover all the costs of the cats for the rest of their lives.

I ended up taking them to the MSPCA. I locked them in the summer porch so I could round them up. They sensed something terrible was happening and howled from the moment I put them in their carrier cases, all during the hour drive to the MSPCA and surrendered them. It broke my heart to sign them over to a guaranteed death sentence. I held my tears back until I was outdoors. I got on the road and drove and drove, crying all the way, until I was so exhausted that I could drive no further. I had reached Harrisburg, PA.

I took another cross-country road trip, this time via the I-40 route. The drive was not fun, just time-consuming. I had formulated a plan in my head to "disappear" when I got to the desert. I was pretty suicidal at this point. Despite doing a lot of footwork, I had no employment prospects.

When I got to Santa Fe, something I might call miraculous happened. I had formulated a plan to drive out into the desert and just keep walking until I died. As I walked around the historic old town of Santa Fe among its Pueblo architecture, I felt enchanted. On the Santa Fe Plaza, an overwhelming sense of calm and comfort enveloped me.

I had had similar experiences elsewhere—in the Swabian Alb outside

Urach, in Chartres Cathedral, in the Cloisters in Manhattan, on a coastal mountain top in Sonoma County, in a grove of fern trees in Golden Gate Park. Sedona, Arizona, is the best known of such places. In such places I feel what was once called "sublime"—a feeling of boundless well-being and security. Artists once strove to capture this in Romantic paintings. Such spaces have also been called "spiritual vortices"—places where the body and heart center in balance and harmony.

This feeling accompanied me everywhere in Santa Fe. One day I drove up to Taos, where this feeling was overwhelming. I found a quiet spot there and sat down and meditated. The desire to kill myself vanished. I felt safe and secure, ready to resume my journey to California. My next stop was Sedona, and indeed, everywhere there I felt engulfed in that vortex of transcendent spiritual connection.

52

When I got to the Bay Area, Bob was living in a condo complex in Sunnyvale. I wasn't about to live in the Silicon Valley, so the apartment-hunting was left to me. I learned that John Musselman was looking to sublet his apartment in Noe Valley, just over the hill from the Castro. He offered us the apartment at the rent-controlled rate he was paying. He and his husband John had moved to Los Angeles and were both working for the LA Opera. The apartment was perfect. It was a 1970s building that conformed to the neighborhood's historic look. Our apartment's east walls were glass, so the place was *very* sunny. We had a view of the back lots, and we could see Mount Diablo way out on the horizon.

When the moving van arrived, I did all the unpacking and setting up of the apartment, a two-bedroom with a dining nook. It cost $10,000 to move our household cross-country, which Bob's new employer fortunately paid.

I applied for job after job, but I got nowhere in my first two years back in San Francisco. I was without income for those two years. I did not even have a checking account. I had to ask Bob for pocket money.

I took two semesters of Spanish at City College of San Francisco, where I fell in love with the language. It had been many years since I had tackled a new language, so it was fresh and exciting. I watched Spanish-language TV to help me along. Every Saturday evening I watched three hours of *Sábato Gigante*. Bob parked himself at the dining room table and chatted online with people who would turn out to be members of the Rainbow Motorcycle Club. Bob had built a whole circle of friends that he never even mentioned to me.

My first inkling had been when he had a bad car accident driving home in the dark one night in Fitchburg. A couple days after he had been hospitalized, I started getting phone calls from people I had never heard of calling to find out how Bob was doing.

While looking for a job those first two years, I did a lot of career-changing footwork. I worked with the Positive Resource Center, an agency that specialized in helping gay men with AIDS trying to go back to work after being on disability for many years. Because of the three-drug cocktail of antiviral drugs, people suddenly stopped dying of AIDS. They had hopes of returning to an active life. I spent three years with the agency, but I did not get a single interview out of them.

Early after my return to San Francisco, I decided to return to gay AA. The first time I went, I went as far as the front door. I was so scared and ashamed, having turned my back on it for ten years. Being terrified, I did not go in. It took me a few more attempts before I had enough nerve to enter the room. Even then I felt very uncomfortable like an outsider for a long time.

I attended AA meetings every day. I got a sponsor, John E., who took me through the Steps again. When I completed the Twelfth Step, John said to me, "You know, you didn't need to quit your job at Mount Ida. It's your fault you can't find work now." His betrayal of my trust after taking me through the steps led me to fire him. It would be many years before I would trust a member of AA again.

I returned to an active spiritual practice. I deepened my involvement in Buddhist practice, meditating daily, joining a gay sangha, and attending weekly group meditation at the San Francisco Zen Center.

I returned to regular Sunday worship at St. Gregory of Nyssa Episcopal Church. The parish was noted for its innovations in the liturgy, incorporating scripts drawn from Eastern liturgical texts and local compositions. Following sharing from parishioners and before the Eucharist, everyone participates in a ritualized dance around the altar, in honor of the "dancing saints."

Father Paul Fromberg's sermons and interpretation of text were stirring and dynamic. Nearly half the congregation seemed to be gay. The parishioners, true to the character of San Franciscans in general, were very diverse, many accomplished in their professional or personal lives, and manifested a strong sense of community. While I was excited to meet so many people who welcomed my own brand of bohemian nonconformity and intellectual passions, I also felt uncomfortable around so much material wealth. I was clearly among the Ivy League class of Episcopalians.

I volunteered as a lay leader with the role of walking in a circle around the congregation and singing out a call to worship. During training, I had led through one practice round. I was very nervous, trying to remember the words and hoping to hit the right notes without musical accompaniment. The following week, as I was putting on my vestments, someone came in and told me I had to fill in for the regular person, who was home sick that day. I didn't have a chance to say no. I was scared with only a single practice run under my belt. But I did it. I even hit all the right notes.

Imagine how I felt when, the following Sunday, the head of the vestry informed me that I was immediately dismissed from my duties. I was informed that the look on my face while I had encircled the congregation was one of terror. That was simply not the message the church wished to communicate. The person ordering me fired remained anonymous. Once again, I felt deeply shamed in front of the entire congregation. I felt this was an unfair and harsh judgment, having only ever practiced once. I never returned to St. Gregory of Nyssa.

I eventually found work by networking in gay AA. An English faculty member from Diablo Valley College in Pleasant Hill, way out in East Bay's extreme edge, told me they were hiring English composition instructors. He told me who to email and where to send my résumé. I had a brief interview and was hired on the spot to teach two classes. Bob continued to pay the rent while I barely got by on my new income.

In the meantime, Bob had found himself a new boyfriend in the ranks of the Rainbow Motorcycle Club, a long-haired gay biker club, which he kept secret from me. Bob was *never* available to me. He claimed he was working seven days a week. When he had the odd bit of time off, he hung out with his long-haired gay biker buddies.

Many nights I waited for Bob to come home. One night he came home late from the bars with no explanation. I asked him how much he cared for me. He refused to answer me at first, but I persisted. He finally confessed he wanted me to have medical insurance, which his employer provided for the two of us.

"Is that all?!" I asked, astonished and enraged. "That's all you care about me?" I was beside myself.

I moved into the spare bedroom and began sleeping there that night. We continued to live together for another year.

I had found a home for myself as a gay man at the Men's Resource Center in Amherst, MA. When I returned to San Francisco, expecting to pick up where I had left off, I found myself having to go back to the end of the line and start over. Most of the people I had known in San Francisco had moved on. Some had retired and were forced out of the City. Many had relocated to Palm Springs.

During the AIDS epidemic, I read everything I could to help me cope as well as how to make meaning out of our experience. One of the most helpful books I read (and which became more so after the epidemic was over, and I found myself living in its aftermath) was Viktor Frankl's *Man's Search for Meaning*. (I had taught this text in my Literature of Death and Dying course at Mount Ida.) Frankl asserted there were only two kinds of people—decent and indecent. There were some decent Nazis and some indecent interred Jews (the Kapo in particular).

I distinguished "angels" (decent people), whose kindnesses turned up unexpectedly. There were indecent people—so many of my progressive gay friends, who had abandoned me and left me to fend for myself in San Francisco, out of fear they might be infected with my "bad luck" and both of my previous two partners, Adam and Bob.

53

During my first two years back in San Francisco, I found no employment. I got no word-of-mouth leads. I got no responses to posted job listings, which I found mostly on Craigslist. I tried the temp agency route that had helped me back in 1979. I couldn't even find an agency willing to take me under their wing. In 1979 all I needed to do was take a typing test, to determine my employability. Now I needed to have proficiency in an array of business software programs. Because all I knew was Microsoft Word, they wouldn't touch me.

I signed up with an "AIDS Back to Work" program, which helped people who had been on permanent disability and out of the workforce for many years, come out of retirement and find work again. I was assigned a career counselor and a job counselor. I worked through the *What Color Is Your Parachute* book (for the third time). I went through hours of lectures and tests, I took the Briggs-Meyer personality test, I took career compatibility tests, and I did workshops, which all helped me to identify appropriate careers for me. In order of compatibility, they were foreign language teacher, English teacher (the two fields I was unable to find work in), grant writer, alcoholism counselor, and priest.

Another series of exercises encouraged me to envision my ideal job. This was documentary filmmaker. When I told my career counselor of my "ideal career," she exploded. "You are out of your mind! Don't even think of trying to do that!" She was, of course, right. That was another long, slow process, most likely keeping me in the same financially marginal existence.

I applied to the New College of California for training as an alcoholism counselor. My application was rejected. The State of California EDD paid for my training as a grant writer. When I went on the job market, I quickly learned that organizations trained their own employees to do this work. I could not get hired as a freelance grant writer without a proven track record.

A friend who was an elementary school teacher had found his job at a private school through an agency that specialized in private school placements. Through his intervention, and apparently as a favor to him, the head of that agency accepted me into their placement program. This resulted in perhaps my most humiliating experience in looking for work up to that point in my life. The agency held a job fair, where all the teacher candidates were interviewed and hired by the human resources person from various Bay Area private schools. One after another candidate was invited to be interviewed and then hired on the spot. I sat there all day long without being invited to a single interview. By 5:00 PM I was the only person left in the room. The agency director finally told me to go home.

On my own I enrolled in a program that trained me in how to become an entrepreneur. It became clear that I had no aptitude for business.

Having come to the end of my list of possible careers, I applied to the Graduate Theological Union in Berkeley to become an Episcopal priest. The Church Divinity School turned me down and passed me on to the Pacific School of Religion, which they felt was a better match for me. The PSR is the most progressive of the seminaries, where openly gay seminarians could expect to find a suitable home. I attended part-time while continuing to teach part-time at DVC. With an addition of a $50,000 student loan that year, I was able to meet tuition and basic living expenses. (Between scholarships, fellowships, Tom Libby's kindness, and mostly part-time jobs, I had been able to put myself through college from freshman year to PhD without acquiring a penny of student loan debt. The GTU loan was for 2009-2010. As of this writing, I have not been able to make a single payment on this loan.)

I went back to grad school when Bob had moved in with his new boyfriend and cut off his financial help. (It never occurred to me to sue him for alimony.) I had started attending the Pacific School of Religion at the Graduate Theological Union in Berkeley. I planned to become an Episcopal priest.

I loved that place so much. Were it possible, I would've easily moved in and spent the rest of my life in the ecclesiastical enclaves up on the hill north of the UC Berkeley campus. I realized that I was not cut from the same cloth as my fellow men. I was not made for this world; except for academia, it had rejected me everywhere.

When Bob and I moved to California, I lost my health insurance and began another forced drug holiday. I could afford COBRA and Bob refused to add me to his policy through Apple. I went without my antivirals and my antidepressant for the next year. A year later I came down with pneumonia, which deteriorated rapidly. Bob put me in touch with his HIV specialist in the Silicon Valley. A friend from Massachusetts happened to be visiting us, and he drove me down to a hospital in Mountain View. The physician saw me and sent me directly to the hospital. He lied about my lack of insurance, which worked long enough to get me admitted. By the time it did catch up with me, Bob had paid for my COBRA.

Once I had medical insurance, I was able to see a psychiatrist again and get back on antidepressants. I met with a Dr. Gorodetskaya who, within ten minutes of asking probing questions about my life story, diagnosed me with "bipolar II disorder," something I had never heard of. It differs from bipolar I, or manic-depressive disorder, in that the polarities are depression and anger (not mania). She explained BPDII was very difficult to diagnose, and then usually only after it had caused the afflicted person to destroy one marriage after another, one career after another. She also stated that sexual promiscuity was another symptom.

It struck me as rather facile to explain away the joy of my sexual adventurism and the horror story of my employment history as caused by mental illness. It excluded my history of childhood sexual abuse. It excluded the abundance of sex as an exuberant celebration of gay liberation. It dismissed the reality of structural social and economic inequalities in a capitalist society. It trivialized the trauma of my experiences as a faculty member at Mount Ida College.

On the other hand this did explain the source of my bottomless anger.

In my online search to find a gay men's group with a sensibility I had found among the men at the Men's Resource Center in rural Western Massachusetts, I came across The Billy Club. (The name was later changed to The Billy Community, as google searches turned up truncheons and cudgels.) I was invited to a monthly potluck at a Billy's home in San Francisco and was very surprised to meet so many gay men I had known from when I previously lived there. Someone there explained to me what the Billys were all about and recounted their history. (Eventually, a version of the early days of the Billys was written down by one of the four founders, Ron VanScoyk. At the time of this potluck in 2005, most of the founding members had died.)

The Billy Community had arisen during the early years of the AIDS epidemic as a picnic. Rural gay men living in the hills of Mendocino, Lake, and Humboldt counties sought a way out of the overall rural isolation and sought a mutual aid, self-help and support group for everyone, living far from the AIDS networks in San Francisco, coping with the medical, practical, emotional, and spiritual needs of (mostly gay) men living with AIDS and the friends supporting them. They began as a picnic. The first was so successful that more were held.

Richard, one of the founders, had a hand-made card business and, since he and his partner Terry affectionately called each other Billy, he called his business The Billy Club and had a rubber stamp with the name and address for his business. Terry used this as the return address for the notices they sent out, having no idea the group would continue. But the name stuck.

Out of the practices and values of the first gay men who came together and from what they learned in their practice of rendering support for each other, arose a sense of community, shared values, and shared rituals—they defined themselves as a "heart-centered community." The central ritual of the Billys is the heart circle. It is a sacred space where every Billy (gay, bi, trans, and queer man) and Billykin (anyone else who shares Billy values) can speak openly and freely—joys, fears, playfulness, hopes, dreams, traumas. It is a safe place to take risks. (Here it parallels the AA model of "What you hear here, who you see here, let it stay here.") Billys practice "radical acceptance."

It wasn't until later that I learned that Harry Hay, a major figure in pre-Stonewall gay activism, had had a strong influence on the early Billys. Harry had lived with the Pueblo Indians in the American Southwest, where he experienced "two-spirit" people and saw that in their society queers played important helping, spiritual and ceremonial roles in society. Harry was unconventional in dress and notably promiscuous. He cofounded the radical faeries, of which the Billy are close kin, and sought to liberate everyone from socially enforced gender roles and restore sacred meaning to conscious acts of love.

Although Harry never attended any Billy event, his partner John Burnside did come after Harry's death. Numerous Billys had also gone to radical faerie gatherings. Bill Blackburn, who has been a guiding Billy elder since I found my way to this community, related how through his having a sexual dalliance with Harry had brought Bill into the (Whitman) gay tribe. This too does not have a name, and I began to describe it as "gay genealogy" when Bill informed me after we had had sex that I was now also lined into this lineage, of one gay man having sex with another gay man, going in a direct line back to Walt Whitman. (It's nice to have something over the Descendants of the Mayflower.)

One way of becoming a Billy is by participating in one of the quarterly

Gatherings. My first gathering in "Billyspace" was a July Gathering at a remote location in coastal northern California. (I think of it as a kind of queer-spiritual Bohemian Club.) An important ritual at the gatherings is the initiation ritual, for me a truly transformative mystical experience. For me it was an intimate soul-baring spiritual experience, where I was clearly and intimately seen by and lovingly embraced by everyone. As I stood in this state and was hailed with the collective greeting, "Welcome home, Billy," I cried with tears of joy. I had felt I had found a home in the gay community living in the Castro, but I now knew that, for the first time, I had truly come home to my *tribe*.

During a Talent/No Talent Show at a July Billy gathering, a young man played a guitar and sang a song he had composed. The song was sadly sweet, his voice a sonorous baritone. He was strikingly handsome. As I listened to one song, and another, a different song began playing in my mind. "Singing my life with his words, killing me softly with his words, telling my whole life with his words" intertwined with his words and with a seed germinating deep within me. I found myself beginning to fall in love.

The next morning the man came to our morning heart circle. Many of us, including me and the man, were naked. When the heart circle ended, I approached the man. His name was Justin Brentwood. He was the youngest Billy and he had been nurtured by the Billy tribe from a young age. Justin had come out in high school and made headline news when he brought his black male lover to his high school prom in Hayward, California. Justin was a poet and journalist and went on to become quite famous.

After the Gathering I began dating Justin. I found my desire for him skyrocketing. I craved his company and his body. Negotiating sex was tricky due to his AIDS phobia. I turned to Ed Wolf for guidance in my relationship with Justin. Justin was not much more than half my age. Ed's partner Kirk Read was also rightly half Ed's age. I found Justin to be more mature than his years, but oddly also very immature. His interest in me turned out to be a passing flirtation and his rejection triggered an obsession in me I had only ever experienced before when John Adams had rejected me. I pursued Justin unrelentingly, while he alternately repelled and seduced me.

One evening he invited me to his place to join him in a bubble bath. With both of us naked in the bathtub, me on top of him, I began to caress him. He pushed me off him and climbed out of the tub, fuming that I had turned the intimacy into something sexual. He cut off communication with me. At the next Gathering Justin confronted me, raging that he was not going to allow me to make him feel unsafe in Billyspace. We made a truce.

In the middle of the Justin drama, I got a call from my sister that Dad had had a stroke and was in the hospital. I didn't have the money or the inclination to fly back East. There was nothing I could do. Dad's stroke was the final straw for my sister, causing her to throw up her arms and give into hoarding. Dad wound up a human vegetable and spent his last years in a bed in this vegetative state. My sister refused to pull the plug. I visited him one last time with my sister and an uncle. Sadly that is how I have remembered him ever since. He was already dead to me when I got word he had passed away.

My next boyfriend was a very sweet man I met on a weekend retreat of the St. Gregory of Nyssa parish at Bishop's Ranch, outside Healdsburg in beautiful Sonoma County. Single men slept in bachelor's quarters. The first night Jim Harding approached me after lights out to ask if he could sleep with me. I welcomed him into my bed. From that point on we began dating. Jim was a polar pocket Bear, short, stocky, furry, and white-haired. He taught at a private school and had moved to San Francisco after being displaced after Hurricane Katrina had devastated New Orleans.

It was unusual for me to be the pursued rather than the pursuer. Our relationship progressed rather tentatively. Jim seemed a rather old-school cultivated gay gentleman. I thought I would be too bohemian for him. When he opened his apartment for a Billy potluck, he seemed ill-matched for the Billy informality. Jim's alcohol-laced cooking proved too risky for me, and I sometimes had to pass on some dishes. I saw we were not compatible for a long-term relationship so I broke it off. I was still married to Bob, and Marlene's generosity was what stood between me and homelessness. I was not about to make myself a burden for Jim.

During my fourth year in San Francisco, I went online for a man to date. I connected with a guy up in Eureka, in Humboldt County. His name was Paul Hirt. We seemed to have a lot of common interests; in particular my commitment to the Billy community spoke to his own brand of two-spirit identity. Paul unpacked his world to me. He introduced me to his friends, a few gay men, a lesbian couple, and a Native American man. Paul was most closely connected to the local Native American community. His yard was set up to host sweat lodges

We began dating. I made the three-hour drive to Eureka every weekend. After six months, we felt we were on sure enough footing to make a go of it. Paul had previously lived in San Francisco and was unwilling to move back to the City. He promised me there was a small gay community in the Eureka area, there were plenty of jobs, and I could start afresh.

Thanks to an angel, I was able to move into Paul's Victorian house, which was weather-worn. All my furniture and possessions fit in. I set up my home office in the spare bedroom. Paul had wiring done to accommodate all my office equipment. He begrudgingly allowed me to have satellite television installed. I had my leather sofa out in the same room.

Shortly after I moved in, the gay men disbanded their social group. I tried to start a Billy group, as there were a few Billys in the area. I soon learned that the gay men who had left the Bay Area for Humboldt County wanted nothing to do with any gay community.

Our home life was routine. We had Taco Thursdays, where Paul prepared the meal. We went shopping weekly. We got together with Paul's friends. We went to the movies once in a while. Paul showed me the grove of redwoods where an important scene in *Star Wars* had been filmed. Paul took me to a hot tub site. He showed me the local cruising grounds. We subscribed to the live performance program at Humboldt State University and saw first-rate performances.

I undertook job work with no enthusiasm. As it became clear that jobs were scarce and lots of locals were looking for jobs that did not exist, I gave up. I enrolled in the College of the Redwoods, the local community college. I returned to learning Spanish and I took the course on the US Constitution. It was a prerequisite for the Teaching Credential program at Humboldt State. I applied to that program to make myself employable as a high school teacher.

As that first year with Paul unfolded, it became clear we were not a good fit. It turned out we had few interests in common. My libido died, which upset Paul a great deal. As the second year of living together approached, Paul pushed me aside. I slept on my sofa in the TV room. I read a lot. (I reread all of Heinlein.) I watched a lot of DVDs, including all of *Buffy the Vampire Slayer*. I was cut off from all of Paul's friends and frozen out emotionally by Paul. I found myself living in total social isolation.

I taught German film and German language in the OLLI program and was paid $50 for teaching each course. I ended up applying to Humboldt State University where I earned a California high school teaching credential. I was banking on getting my teaching credential as a way to move out and move on. I was assigned to two master teachers, under whose supervision I would do my student teaching. I was assigned to the only German teacher in Eureka, who I had subbed for during my first year. We already had a cordial relationship. Finding a willing English teacher was much harder. I had asked the Eureka High liaison to be my master teacher, but he declined, saying he had too many commitments that semester. (He was the faculty advisor to the high school's Gay/Straight Alliance. He was straight and so were all the GSA student members.)

Another English teacher consented. He took me aside, informing me that he would not permit me to come out in any of his classes. I was taken aback. I thought Eureka was more tolerant than that. My understanding of California law was that this was illegal. Instead of fighting him, I reported this to the faculty at the university, who sought to find me someone else to work with. I ended up being assigned to work with a woman who taught in the Specialized Program. This was a parallel track for students who had problems fitting in. They had their own teachers and their own building. The students I worked with did not trust me—I was an unfamiliar outsider. I ended up correcting their essays and playing dodgeball with them. I learned nothing about classroom teaching.

I applied to numerous California high schools to teach English. With the encouragement of the university faculty, I applied to teach in Specialized Programs and in the state prison system (where positions are often difficult to fill).

I did not receive a single interview.

54

An old friend from Brooklyn, Al Baccara, had relocated to the Palm Springs area. David and I had met him through an ad in *BEAR*, and we hosted him on his first visit to San Francisco. Al and I had remained good friends over the years. He'd stay with me in San Francisco, and I'd stay with him in Brooklyn. He had been an ideal guest.

Al made several trips to California and tried on living in each of the places he visited before deciding to settle down in the Coachella Valley. When he landed a job teaching junior high school math, he bought a McMansion in a gated community on the edge of Indio, a traditionally Latino city on the east side of Coachella Valley. He could afford a lot more house there, and Palm Springs was a 20-minute drive.

At Al's invitation I visited in Palm Springs prior to my move. He had praised Palm Springs to high heaven. He took me along to a string of Christmas parties he had been invited to and introduced me around. He showed me his warm and welcoming gay community. It looked very promising to me.

I moved once again, and with the help of an angel brought all my furniture and earthly possessions with me. Some stuff fit in Al's house. My bed and chest of drawers, my office furniture and equipment, and my DVD library all fit. I had my own bedroom and I shared the office room and a bathroom with Al's other roommate Robert. (Robert was congenial. He worked on the maintenance crew of a casino. He and I went out for breakfast together once or twice a week at the diner at a nearby strip mall.)

Everything else was put into storage in another house standing empty. Al had persuaded his parents, who lived on Long Island, to buy a second home in his gated community. This they did, and it stood empty and unused, with all the utilities on and the house kept air-conditioned year-round.

Al invited me to watch TV with him, but his primary viewing fare was cooking shows. He invited me to sleep with him, which I declined. Bill split the cost of the utilities three ways. I had cable and internet. Air-conditioning was at least as expensive as heating fuel elsewhere. It ran constantly because of the desert heat. Al would not charge me rent until I found a job.

Everything happened in Palm Springs—gay AA meetings, gay bars and restaurants, an Episcopal church, and the Desert AIDS Project, where I got all my medical care done. I drove to Palm Springs every day. I saw a therapist. I joined a weekly movie group at the DAP. They served pizza. A few other guys would show up. As soon as the pizza arrived, they would grab several slices and leave. I was the only person who actually stayed and watched the movies.

If Al was home when I was using the kitchen, he would follow me around telling me to wipe up any spills as soon as they happened. When Al discovered Robert's truck had leaked oil on the pavement on the street, he commanded Robert to clean it up. I went with Al to synagogue a couple of times, where he was very involved with the politics there. Al went out to the gay bar that had karaoke all the time, and often brought a trick home. He got together with his friends, the men he had introduced me to. But I was never invited to join them. When Al organized his friends to go to the Palm Springs Gay Pride March, I asked if I could join them. I went along, but found myself standing alone behind a slim palm tree trunk while Al and his friends all sat in a row in lawn chairs they had brought along. They took photos of each other, as I watched from the sides, obviously invisible to them.

It quickly became clear to me that Al had reduced me from "friend" status (a social equal) to "tenant status" (social inferior). I was never included in Al's social life. (I had hoped to make friends among Al's friends that I had met on my Christmas visit.) I told Robert about this, and he said Al had done the same thing to him.

My job hunting continued when I moved to Palm Springs. Relying on my freshly minted high school teaching credential, I applied to teach high school English in several school districts. Al chirped cheerfully about how we could be teaching at the same school. Once again, I did not get a single interview. I turned to Craigslist and submitted applications (which had now been replaced by extensive online questionnaires). These were all minimum-wage jobs. Again, nothing.

Al "suggested" I shave my beard off, as he believed that would make me look younger. I did so to appease him. However, since I never came face-to-face with any potential interviewers, no potential employer had ever set eyes on me. I signed up with the California EDD and was assigned a caseworker to help me find a job. His name was George Puddephat. He was also gay and very involved in the gay leather community. George followed my lack of progress. He even took me in person to Bear Ware, a shop that sold Bear merchandise. He introduced me to the owner and told him I was the Bear history guy. George suggested having me clerking there would be a boon to the business. But the store owner had zero interest—he couldn't have been more nonplussed. Soon I gave up looking for work, once again in total despair.

As this first year in Palm Springs unfolded, it became clear that I was not going to find work. I could not live with Al indefinitely rent-free. I hated living in the desert—I found its landscape dreary and depressing. I did not care for having to drive 25 miles to Palm Springs every day. I did not find its gay community particularly welcoming. (In Palm Springs I ran across many of the gay men I used to know in San Francisco; in Palm Springs they had no time for me.) When Al gave me a lecture on how to properly use the toilet, I had had enough of living under his roof. I gave him all my Arts and Crafts furniture, including several original Stickley pieces in exchange for unpaid rent.

I had been having weekly phone chats with my sister over this year. When my Palm Springs experience had become intolerable, I asked her if I could move back to McGraw, New York, and live with her.

55

I packed up all my clothes and a few other valuable items that would fit in my car, leaving most of my possessions in storage in Al's care, and headed back to McGraw. When I arrived, I found Sylvia had become a hoarder. She also had a dozen cats. The house reeked of cat shit and piss. Every room was packed full, leaving just a fire path through the rooms. Sylvia had assigned me the downstairs bedroom but had not cleared any space for me. I left my stuff in my car overnight until Sylvia cleared a few drawers and part of the bedroom closet for my stuff.

I framed my life in McGraw as the staging ground where I could prepare myself for the next chapter of my life. Other than Sylvia, I knew no one there. I set about seeking ways to meet people. I began attending AA meetings every day. I drove to Syracuse to attend the only weekly gay AA meeting. Most attendees were not queer, but straight, and attended because the meeting was thought of as "cool." I attended the only gay AA meeting in Ithaca, which turned out to be the final gay meeting session there. It was disbanded due to lack of interest.

I got a sponsor. It was the first time I ever had a straight male sponsor. On the positive side, Tom T. pointed me toward service beyond the meeting level. I got involved at the district level. (There are no leaders in AA, only trusted servants.) I held every service position within several individual meetings. I came to understand how AA's inverted government model worked (as in anarcho-syndicalism, the power rises from the ground up). But I found the egos on display at the governance level more than I could tolerate. Since there was no money or fame involved in being a leader, I failed to grasp the apparent need of individuals who craved power in anonymity for power's sake alone.

Despite meeting and working with many, many people in AA, I never made a single friend. I was much in demand in my service roles. I gradually came to recognize that I was respected, even admired, for the quality of my sobriety. But no one was willing to accept my invitation to a meal or coffee with me outside of the context of a meeting. I tried testing the validity of this conclusion. I invited an entire noon meeting (some 30 people) out for ice cream at my expense following the meeting. Not a single AA accepted my invitation.

I experienced two kinds of AA contact outside of meetings. Whenever I held a service position, I got calls from people needing to do business. I gave people rides to meetings. I filled in on a moment's notice if someone was unable to chair a meeting. I met my sponsor for dinner every Tuesday night before a meeting. He invited others to join us, and these people often came. People I invited never showed.

Over time I reached out to this sponsor and a couple other AA old-timers I trusted seeking understanding as to why I was finding no social connection in AA. The old-timers shrugged me off. My sponsor told me, "Stop being gay and find a nice girl to settle down with."

I mounted another job hunt. I submitted applications for advertised positions (mostly adjunct) at colleges and universities in the region. I sent my C.V. to their English and German departments. I applied to advertised positions in Cortland County high schools. I never heard back from anyone. I applied, my heart filled with a mixture of feelings—dread, foreboding, anger, embarrassment, frustration—to a handful of minimum-wage jobs, knowing full well I would not hear back from any of those people either.

I discovered there was a Cortland LGBT Center, which had a gay men's monthly potluck dinner. I started attending the monthly meals. There was a core group of four guys who regularly showed up. On occasion someone else would come. Such individuals never came back after their first visit. Every potluck followed a predictable pattern: One member, who always drew the group's attention, would lay out the most recent experience of how he had been victimized. The other members would offer him helpful suggestions, which he never followed. This scenario became a broken record. I spoke with other men at SAGE who had visited the Cortland group and cited this dynamic as the reason they never went back. The Cortland men sometimes wondered aloud why their group never attracted more men. After five years, my patience with this group wore out and I quit going.

I discovered SAGE Upstate in Syracuse. I joined their writers' group, joined the gay men's support group (which served as my only local "gay community"), and attended monthly potlucks and quarterly dances. I started a monthly Saturday movie matinee group. I served on the board of directors. Again, I made no friends. Obviously, there was no dating pool for me there.

By this time it had been fifteen years since my *Bear Book* had been published. My fifteen minutes of fame as the Bear historian of record had come and gone. While Bob and I lived in San Francisco, John Burrows formally invited me to come to P'town Bear Week and give a presentation on Bear history. Five years later, Gary Turner brought me to P'town Bear Week as his guest. Freddy Freeman, who organized a semi-annual "Bear Your Soul" weekend event at Easton Mountain in the Adirondacks invited me to speak about early Bear history. The last time I spoke in an official capacity as the Bear historian was when I was interviewed by the *Los Angeles Times*.

By that time, the *Bear Book* and *Bear Book II* had passed from memory. Most Bears had no idea that a history of the Bear community had been written. I heard numerous stories, fabricated out of thin air, explaining the history of Bears. I was even lectured by one of the Cortland gay potluck guys that he was a Bear and I was not. The Bear community had gone mainstream since the publication of my books, and much had changed in the Bear community and Bear identity. Bear clubs had come and gone. IBR no longer took place, and P'town Bear Week had become the preeminent event. There were bar events every weekend somewhere in the world. A Bear circuit had arisen and muscle Bears had emerged at the top of the social hierarchy.

I had dropped out of the Bear community by then. I was now poor and living in Cortland, with no means to travel to Bear spaces. I was both disappointed and disgusted by what looked to me like the Bear community becoming exactly what they had started out as an alternative to—socially exclusive and reveling on conspicuous consumption. I was serious when I said I was now too poor to be a Bear.

In an effort to document the evolution of Bears since my books had been published and to understand where Bear values actually now were, I put out a call for submissions for *Bear Book III*. I contacted everyone I personally knew and sent the call to online websites that had a Bear readership. I was taken aback that none of the online Bear groups or Bear merchandisers were willing to post my call. I was very discouraged that I never heard back from a single person I had personally reached out to. That put an end, in my mind, to my relevance to Beardom.

I began auditing literature and Spanish courses at SUNY Cortland. My efforts to continue learning Spanish continued to be sabotaged. Because senior auditors are at the bottom of the list and there are far more students wanting to take Spanish than there are sections of Spanish being offered, I often was not able to move on to the next level course. (Auditors came last in the pecking order.) I would have to go back and repeat the level I had last taken because I had forgotten so much over the one-year wait to get into a course. The last time I tried to get into a section, the instructor turned me away, saying he did not permit senior auditors because his experience had shown him that we are too old to learn. (I filed a formal complaint of illegal age discrimination with the college's diversity office. They informed me they would forward it to the employment office. After six months, I had heard nothing. I contacted both the Diversity and Human Resources offices, and both told me they had no record of my complaint. They suggested I resubmit my complaint. I got the point that I was wasting my time.)

One of the reasons I wanted to learn Spanish was to prepare myself for the possibility of moving to a Latin American country. During these McGraw years, as evidence mounted that I would never find work and probably never make friends here, I investigated every possibility I could think of to leave Central New York. I researched Germany, Britain, the Netherlands, and Canada as countries to emigrate to. My income fell far short of the required minimum to qualify. I considered Latin America. I was either too poor or the country too politically unstable. A Facebook "friend," who was an expat in Ecuador, encouraged me to investigate moving there. I found it too politically unstable. I had no interest in any American expat communities. These were enclaves of people who typically never learned the language, didn't mix with the locals, and as my contact in Ecuador described them, all watched American TV and complained about how much they missed the US.

I looked into low-income housing in several places where I would consider living. There was no housing in New York City, South Florida, or the Bay Area. I applied to the Desert AIDS Program for housing in Palm Springs. I was put on the waitlist and was told an apartment would become available within 12 months. After three years nothing had opened. Eventually I had come to the realization that I could never tolerate that desert heat.

Cary Randolph, my editor at Haworth Press, lived in Binghamton with his husband. When I first moved back to McGraw, he invited me down a few times. He showed me the carousels Binghamton is noted for. We went on an open-house tour of the local churches. We went to the movies once. He and his husband drove up to Cortland for dinner once.

After a while, Cary became available for a monthly dinner with me. We met at Aiello's, an Italian restaurant in Whitney Point, halfway between Binghamton and Cortland. When I pushed him to get together more frequently to do other things together, he pushed back saying he was very busy—he had a full-time job. Increasingly, he conveyed the impression that he felt put out by even our monthly dinners. Several times, after agreeing upon a dinner date, he would message me a couple of hours before the dinner date that he was unexpectedly unavailable. I stopped reaching out to him, but always accepted promptly any time I heard from him.

Old friends had given me the email addresses of friends of theirs on faculty at Cornell or SUNY Cortland, urging me to reach out to them. I emailed perhaps a dozen local academics, introducing myself and offering to meet for coffee. I never got a single response.

I started attending weekly services at Grace and Holy Spirit Church in Cortland. This was the church I had been confirmed in when I was 13. I attended on a regular basis and went to coffee hour following service. Grace is a "welcoming" church, meaning it is gay-friendly. The priest, who everyone called Father Pete, was openly gay himself. Father Pete proclaimed in every Sunday service that the congregation was proud to "welcome the stranger in our midst."

This struck me as ironic as no one ever talked to me at coffee hour. I didn't understand what was so welcoming about ignoring me.

I turned to the internet for connections. I could think of no other way of meeting local gay men. In the beginning I communicated with married "bi-curious" men, looking to hook up for no-strings-attached sex. As soon as I proposed meeting in person, every one of these guys stopped communicating with me. I became willing to travel some distance to meet a guy. Again, as soon as I proposed meeting face to face, they dropped me. I learned this was called "ghosting" someone. In our new world of virtual reality, virtual friends, and virtual communication, ghosting was the socially accepted standard for (not) dealing with other people.

For medical care I went to my family's doctor in Cortland. For HIV/AIDS I went to the HIV clinic at Upstate University Medical Center in Syracuse. I found the HIV people to be friendly, up to date on HIV and on health issues of gay men. They kept on top of my sexual health. One day I challenged my PCP about her lack of AIDS knowledge. Her response was to storm out of the examination room. Dr. Reddy, my HIV specialist, offered to be my PCP. I accepted and I never saw or spoke to the local country horse doctor again.

I made numerous other attempts to make connections and gain traction. They all followed the same pattern I have described here. I found myself going to all these places to avoid being alone and stuck in my sister's house. Living in the midst of all her stuff (how can I describe the dump, the hovel, the disaster area?) was very disheartening. I had offered to clean up her house, but she flatly refused. I offered to do the dishes every day (which would have cleared enough space to cook in the kitchen), but she refused. Going to all these places every day in order to get out of the house to avoid being physically alone, only backfired. I felt invisible, at best, but more often judged, rejected, and shunned. I ended up feeling worse when I left than when I arrived.

My long-time sleep problems bloomed into intolerable insomnia. I could not fall asleep or stay asleep. At best I would get two hours of sleep. I kept the TV on—for company and to have something for my raging brain to focus on.

Increasingly, the mood swings between anger and despair, allegedly caused by the bipolar disorder for which I was already taking the legally permitted dosages of psych meds, turned into a daily rollercoaster ride. My despair became suicidal; my anger became rage. These mood swings exhausted me. I struggled to hide this and tried to present as calm a demeanor as I could summon. I had no one to turn to and I used Facebook to vent. I raged on and on and said all sorts of things utterly inappropriate in a public space. And what I did say was still the tip of the iceberg of what I was feeling.

I stopped taking my meds. I stopped bathing or changing my clothes. I stopped taking care of myself. I only ever became aware of this when people complained that I stank. A guy in my SAGE group told me the group members couldn't tolerate my smell. My AA sponsor told me that I didn't have any friends in AA because I stank. (But why, then I wanted to know, did anyone want to be my friend the three years before their thoughtless cruelty had caused me to give up on taking care of myself?)

One day, at my wit's end, I called 911 and asked for Suicide Prevention. My psychotherapist had instructed me to call 911, which was not a suicide hotline, if I ever felt that close to killing myself. The person taking my call did not forward my call to Suicide Prevention but began asking me for personal information—my name, my address, whether I was alone. I hung up immediately, regretting having followed the therapist's advice. Fifteen minutes later two armed uniformed policemen showed up at my front door. I refused to let them in and I assured them I was okay.

56

During these years in McGraw, I was very fearful of being isolated and lonely. The first two years or so I kept myself as busy as I could with my social involvements. The rest of the time I watched TV. I convinced Sylvia to get internet service, which I paid for. I used Facebook again to vent my frustration, anger, and loneliness in lieu of having a confidante. I used Bear Forest, a Bear-oriented gay hookup site to look for someone to date and to look for friends nearby. None of the gay men I had met at SAGE or the Cortland potluck introduced me to any of their friends and there was no other way to find gay men in person. (I often introduced people I knew to each other if I saw they had something in common and would benefit from knowing each other. I naïvely believed this would happen to me in Central New York.)

I made three connections through Bear Forest. The first one was a guy in Ithaca. He invited me to Sunday dinner with his husband at their house two or three times. Then the invitations stopped. He would email me once a month saying they were busy, but they would have me over next month. This went on month after month for two years. Then he ghosted me.

The second guy I seemed to strike a connection with lived in Albany, a three-hour drive from Cortland. I drove to Albany to spend a weekend with him and start to get to know each other. The first thing he did after he let me in his house was tear my clothes off and have sex with me, which was the third rape in my life. After that, he took me out to dinner. That night

I didn't sleep a wink in a recliner watching TV. In the morning he came downstairs and announced to me, "You're too multifaceted for me to date." He then parked himself in front of his computer and went back to looking for his next trick. After waiting two hours for him to return his attention to me, I asked him when we would have breakfast. He informed me he didn't eat breakfast and went back to the computer. At that point I got my backpack and told him I was not staying the weekend and was heading back to McGraw. He thanked me for coming and gave me a kiss goodbye.

I thought I had heard every excuse for why I was unacceptable for someone to date. But being "too multifaceted" took the cake.

I also met Hank Dobson, who became the first (and only) friend I made locally. We crossed paths at SAGE, just as he was moving from Syracuse back to Binghamton and I was starting to go to SAGE. It was a fluke that we happened to be there at the same time. Our connection was movies.

When I turned 62, I retired formally and filed for Social Security so that I would have steady and stable, if inadequate, income. I continued to receive money from an angel, and after my Social Security kicked in, I started setting some of that aside as an emergency fund.

Another guy I connected with was named Phil Driver. He lived in Brooklyn, was on permanent disability, was passionate about classical music, and had only come out as gay around the age of 50. We were roughly the same age. Our online exchanges turned into phone calls. I enjoyed talking to him immensely.

By my fourth year in McGraw, my connection to Phil had grown into something more. He invited me to visit him in Brooklyn. I took the Greyhound down to Manhattan a few times to spend a long weekend with Phil. These visits were vacations in Manhattan for both of us.

Then on one call with Phil, he said he wanted to ask me something.

I said, "I think I know what you want to ask. You want to marry me, right?"

"Yes," he said.

I had just booked a flight to London to visit Ken Ratcliffe using money from my emergency fund. I spent two weeks with Ken in London. We went to art museums every day. I sent Phil a postcard every day. He called me on the phone, often just to say hello, every evening.

Once again, I packed up my car with my clothes and a few essential items. I shipped my books and DVDs ahead of me to Brooklyn. I used GPS to guide me across the City. As I drove down the interstate in Pennsylvania a sign appeared: "Lincoln Tunnel Straight Ahead." GPS then directed me to an exit in Pennsylvania, sent me in a huge loop through the hills and brought me back to the exit it had sent me from. This happened two more times. I finally ignored the GPS and followed the freeway signs. GPS sent me through Lower Manhattan and through Friday afternoon rush hour. The drive was terrifying.

When I got to Phil's apartment, I found all my book and DVD packages sitting outside his apartment door. Phil was a hoarder like my sister. Like my sister, when I arrived, I found that Phil had not made any effort to make room for my stuff. In fact, I never unpacked my suitcases. My books and DVDs remained in their shipping boxes in the middle of the floor.

I noticed within a few days that Phil was somehow different. I told him, "You seem to be a completely different person from who I was dating."

Phil laughed it off and said, "I'm still the same person. You must be imagining things."

But he *was* different. He accompanied me everywhere. He started asking me to pay for his meals. We ate every meal out. He asked me for subway fare. He asked me for money to buy him books and whatever else caught his eye. He would give me something he had bought with my money and tell me it was a gift from him.

His requests turned into demands. Once in a while, he would offer to pay me back. But before the money turned up, he would erase his debt by billing me for expenses—repairs to the furnace, new light bulbs, doing my laundry for me.

Phil had been present when I opened my bank accounts so he knew exactly how much money I had, including the emergency fund that I deposited into my savings account. He began telling me the plans he had for spending every penny of that money. We were going to have a wedding and reception I would pay for. We would go on a cruise in Norway for our honeymoon, which I was would pay for. He was going to remodel his kitchen, which I would pay for.

I said nothing when he articulated these visions. I was willing to pay for his meals and subway fare. I tried putting my foot down with his demands for money for impulse purchases. We began to argue about money. This escalated to the point that he would threaten to toss me out into the street if I didn't give him the money. He informed me that his mother was suspicious of me and accused me of taking financial advantage of Phil. He made clear he encouraged her to believe this, all the while failing to mention that I was supporting him.

Our days were pretty low-key. I would wake up and make myself a cup of coffee and have a bagel. Phil kept the bagels in the freezer, so I would thaw one out in the microwave then toast it and add cream cheese. Then I'd go back to bed and watch morning TV until Phil woke up. I gave up trying to wake him up or get him out of bed because he would say "Fifteen more minutes," and then turn over and go back to sleep for two or three hours. He rarely got up before noon.

When Phil woke up, I'd have showered by then. He'd take a shower and get dressed. Sometimes, when he was particularly overmedicated (he was always overmedicated), I would have to help him dress.

He'd ask me what I felt like eating and we'd choose a restaurant. We'd walk past the rows and rows of the apartments of our Hassidic neighbors, then under the Marcy Avenue J train subway station, and north along Bedford Avenue.

Our neighbors—men in black suits, black hats and *payos* (sideburns), their wives in dark, modest dresses, wearing head coverings, and with their children—tended to go no further north than the Marcy Avenue station. North of that trendy hipsters crowded the streets. Phil and I always stood out as the only people over 30 in the neighborhood. Bedford Avenue was lined with twentysomething restaurants, boutique shops, micro art galleries and bars in refurbished factory and warehouse buildings. There was a wide range of ethnic restaurants to choose from. After lunch we always went to Martha's Country Bakery for dessert. The waitresses all came to know us, put our order in before we sat down, and occasionally brought us extra desserts as a thank-you for our patronage.

Then we'd go back home. I would watch TV in bed, and Phil would listen to classical music on the radio in the front room for the rest of the day. This pattern was routinely broken up by doctors' appointments in Manhattan. We saw the psychiatrist every week. Because it was such a schlepp from Williamsburg, our appointments were back-to-back. The shrink constantly tweaked my meds—increasing or decreasing one med or another, sometimes adding a new one or replacing another.

I became overmedicated much of the time as well. For several weeks, I had trouble keeping my balance and fell down often, having a hard time getting up or walking on my own. I fell once leaving our apartment and a neighbor called an ambulance.

Another time I fell down in Martha's and an ambulance was called. After that, our waitress always asked if I was doing okay.

I was also on Klonopin for anxiety disorder. Mainly I took it to quell the anxiety enough to be able to fall asleep. The drug gradually stopped working. One night, I kept taking two more pills, over and over until I had taken 18 pills. Fearing I had overdosed, I called an ambulance. It was 3 AM or so, and Phil was sound asleep.

I remember being strapped into a gurney and loaded into the

ambulance. The next thing I remembered was waking up the next day in a locked psych ward. I was sleeping in a bunk bed in a men's dorm room. I was dressed only in a hospital gown. I didn't have my dentures. (A while back I had suddenly had to have my teeth pulled and dentures made, which an angel miraculously paid for.) There were also women in the ward. Everyone else there was younger than me, in their 20s and 30s.

There was a TV behind a glass wall inside the nurse's station, which the nurses controlled. We were served small servings of bad food. I got soft food because I had no teeth. I got some of my meds. It was not clear to me how they figured out what I was on.

Eventually Phil located me and came to the hospital. Based on Phil's vouchsafing for me, they were willing to release me into his care.

After a subsequent overnight in another emergency room I had been admitted to, Phil was not able to find me. I was released wearing only the underwear I had on when the ambulance picked me up. I requested street clothes and was given a pair of pants and a pair of shoes. I had to go to another building to get the paperwork for a subway ticket home. I looked homeless. No one in the subway gave me a second look.

I took Phil to an occasional matinee at the Angelika arthouse cinema on Houston Street. I took us out to a few art museums. I joined the Goethe Institute and borrowed four or five DVDs of German-language films every week.

I went to AA meetings, and Phil always accompanied me, even to closed meetings (where only self-identifying alcoholics were permitted to attend). I tried a couple of meetings in Williamsburg. The attendees were all young hipsters, who whined about "luxury problems." I tried several gay meetings in Manhattan. One was full of old-timers who were friends with each other and had been meeting there for decades. I took the names of potential sponsors from a list posted at each meeting. I never met any of these sponsors face to face. We always talked over the phone. The only one who seemed a good fit got drunk and had to terminate the sponsoring relationship. I started attending meetings daily in the Rainbow Room off Times Square. The meetings were always packed. Lots of tourists came. There was little consistency in attendees. I exchanged numbers with a few regulars, but none sustained contact with me.

Phil sang in a large chorus and in an acapella group who sang "evergreen" pop songs. He insisted I join the acapella group. The chorus director noticed I often sang off-key. He told Phil privately that I was no longer welcome.

When my Medicare Plan D coverage was cancelled because I had moved to Brooklyn, I could no longer afford my medications. I stopped all medications. One evening an itch started on my right leg. It did not go away. Over time the itching spread all over my body. It was particularly intense above my neck—in my ears, in my eyebrows, on my eye lids, on the back of my neck, but also on my toes and the tip of my cock.

Shortly after that Phil disappeared. He had gone to a chorus rehearsal and never came home. His sister called me a couple of days later to let me know he was in a mental hospital for observation.

Meanwhile, Phil had threatened me one time too many to kick me out of his apartment for refusing to give him money he was demanding. I decided to leave him. I spoke to my sister and arranged to move back in with her—temporarily. I had called both Cary Randolph and Hank Dobson to see if they could drive down to Brooklyn and drive my possessions and me back upstate. Hank refused flat out, saying he could not handle Manhattan's traffic. After agreeing initially, Cary also withdrew his offer for the same reason. I made arrangements with a Brooklyn moving company. I booked a ticket with Greyhound. For weeks I worried about telling Phil I was leaving. I kept pushing the time further away. As it turned out, he was in the hospital on my moving day so I never had to tell him in person. I left him a note and my set of keys when I left.

Having left my keys in Phil's apartment and pulled the locked apartment door behind me, and with the moving van parked halfway down the street, I was stopped on the front stairs outside Phil's apartment by two hostile and aggressive uniformed cops. They told me they had gotten a call from someone who reported someone was burglarizing the apartment. I explained I was moving out.

They demanded my ID. I gave them my driver's license, which still had my McGraw address on it. They rejected that. They asked me for a utility bill with my name and this address on it. I explained no utilities were in my name. They demanded I let them in the apartment. I explained, once again, I was in the process of moving out, and I had left my set of keys in the apartment, which was now locked.

By then a crowd of neighbors had gathered and an upstairs neighbor was standing at the top of the stairs watching the scene. I yelled at her, "Why did you call the police?" She said her husband had called. I fumed. These people had seen me and Phil come and go out of the building every day for six months.

The cops asked the crowd if they knew me. They said yes, I lived there. I told him the movers were down the street. One of the cops walked to the moving van and confirmed they were moving me out. In the end one of the cops apologized to me, saying, "Sorry to have treated you that way. But we have to be careful."

I hustled to get to Port Authority to catch my bus to Cortland. Like the parking ticket left on my car on the eve of my departure from San Francisco to Boston, this bit of nastiness made me eager to get the hell out of Dodge.

57

When I got back to Sylvia's in McGraw, I discovered she had had the movers leave my clothes in a pile on my bed and all my boxes in the garage. The overcrowding of her hoarding had gotten worse. Moving back and forth between two hoarders was taking a toll on me. Being back in McGraw was very dismaying. I girded my loins and summoned my mental and emotional strength (what was left of it) to start over one more time, to make one last good faith effort to make living in Cortland tolerable. I had not yet made lemonade out of these lemons and I certainly was not smelling of roses.

I applied to the Cortland Housing Authority for low-income housing. Once again, I started attending AA meetings daily. I also started going to Grace Church every week, and I joined the church choir. I returned to the men's support group at SAGE. I volunteered to serve on the advisory board at the Cortland LGBT Center. I started attending the Cortland gay men's monthly potluck, where the same dysfunction was in full operation. I joined the Ithaca Gay Men's Chorus. (Calling it "gay men" was somewhat misleading as its membership had definitely become "queer." There were numerous transmen and the director was a lesbian.) I became a member of the Binghamton German Club and went to Friday dinner every week.

After an astoundingly short waiting period of five weeks, I was offered an apartment in a high-rise in downtown Cortland. I had been worried about which housing I would be given. Much of it was rather depressing. The building was clean and safe. A designated parking space was included. My apartment on the seventh floor was very small, but cheerful and bright, and it had a beautiful view of the historic Cortland County courthouse and the hills to the east. I woke up to the rising sun.

Moving in was a challenge. Sylvia gave me the bed I used in her house (and the one Mom had died in), my old kneehole student desk, and a bookcase. I approached Father Pete at Grace Church for help from the congregation. He posted an announcement and let me know he had heard from several parishioners—one man offered his truck and three others offered furniture. However, when I pressed him to set a date to collect this furniture, he informed me he couldn't find anyone willing to help move the furniture. He just sighed and shrugged it off. I felt brushed off.

My friend Hank gave me a small kitchen table that was the right size for my tiny apartment. My new AA sponsor offered to go with me to secondhand shops, but that promise never materialized. I began buying furnishings as I had the money to do so.

I adopted a kitten from the SPCA. It was listed as a female. I told the SPCA I was sure it was a male and named him Schuyler. When Schuyler came back from his first visit to the vet and had been neutered, he was now registered as male. On paper at least, my cat was transgender.

To symbolically celebrate my new attempt to start over, I planned a housewarming party. I sent out invitations a couple of months ahead to enable people an opportunity to plan for it. I took great pleasure in thinking about the party, planning it, buying a bottle of wine, a six-pack of beer, and dishware here and there.

The housewarming was very pleasant. About half the people I had invited showed up. I noted that none of the Cortland gay men, none of the academics, and none of the lesbians I had invited came. All of the people I had planned to introduce to each other were no-shows.

A year after the party Sylvia and my friend Hank were the only people still in touch with me.

As time went on, everything remained fixed in the same old pattern. At Grace no one continued to talk to me at coffee hour. No one in AA was willing to get together with me at "arm's length" over coffee. Only one of the men from my SAGE group and none of the men from the Cortland gay men's group had shown up for the housewarming, so I withdrew from those activities. At the German Club, nothing came of the German class I had offered to teach. I had joined the German Club chorus, and that met for rehearsal exactly once in a year's time. I had an occasional conversation over Friday dinner, but it seemed no one actually spoke German and it was clear no one had any interest in learning.

In order to avoid being alone, I returned to having an activity for each day of the week. My fear of ending up a "poor, old, single, friendless fag" had been realized. My fear of precisely this fate had compelled me to flee from Cortland as a teenager and find a place where I belonged and where I expected I would find friends, peers, happiness, love, and acceptance. The world had changed so much and the growing acceptance of homosexuals and the integration of us into mainstream society had progressed so far that it seemed impossible to me that my destiny could resemble in any way the bleak and lonely life CBS had broadcast back in the 1960s.

I focused my rage alternately at other people for rejecting me and at myself, blaming myself for being blind to something fundamentally wrong with me, something that was obvious to everyone else. The self-loathing is what prevented me from lashing out at people. Freud would say that I had made myself so loathsome, so self-isolated, so self-obsessed that no one could possibly love me. Sadomasochism is a private, guilty pleasure.

My striving to foster a sense of hope gave way to ever deepening anger and despair. My mood oscillated between the two, sometimes being filled with both at the same time. Sylvia suggested I try smiling more and learn to engage in small talk. An AA I took into my confidence suggested that I should basically change my personality—make myself into an extrovert.

The election of Donald Trump and his four years of insanity fueled my rage. Every morning I would wake up and check the news to see what new outrageous thing he had said or done over the last 24 hours. Each time it seemed he could not outdo himself. Yet every day he did.

I took to going for long drives in my car. These grew into day trips. When I reached the turnaround point, I would have a late lunch. I would set out full of anger and despair, and it usually took hours for me to calm down. My ruminations had taken on a life of their own. My mind turned every negative thing that happened to me into a trick god was playing on me. I was now Tantalus with god tangling enticing grapes before me, and then snatching them away as soon as I took the bait. I saw god as a pure sadist. I pleaded for him to stop. I pleaded for him to let me know what unforgivable transgressions I was guilty of, so that I would at least understand a purpose in my torment. Previously I had prayed to have my life back, to have a partner, to have friends, or to have enough money to travel on (so I could forget I had no friends), or at the very least to let me have a reason for living.

Much of my past came up, emotions and trauma I thought I had worked through and left behind. I found myself still grieving the loss of John, my "one and only 'true' love." I cried and cried for nearly two years of those road trips. I played CDs full of love lost, love betrayed, love missed over and over. Patsy Cline, the Mavericks, ABBA, k.d. lang, Garth Brooks,

"Cry Me a River," "The Man I Love," and all those 1950s and 1960s pop songs of love thwarted and love lost.

Gradually, the despair was replaced by anger. I began dwelling more on Bob's betrayal. I twisted my entire relationship history to read as a series of heartbreaks and betrayals. I posted on Facebook I was tired of being the "practice boyfriend," noting that all of my past partners were still together with the man who came after me or whom I had been left for. Having no confidantes, I used Facebook as the place to vent all my rage and despair. I made sure to savor every ounce of masochistic pleasure. I found validation in Stephen Crane's poem "In the Desert."

> In the desert
> I saw a creature, naked, bestial,
> Who, squatting upon the ground,
> Held his heart in his hands,
> And ate of it.
> I said, "Is it good, friend?"
> "It is bitter—bitter," he answered;
> "But I like it
> "Because it is bitter,
> "And because it is my heart."

When I could afford to upgrade to an iPhone, I started taking photographs on my day trips. The trips shifted from being a private space to dive in and savor every bitter memory I could conjure, to a place where I could pretend that I was on vacation from my life in Cortland. I fantasized sharing my drives with my partner by my side or waiting for me at home. But more and more my focus shifted on the photography and visits to interesting places.

In the aftermath of the catastrophic relationship in Brooklyn (I never mentioned the man's name and referred to him as "Mr. Whackadoodle"), I became wary of online connections. There seemed to be a major shift online as well. I no longer heard from any local men (who had all ghosted me as soon as I suggested we meet in person). Instead, the guys who contacted me were very young (or at least used the photo of a young guy in their profile), were located far away, and some even outright professed their love for me.

English was clearly not the first language of many of them. None of them even seemed to take the time to read my profile. A pattern emerged, with slight variations. "Where are you located?", "Are you single?" "Are you a top or a bottom?" "How long have you been on this site?", "How long have you been single? And why?" and the like—mostly information given in my profile. More and more guys would address me as "dear" in their first communication. More and more stated they "loved" me without knowing anything about me. More and more wanted to switch to communicating by WhatsApp, Hangouts, or other online mediums. A few I gave my email address to. Fewer still I exchanged phone numbers to text with. Some ghosted me at that point. All I could figure out was they were "trophy hunting" and only wanted my contact info as a souvenir.

The rest were all clearly scammers. I found myself at the receiving end of long, gushing letters professing love, letters that sounded like a 13-year-old girl in the throes of puppy love. The letters were interchangeable. Only once did I keep leading a guy on, pretending I was believing him. We progressed from his gushing letters to phone calls. He spoke with a thick Russian accent. He claimed he lived in Stockton, California. When I asked him about his accent, he explained that he was originally from Russia (never specifying where in Russia) and had come from a broken home. He was 19 when his mother died, and he moved to California. He said he had a computer business and directed me to his business website, which showed an upscale computer store.

Then the inevitable happened. A shipment of computers was allegedly being held up in port. He desperately needed $50,000 and wanted me to give it to him. At this point I blocked all points of contact with him. I researched the name he used. I found there actually was a man by that name with a computer shop in Stockton. I called him and told him someone had stolen his identity and was using it to scam people.

During these years of ever-increasing despair, I became obsessed with my death. For the second time I had come to a state of social death. The price of long-term AIDS survivorship was unbearable.

I returned to a mental place I had been in when my demise from AIDS seemed imminent. I spun fantasies of being forgotten. I thought of how once famous people had ended up forgotten and impecunious, dying poor and forgotten. Louise Brooks, a celebrated star in 1920s German films, became an alcoholic and died forgotten in Rochester, New York. Kate Smith, celebrated for her rendition of "God Bless America" first recorded in the 1940s, became incapacitated by diabetes and then mental decline, spent her final years under the care of a live-in nurse and died in Raleigh. Even though she had been anti-racist before that word was coined—she famously called for racial tolerance in a nationwide radio broadcast in 1945—she was deemed a racist and a statue of her in Philadelphia was taken down.

I thought of Vincent van Gogh and his sad life, how he had died poor, mad, and unrecognized, his artistic genius too far ahead of its time. I thought of Benny Hill, often thought of as an embarrassingly adolescent-like joker, dying alone in his apartment watching TV, his body lying there for days before anyone thought to check in on him.

I thought of Alan Turing, the British codebreaker whose efforts helped win World War II, who was later discovered to be homosexual and forced to choose between prison and chemical castration. He chose the latter and was believed to have died by his own hand.

And I thought of Oscar Wilde, whose story is well-known. His fame as a celebrated author did not help him when he was discovered to be homosexual. He also died impoverished and living in exile in France.

I certainly had not became famous. It was no doubt laughable that I could ever think of myself in terms of the public shame of these people's fall from public grace. I wondered how long my body would lie dead in my apartment before it was discovered. I thought the most likely scenario would be someone from the Housing Authority showing up to find out why I hadn't paid my rent.

I took comfort in knowing my papers and the original BHP files were permanently archived at Cornell. One day some researcher would chance upon them. Nonetheless, I felt acute anxiety, propelling me to try to get some of my life story recorded on film. Toby Myers, who produced an online comedy series called *Where the Bears Are*, contacted me to be interviewed for a documentary he was working on. I did the interview via Zoom and iPhone. It was tabled.

Joe Grossman forwarded me the web site of a man in southern California who filmed interviews of individuals who had played a role in early gay activism. He was happy to interview. He set up a trial interview to check the quality of a zoom interview. He reported that the quality was not good enough to bother with. He wrote me, "I'm so sorry. You deserve better." I wrote back, saying, "I've been told that more than once."

By a fluke I happened to catch a last-minute post on Facebook announcing that long-term (pre-HAART) survivors of AIDS were being sought for a documentary about to be made in New York City. I had only a few days' notice to get down there. I emailed Ted Matson, the filmmaker, and let him know I was available. He asked me to participate. I scrambled to find someone in New York I could stay overnight with. No one was available, so I booked a round-trip Greyhound ticket to go down for just the day. I would have plenty of time to kill before my scheduled interview. I contacted AA, hoping to hang out at the Rainbow Club. But the building was closed due to Covid. I opted to go to MoMA instead.

After going to the museum and having a quick bite to eat, I walked to the address Steed had given me. When I got there, it turned out to be a hardware store. I thought maybe I was turned around and had mistakenly read "east" instead of "west." I set out on a very long walk to the other side of Manhattan. I was constantly winded. I had waves of vertigo and had to stop and hold a lamp post or the side of a building to keep from falling over. I was drenched with sweat. When I got to the new address, or where it should have been, I found nothing. I headed back to the west side address. I asked a salesclerk in the hardware store if he knew the place I was looking for. He took me outdoors and pointed to a small door that led upstairs. The studio was on an upper floor in the back of the building. I arrived at precisely the time my interview was scheduled for, drenched in sweat and out of breath. Steed was running behind, which left me a half hour to dry off, rest, and compose myself. I found it odd that Steed did not do any paperwork, securing legal permission to use our interviews.

The interview went well. Ted seemed to find my story so compelling (I thought) that he interviewed me for three times the length he had allotted. When his interview was aired online, I discovered it might better be called an extended public service announcement. My interview had been reduced to ten seconds of a talking head. I felt misled.

58

During my first year back in Cortland, after I had moved into public housing, I saw clearly that I was stuck. Attempting yet again to start afresh left me feeling like I was trapped in a *Twilight Zone* episode of *Groundhog Day*—every day was the same. I took to cursing people under my breath, openly flipping the bird and mocking people (to myself) for being oblivious to my private castigations. That first year in my building I had tried to be friendly and said hello to everyone I saw. Almost without exception, they ignored me, leaving me feeling invisible. I christened my building The Zombie Hotel, where we were all already half-dead.

I began withdrawing from each of my commitments, ceasing showing up and subjecting myself to the increasingly painful experience of feeling invisible. I felt I had been judged, found unacceptable, and rejected as *lebensunwertes Leben* (Hitler's classification of Jews—"life unworthy of life").

Suddenly Covid appeared, quickly becoming a global pandemic, and society shut down. My process of social withdrawal was taken care of for me. Now I was forced to live not only in social and emotional isolation, but also physical isolation. The world joined me in what had been my private hell.

This nearly two-year-long shutdown would prove to have a silver lining for me. Finding myself immediately and completely cut off from every social interaction, my emotional pain and my recriminations of others and myself ceased. As the cliché had it, it felt so good when I stopped hitting myself with a hammer.

More gradually my intense mood swings between rage and suicidal despair played themselves out. When I stopped feeding them, they diminished and vanished. I began to feel an inner peace I had not known in many years. My insomnia gave way to full nights of sleep. Waking up feeling nauseous and on the verge of throwing up lessened. My initial waking thoughts of hurling myself out of my seventh-floor window began dissipating.

I continued to live in fear of total physical isolation. Around the time the shutdown was being lifted my surgeries, which had been postponed, were scheduled. I had three minor, yet debilitating, surgical procedures in a row, beginning two days before Christmas and ending in the spring. I found myself unable to care for myself, barely able to get myself out of bed to go to the bathroom. I was sent home the same day of each of my surgeries, when I really should have been kept in the hospital until I could take care of myself. The surgeons told me to have my neighbors check in on me. At that point my neighbor on both sides of my apartment had moved away and the apartments were empty. They had both told me they had had enough of Cortland people and were getting the hell out of there. (Several people had asked me how many people live in Cortland. When I googled to discover that Cortland had a population of 17,556, I came across this: "Is Cortland a good place to live?" "It is one of the most depressing and inhospitable places to live and/or visit.")

I finally hit emotional bottom. My worst fear had come true.

And then it suddenly dawned on me. If worse came to worst, I could always pull the emergency cord in my apartment. (There was one in my bedroom and one in my bathroom.) Or I could call 911 on my iPhone, which I always kept within reach. If I died, I died.

I had had enough of retirement, which a therapist had told me I never adjusted to. I had had enough of seeking meaning by trying to gain traction through social and volunteer commitments, through trying to find someone to date, through trying to make friends. Except for befriending Hank, this had all proven futile, useless, and misguided.

I had felt unwanted. I felt I was of no use and my life was meaningless. I had no purpose in life. My efforts to find new purpose had led to this grand nothingness. I had to create meaning for myself. At the base of all this I felt a deep shame, which I thought I had left behind long ago.

I vowed to bring myself out of retirement, step by step. After the protracted social isolation, I took tentative and judicious steps venturing back out among people. I had succumbed to social death in the aftermath of the AIDS epidemic, an experience circumscribed to the gay community and still oblivious to the general population. I had succumbed a second time to social death in the aftermath of the Covid pandemic, an experience I shared with the entire world. This time, I thought, people might begin asking whatever happened to the "forgotten generation" of long-term (pre-HAART) AIDS survivors.

Seeking to find my way back to a purpose-filled life, Viktor Frankl once again proved my guide. As Buddhism teaches, life is suffering; we only have power over how we understand that suffering. AA teaches, in the words of Abraham Lincoln, that "most people are as happy as they make their mind up to be." As students of the history of Nazism have pointed out, how people deal, or fail to deal, with the rise of authoritarianism in Trumpist America, "what you are doing today reveals your true character—what you would have been doing living through the rise of Hitler." I abandoned my hope of finding a life companion again. This has given me great peace of mind. But I cannot live feeling completely unloved. My high school friend John Alexander repeatedly reminded me that I have friends and I am loved, even if they are not in my daily life.

Above all, humans are meaning makers. We need to have meaning in our life to survive. I have successfully survived my multiple traumas by bringing my focus back to hope, to having responsibilities, to having choice (restricted only by limited income and encroaching old age), and to finding beauty in nature and art. My photography has become a major source of joy in my life.

Zoom had opened doors back into engagement with my California life. For a while I participated in gay AA meetings in San Francisco. I attended some Sunday services at St. Gregory of Nyssa. I reached out to all my old friends (for whom I still had an email or street address) and renewed and deepened some of them. Those who did not respond to me I let go of. I reconnected with my beloved Billy community and joined an online support group for single Billys.

I was very disappointed and discouraged that no one had ever picked up the work with Bear history after I retired. My own anger and disappointment with what I saw the Bear community had turned into dissipated, and I sought to catch up on how things had developed since I had dropped out of all Bear circles. I was heartened to see that the community had bifurcated. While the A-list Bears had carved out their niche at the top of the social hierarchy, most Bears had remained true to the celebration of early Bear values. This was abundantly apparent among Bear clubs in Europe. I put out a call for a BHP Reboot to resume documenting Bear history in the digital age. A small but committed group of individuals (including a Black

Bear and a transbear and a British Bear) with a range of professional skills necessary for the project has formed, and our work continues.

Coming out the other side of so many years of finding no logical reason for being in Central New York aside from economic necessity, I began to see those years to have been a path leading me, however slowly and inscrutably, to the next chapter in my life. I was able to return to working on my memoir. I write essays to sort out my thinking on various aspects of my life.

My frequent photo safari day drives took focus as my photography got better, coming up to professional standards and, with the encouragement of my friend Chris Komater, a professional fine arts photographer and conceptual artist, and my former roommate Tom Libby, a trained art historian and art dealer, the idea for a book of my photographic work took shape.

I began reading widely in literary theory, reviewing what I had struggled to understand as a graduate student and bringing myself up to date with how literary theory and queer theory had evolved since I had stopped actively learning them when my coursework at Berkeley had ended. My sole, and intermittent, contact with that world continued as I audited classes at SUNY Cortland taught by Tyler Bradway. This began with a graduate course on recent science fiction, which Tyler had us read queerly. Then came a course on LGBT literature, where I found my own life experiences living through and at times helping to create being taught as "ancient" history. I offered myself as a primary resource; students were incredulous when I assured them that life for gay and lesbian people really had been exactly the way history said it had been. During the shutdown I was unable to audit Tyler's Literature of AIDS course, but was invited to come in person for an entire class to share my experience of living through and surviving the AIDS epidemic in San Francisco and answering the students' many questions candidly. (I think I blew the class away. But it left me physically and emotionally utterly exhausted.) Most recently, I audited Tyler's class on literary and cultural theory. I found it very helpful to be able to follow the arc of development of the theories I had struggled to understand as they developed while I was in grad school. I had already worked to put these theories into plain English as part of my project in this memoir, and found Tyler's understanding of them, as I have long held, are (usually) interesting and (usually) helpful—"the right tool for the right job," as I put it.

I have long been upset to watch professors of literary and especially queer theory. These theories are quite complex and couched in dense language, impenetrable to the layperson. Rather than embracing the people and cultures who they are writing about—and queer theory started out seeing itself as outside the academy, challenging the authorly of academia—queer theory scholars used their arcane knowledge to consolidate their power within elite educational institutions and to promote their own academic careers, sometimes attaining the height of privilege as star status in the world of academic celebrity. (In plain English: The greater their social status and privilege in elite professional circles, the more entitled they feel to act like assholes, beyond the reach of accountability.)

59

I have stopped pleading with the fleas in my fur collar. Some kind of seismic shift has taken place. Once I let go of my obsessive focus on all the negativity that seemed to surround me, I was able to remove my "Cortland blinders" and look over the fence and reach out to the larger world out there. As I reconnected with old friends, as my anger and despair dissipated, as I let go of my pointless busy-ness, as my perspective shifted, I began to move forward again. I began noticing and paying attention to the positive things, no matter how little, I was now seeing.

On the rare occasions I cross paths with people I knew from AA, Grace Church, the gay men's potlucks, or other places, I cheerfully return a hello, if one is forthcoming. Those who ignore me, I ignore in return. When I have found myself in the presence of someone who upsets me, I quickly move on. I do not engage with the negative self-talk that such encounters trigger within my mind. My fellow "half-dead" neighbors, who had responded to my hellos by ignoring me, have begun to say hello. A few even greet me with, "Hey, Bear. How you doin'?"

In 2020, my libido returned. I realized this when I started having wet dreams. Of the three postponed surgeries I went through, one was to have my hydrocele drained. What had begun as a testicle the size of a golf ball had grown in three years to the size of a large grapefruit. The surgery was no longer a matter of aesthetics, but a necessity. With my libido fully intact, I wanted to be able to have sex in the unlikely event I ever met a man sexually interested in me.

I continue to maintain my profile on several gay "dating" sites. It has been years since I have encountered someone on any of these sites who is not a "bad actor." It seems bad actors have driven men legitimately seeking social or sexual connection away.

I gave job seeking one last go around. Sylvia had told me TC3 offered Russian because the college had a native speaker on staff. She said German was still in the catalog. So I emailed the head of the humanities program and suggested I teach German. They could list the course in their class schedule and see what happens. My argument went they were taking no risk, this would cost the college nothing. I never heard back from TC3.

Tyler told me SUNY Cortland was always scrambling to find adjuncts to teach Freshman Composition classes. The college maintained an open call for an adjunct pool of composition instructors. I had submitted my application for this call twice before, but Tyler encouraged to apply again. I emailed the faculty member in charge of hiring and explained I was applying but had questions concerning the fact that I was retired and had not taught in several years. She responded quickly, informing me that the English Department had no openings. This was obviously illegal age discrimination. I took a little pleasure in having, finally, caught someone in their lie. With that, I *finally* accepted the fact that I would never teach again.

One of my solitary pleasures had been going to the movies every week. I appreciated Cinemapolis, the arthouse cinema in Ithaca. It was one of the few cultural perks in Central New York that measured up to "big city standards." As the Hollywood fare continued its downward spiral of replacing profit over good moviemaking, I found myself walking out of one film after another. During the shutdown I shifted to watching DVDs and subscribing to streaming services like Netflix or Hulu. I gorged, watching one or two movies a day, until I killed my passion for film watching.

My reading to catch up on recent developments in literary and queer theory expanded into my old voracious reading habit. I read everything by responsible truth-tellers recounting the horrors and insanities of Donald Trump and his world. I read up on current events and on politics. I read to see what had happened to gay left thought and Marxist literary theory.

Although Marx notoriously proclaimed, "religion is the opium of the masses," his quest for a better society (I find the vision of a "workers' paradise" rather short-sighted) suggests an idealism, an altruistic spirit. Perhaps this impulse is what draws me to left politics and repulses me by what John Kenneth Galbraith describes the "modern conservative," whose moral philosophy is "the search for a superior moral justification for selfishness."

I was long familiar with the fallacious thinking of so many Americans who believe that democracy and capitalism are two sides of the same coin. With the emergence of China's system of authoritarianism and capitalism, Americans are beginning to understand that capitalism does not guarantee democracy.

I audited Nikolay Karkov's course on Marxism. I saw clearly the problem of what do you replace capitalism with? The Soviet Union had replaced free enterprise capitalism with state capitalism. China has now embraced free market capitalism and integrated it into its authoritarian state. Toward the end of his life Marx, who had wrestled with this dilemma, was starting to explore the structure of Native American societies as a vision for a post-capitalist society.

I revisited Martin Duberman's *Has the Gay Movement Failed?* Several things stood out for me. Writing as a highly privileged, highly educated, cisgender gay male, he seeks to find a balance between the dreams and goals of the old gay left and the mainstream successes of bourgeois gay assimilationist politics. Duberman and people like him (and me) were precisely the kind of person the original gay movement sought to help. It left out people of color and the (working) poor. The AIDS epidemic was the death of gay left politics, as the sexual practices of gay liberation, the liberation of a minority group defined explicitly by their sexual practices, was blamed for the cause of the epidemic.

As reformist queer politics has sought to include more queers of color and nonbinary queers under the umbrella of inclusion and bourgeois respectability, the poor have remained outside the umbrella. Even for queer reformists, old queer people remain invisible and poor queer people remain unacknowledged. Indeed, once again as the queer outsider has become a bourgeois insider, they remain either hostile (at worst) or indifferent (at best) to those of us who are lacking in queered respectability. The safety and comfort of teaching or studying queerness in increasingly expensive college or university classrooms becomes ever more obvious as the gap between the haves and have-nots in American society has become cavernously wide and deep.

A liberal arts education, including the study of literature, once considered necessary to be a well-rounded and well-informed citizen, has been jettisoned as a waste of time, making colleges and universities narrow technical schools teaching only skills that will make money. The cost of a college education has become so prohibitively expensive that one must train for a career that will make enough money to pay off student loans. Today's cultural obsession with fame, power, and wealth predates Trump. How does learning about queer history or experiencing the pleasure

LES K. WRIGHT

of queering texts help a working-class queer, most likely working two minimum-wage jobs and worrying about car repairs? In the current feel-good propaganda of "If I can see it, I can be it" (arising in the aftermath of the Black Lives Matter movement), how many young working-class queers can see themselves as hedge fund managers or vacationing in P'town?

60

I love my apartment. It is clean, safe, cheerful, sunny, and cozy. My rent is based on my income, safely removed from market forces. I have a spectacular view. I have a cell phone, a computer, and internet access. There are two emergency cords in my apartment. I surround myself with things that give me comfort—plenty of books, plenty of DVDs and CDs, a well-stocked kitchen, plants, and my cat. Having neither a roommate nor a partner, I have decorated my home to my taste. There is much to be said for being surrounded by the beauty of art and nature. I am a quiet neighbor and mind my own business. Who cares if we are all being warehoused here? Some of my neighbors are obviously killing time until their time comes to go.

In America today the more money you have, the more freedom you can buy. Some things do not have a price tag on them—love, friendship, use of one's imagination, and creativity, for example. Age prevents me from restarting my teaching career. Poverty prevents me from choosing where I live. Hardly anyone I know has been able to afford to stay in San Francisco.

Someone once wrote that the deepest pains everyone experiences are longing for impossible things, nostalgia for what never was, the desire for what never could have been, and regret over not being someone else. My worst fear is that my life may have had no point, that I didn't live up to my potential, that I have been a person of no consequence. A local AA elder once told me, "Don't let the bastards get you down." I also learned in AA that "Why?" is not a spiritual question.

LES K. WRIGHT

ABOUT THE AUTHOR

Les K. Wright is an author, literary scholar, gay historian, gay activist, and photographer. He grew up in upstate New York, lived and studied in West Germany in the 1970s, and completed a PhD at UC Berkeley in 1992. He is a founding member of the LGBT Historical Society of San Francisco, founder of the Bear History Project, and editor of *The Bear Book* and *Bear Book II*. Infected with HIV in 1981, tested positive in 1986, and diagnosed with full-blown AIDS in 1991, he is a long-term (pre-HAART) AIDS survivor, a member of the forgotten generation of PWAs. He has taught English, Humanities, and German at several colleges and universities in New York, Massachusetts, and the San Francisco Bay Area. After retiring from teaching and becoming an economic refugee from California, he continues to work as an independent scholar and returned to photography.

CPSIA information can be obtained
at www.ICGtesting.com
Printed in the USA
LVHW030817080223
738923LV00001B/4